Nelson English

Language & Writing **10**

Don Aker

David Hodgkinson

NELSON

THOMSON LEARNING

Australia • Canada • Mexico • Singapore • Spain • United Kingdom • United States

NELSON
TM
THOMSON LEARNING

Language & Writing 10
by Don Aker and David Hodgkinson

Director of Publishing:
David Steele

Publisher:
Carol Stokes

Executive Editor:
Jessica Pegis

Managing Editor:
Norma Kennedy

Supervising Editor:
Debbie Davies-Wright

Series Editor:
Chelsea Donaldson

Production Editors:
Laurel Bishop
Franklin Carter
Susan Ginsberg
Julia Hubble

Art Direction:
Anne Goodes

Media Consultant:
Nora Quinn

Composition:
Erich Falkenberg

Production Coordinator:
Julie Preston

Permissions:
Vicki Gould

Printer:
Transcontinental Printing Inc.

Reviewers
The authors and publishers
gratefully acknowledge the
contributions of the following
educators:

Sandie Bender
Ottawa, Ontario

Mike Budd
Windsor, Ontario

Owen Davis
London, Ontario

John Dewar
Saskatoon, Saskatchewan

Rocco Di Ianni
Burlington, Ontario

Lynn Ibsen
Ajax, Ontario

Gerard A. Lavelle
Gloucester, Ontario

Pat Remmer
Brockville, Ontario

Brent Robillard
Smith Falls, Ontario

Lori Jamison Rog
Regina, Saskatchewan

Jim Satterthwaite
Vancouver,
British Columbia

Cheryl Schindler
Scarborough, Ontario

Mary Lou Smitheran
Brockville, Ontario

Terry Swift
Erickson, Manitoba

Gina Tousignant
Brampton, Ontario

Peter Weeks
Stettler, Alberta

**Canadian Cataloguing in
Publication Data**

Aker, Don, 1955-
Language & writing 10

(Nelson English)
Includes index.
ISBN 0-17-618711-1 (bound)
ISBN 0-17-618720-0 (pbk.)

1. English language – Composition
and exercises – Juvenile literature.
2. English language – Grammar –
Juvenile literature.
I. Hodgkinson, Dave. II. Title.
III. Title: Language and writing ten.
IV. Series.

PE1112.A393 2000   428.2
C00-930021-X

Welcome
to *Nelson Language & Writing*

Welcome to *Nelson Language & Writing,* specially designed to boost your language skills and improve your writing. Here is what you will find inside ...

Variety! Each section focuses on one genre—narration, description, exposition, or persuasion—and is divided into three units. Every unit contains a model or models that illustrate a particular writing form and that provide a basis for the lessons that follow.

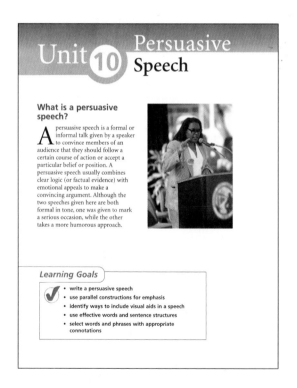

Unit 10 Persuasive Speech

What is a persuasive speech?

A persuasive speech is a formal or informal talk given by a speaker to convince members of an audience that they should follow a certain course of action or accept a particular belief or position. A persuasive speech usually combines clear logic (or factual evidence) with emotional appeals to make a convincing argument. Although the two speeches given here are both formal in tone, one was given to mark a serious occasion, while the other takes a more humorous approach.

Learning Goals

✓
- write a persuasive speech
- use parallel constructions for emphasis
- identify ways to include visual aids in a speech
- use effective words and sentence structures
- select words and phrases with appropriate connotations

A brief introduction helps you get your bearings ...

This feature previews the language and writing skills you'll be learning.

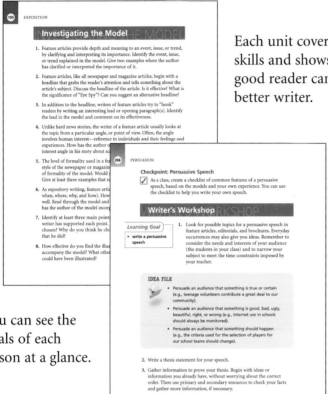

Each unit covers reading skills and shows how being a good reader can make you a better writer.

We've included lots of activities that allow you to practise new skills.

You can see the goals of each lesson at a glance.

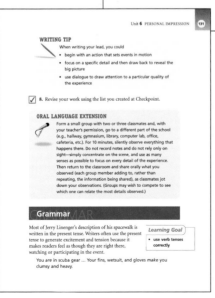

Extend your reading and writing assignment to include listening and speaking skills.

Grammar, Mechanics & Design, Usage & Style, and Word Study & Spelling lessons are related directly to the models and/or to the writing tasks you're working on.

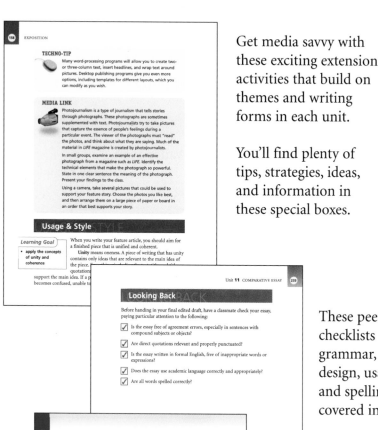

Get media savvy with these exciting extension activities that build on themes and writing forms in each unit.

You'll find plenty of tips, strategies, ideas, and information in these special boxes.

These peer-editing checklists highlight grammar, mechanics, design, usage, style, and spelling topics covered in each unit.

At the end of each section, you get a chance to review and apply what you've learned about the genre.

Contents

Description 88

Becoming an Effective Writer

Writing is easy; all you do is sit staring at a blank sheet
of paper until the drops of blood form on your forehead.

—Gene Fowler

Author Gene Fowler's comment about writing does not seem overstated to
anyone who has sat waiting for the words to come. Few things are more
intimidating than a blank sheet of paper. And few things are more
frustrating than a page filled with words that don't say what you mean.
These feelings of fear and frustration usually result when people think of
writing as a kind of dictation—simply recording on paper the ideas they
already have in their heads. But writing is not merely the act of recording
what you know—it is a *process* by which you *discover* what you know,
identify what you need to learn more about, and find ways to share your
understanding with others. As novelist E. M. Forster put it, "How do I know
what I think until I see what I say?"

The Writing Process

No two authors write in exactly the same way. For example, some authors
need to plan in great detail what they will write before attempting a first
draft, while others prefer to begin writing the first draft as soon as possible
to discover what it is they need to learn about their topic. However, most
completed pieces of writing have gone through similar stages, which are
illustrated in the diagram on the facing page.

At this point in your schooling, you already know that the five stages
shown in the diagram on the following page seldom, if ever, occur in
isolated, sequential steps. The diagram illustrates that writing is more often
a recursive process in which the writer flips back and forth between these
stages. For example, many writers revise their writing while in the process
of drafting their pieces, and most writers find and correct writing errors
long before they have a final draft ready to be proofread. Sometimes writers
are in the middle of a draft when they discover that they need to collect
more information about their topic before they can proceed. They may
even discover while revising a piece that it really doesn't accomplish what
they initially set out to do, and they have to go back and rethink what their
original purpose was. All of this is part of the process of writing—and the
process of becoming an effective writer.

However, writing is not the sort of subject where following a set of rules will automatically bring success. Going through the process is not an end in itself; it is a means to the end of communicating effectively with the reader. To achieve that goal takes time, practice, and an attention to detail that will transform your half-formed ideas into strong, clear, understandable prose. Success will come as you look for opportunities to develop the characteristics of strong writing.

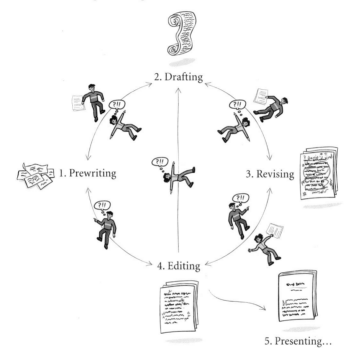

Strong Writing

Strong writing has a definite purpose and presents information and ideas that achieve this purpose. Note how the following excerpt from a physical activity leaflet proves that adopting a physically active lifestyle is easier than you may think:

> Physical activity doesn't have to be hard. Build physical activities into your daily routine.
>
> - Walk whenever you can—get off the bus early; use the stairs instead of the elevator.
> - Reduce inactivity for long periods, like watching TV.
> - Get up from the couch and stretch and bend for a few minutes every hour.

- Play actively with your kids.
- Choose to walk, wheel, or cycle for short trips.
- Start with a 10-minute walk—gradually increase the time.
- Find out about walking and cycling paths nearby and use them.
- Observe a physical activity class to see if you want to try it.
- Try one class to start; you don't have to make a long-term commitment.
- Do the activities you are doing now, more often.

Strong writing adds to the experience of the reader by saying something new, or something old in a new way. For example, here is how astronaut Jerry Linenger describes an experience most of us will never have (walking in space) in terms all of us can relate to.

> You need to work with your hands. You let go. You depend on the two tethers you placed on handholds to hold. You rotate, twist, and float—all randomly and uncontrolled—still the cliff is falling and rotating. You know you are falling with it; you tell yourself surely you are falling with it because you just attached your tethers; yet it is difficult to discount the sensation that you are moving away, alone, detached. You feel as if you are at the end of a fishing pole, which gets longer and longer and thinner and thinner at the end, and you, the fish, are hooked to its flimsy end. It sways back and forth; you, being attached, sway back and forth. The pole no longer looks rigid and straight, but rather like a skinny S-curve. You are hanging to the thinnest limb of the tallest tree in the wind. The tree is falling. You convince yourself that it is a strong oak, that the limb will stay attached and not fracture, and that the forest bottom is far away.

Strong writing has structure—a definite beginning, middle, and end, and a logical progression from one to the next. Events or ideas unfold in a sequence that makes sense to the reader because the writer has taken care to make connections between what has come before and what will follow. Note how the use of transitional expressions in the following passage helps to move the writing smoothly from one idea to another.

> Another cause of resistance is the overuse of antibiotics in agriculture, where they are routinely fed to livestock. Farmers do this for two reasons. First, they are used to cure diseases in animals. Second, they are added to livestock feed to make the animals grow bigger.

Strong writing has voice, the sense of one person speaking to another. The writer's tone, syntax, and word choice reflect the unique personality of the person behind the pen or word processor. The following ironic account of how one student discovered her talent as a procrastinator reveals a clear, recognizable, individual voice.

> It was shortly after I began high school that I realized I was a natural procrastinator. Soon after I made this discovery, others began to notice my penchant for putting things off. My skills really surfaced in grade nine when I was given a French project. My teacher assigned the project in February. It was due in May. I did not work on it in February and March because ... well, it was too cold. In April it was rainy and in May, a week before the project was due, it was warm. Finally, the night before I had to present my project, I got to work. I researched, wrote up, translated, and created an attractive poster, all after dinner (because a *Family Ties* rerun was on after school). I worked two hours past my bedtime. My life as a true procrastinator had begun.

Strong writing reveals a sense of audience. Appealing to the reader's interests or needs, providing sufficient information to make a point of view understandable, and fine-tuning arguments to make them appealing to the uninformed, uninterested, or even hostile reader are all aspects of this type of writing. In this opening paragraph of a feature article, the writer draws his readers' attention by describing a common frustration.

> By now, you are buried in passwords. There's one for your PC, one for your ATM [automated teller machine] card, one for your long-distance calling card, one for your voice mail, one for your Internet-access account. And that's before you even start talking about all the passwords you use on the Internet for everything from buying books, to checking e-mail, to trading stocks. On and on and on it goes. A seemingly endless stream of secret codes designed to tell the multiplying machines in your life that you are you.

Strong writing is concrete and selective, relying on specific nouns and verbs and using modifiers sparingly. Note the emphasis placed on concrete words in this screen adaptation of *Romeo and Juliet*.

> With the diva's spiraling final notes, the ballad concludes. The crowd cheers and screams in applause. An avalanche of balloons, tinsel, and

confetti rains down from the roof. The light dims. Juliet has her back against the arch, her eyes search the darkness, but the boy is gone.

CLOSE ON: Juliet. Suddenly: A gasp; Juliet's eyes widen, shocked. In the dark, a hand has shot out from the folds of cloth in the curtained archway and clasped hers. Juliet barely dares breathe.

She glances furtively to Dave Paris. He watches the stage.

Slowly, Juliet turns toward the hand; there through a break in the curtain she can see eye, cheek, and lips of the mystery boy. As the diva continues her curtain call, Romeo, ignoring the dangerous proximity of Dave Paris, manoeuvres his lips to almost touch Juliet's ear. He whispers as he brings her hands to his lips.

Strong writing is colourful. It "shows" rather than "tells," using examples, comparisons, and figurative language to paint vivid mental pictures of its subject. The following short-story excerpt uses all three methods to convey a powerful impression of a recurring nightmare.

He'd be doing something ordinary—getting off a bus, walking up his front steps—when he would catch a flicker of movement from the corner of his eye. He'd turn, and there'd be a glimpse of something dark sliding around a corner or dipping down behind a wall.

The glimpse always shot him through with a bolt of white terror. He would back up, turn around, edge off in another direction. But if he fled the house, it would be lurking in the yard. Get back on the bus, and it would come snuffling at the automatic door. Try to outrun it, and he would feel its breath bursting hot on the back of his neck.

At the end he would be trapped, hedged in, the bear stalking closer and closer. That was the worst part: it seemed to *enlarge* itself toward him, like a dark balloon swelling across his field of vision, or as if he were a lost spacewalker falling toward a vast dark planet.

And then, the instant before it touched him, when he was sprung tight as a musical saw, there'd come a high-pitched whine, loud enough to make his teeth buzz, and he would burst out of the dream, sweating and gasping, his muscles weak as blue milk.

Strong writing is rhythmic, flowing smoothly from one sentence to the next with the natural cadence of human expression. Strong writing avoids repetition—except for effect—by including a variety of sentence lengths and beginnings. Note the rhythm of the language used in the following speech:

Books have been written about the courage shown in war; and soldiers, sailors, and fliers deserve all the honour they receive. Often they spent years in peril, fighting to preserve freedom.

But most of your acts of bravery took place without the clash of war, and without the stimulus that self-defence can give to courage. You had little if any help, little to gain, and possibly a life to lose. More than the bravery of battle, you showed the courage of giving and self-sacrifice; and that can be an equal or a greater courage.

Some of you may say that others would have acted as bravely. But the rest of us can never be certain. The hope of courage lies in every heart, together with the fear that we will fail.

The true hallmark of strong writing, of course, is the connection it establishes with the reader. Strong writing elicits responses such as "Of *course!* That's *exactly* what I saw/heard/felt/tasted/smelled"; "Hey! I've never *thought* of that"; "I wish *I'd* written that"; "How does this writer know me/my family/my life so well?" The 12 units in this book are designed to assist you in strengthening your own writing so that it elicits responses similar to these.

Accurate Writing

In addition to all these characteristics is another, equally important attribute of strong writing: technical accuracy. Like static that distorts music on a radio, errors hinder the communication of ideas in a piece of writing because they draw the reader's attention away from the content. Trying to identify the significant point in a convoluted sentence or attempting to decipher misspelled words interrupts the flow of meaning and can lessen the overall impact of a piece. Paying attention to the conventions of grammar, mechanics, usage, style, and spelling helps ensure that a piece will achieve its intended purpose.

Unfortunately, these finishing touches can often be as daunting to writers as the blank page they started with. That is why the units that follow contain short lessons and activities that are related to the model and your writing task. As you work through the various components of each writing assignment in the units that follow, you will see that strong writing comes with practice and determination. Just as a basketball rookie improves his or her skills with each lay-up, each foul shot, each defensive manoeuvre, so too will you improve your skills at writing strong narrative, descriptive, expository, and persuasive pieces.

Narration

Narration, the telling of a story, is an integral part of the human experience. Few of us will write the "great Canadian novel," but every one of us tells stories daily, whether recounting a humorous anecdote over coffee or sharing in an e-mail an event that has personal significance. We tell stories not only to convey information about an experience but often to make sense of it—in effect, to make sense of the world around us.

This section contains three different forms of narrative writing: ballad, short story, and excerpt of a film adaptation of a literary work. Although they look distinct on the page and are written about different subjects and from different perspectives, they all engage the reader in the process of discovering "what happened next."

Features of Narration

- A narrative is a story developed from an event or series of events.
- Narratives usually involve a character in conflict.
- Details of character, setting, conflict, and plot are usually chosen and ordered in such a way as to develop a main theme or idea.
- The beginning of the narrative usually establishes the characters, setting, and mood.
- The middle of the narrative describes events in which the character deals with the main conflict and other minor conflicts.
- The end of the narrative usually tells how the conflict is resolved.

Learning Goals

- use a range of sources to gather information and explore ideas for your written work
- identify and use literary forms appropriately in writing a ballad, a short story, and a film adaptation of a literary work
- use a variety of organizational techniques to present ideas and information logically and coherently
- revise your written work independently and collaboratively to improve clarity, coherence, and style
- edit and proofread to produce final drafts using correct grammar, mechanics, usage, and spelling
- use knowledge of vocabulary and language conventions to write competently and effectively
- develop listening, speaking, and media literacy skills
- read a variety of fiction, such as ballads, short stories, and film adaptations
- identify and understand the elements and style of a variety of fiction

Unit ① Ballad

What is a ballad?

A ballad is a poem that tells a story in a simple but dramatic way. In the past, ballads were sung as a means of passing along stories from generation to generation. The traditional ballad form later evolved to include literary ballads. Included in this unit are three ballads: the first two were written in the nineteenth century (although they are set in a much earlier time), while the third is a modern folk ballad.

Learning Goals

- write a ballad
- identify and use parts of speech correctly: nouns, verbs, adjectives, and adverbs
- use commas correctly
- investigate the use of metre in poetry
- use a dictionary to find the etymology of a word

Lochinvar

BY SIR WALTER SCOTT

O, young Lochinvar is come out of the west,
Through all the wide Border his steed was the best;
And save his good broadsword he weapons had none,
He rode all unarm'd, and he rode all alone.
So faithful in love, and so dauntless in war,
There never was knight like the young Lochinvar.

He staid not for brake, and he stopp'd not for stone.
He swam the Eske river where ford there was none;
But ere he alighted at Netherby gate,
The bride had consented, the gallant came late;
For a laggard in love, and a dastard in war,
Was to wed the fair Ellen of brave Lochinvar.

So boldly he enter'd the Netherby Hall,
Among bride's-men, and kinsmen, and brothers, and all:
Then spoke the bride's father, his hand on his sword,
(For the poor craven bridegroom said never a word.)
"O come ye in peace here, or come ye in war,
Or to dance at our bridal, young Lord Lochinvar?"

"I long woo'd your daughter, my suit you denied;—
Love swells like the Solway, but ebbs like its tide—
And now am I come, with this lost love of mine,
To lead but one measure, drink one cup of wine.
There are maidens in Scotland more lovely by far,
That would gladly be bride to the young Lochinvar."

The bride kiss'd the goblet: the knight took it up,
He quaff'd off the wine, and he threw down the cup.
She look'd down to blush, and she look'd up to sigh,
With a smile on her lips, and a tear in her eye.
He took her soft hand, ere her mother could bar,—
"Now tread we a measure!" said young Lochinvar.

So stately his form, and so lovely her face,
That never a hall such a galliard did grace;
While her mother did fret, and her father did fume,
And the bridegroom stood dangling his bonnet and plume.
And the bride-maidens whisper'd, " 'Twere better by far,
To have match'd our fair cousin with young Lochinvar."

One touch to her hand, and one word in her ear,
When they reach'd the hall door, and the charger stood near;
So light to the croupe the fair lady he swung,
So light to the saddle before her he sprung!
"She is won! we are gone, over bank, bush, and scaur;
They'll have fleet steeds that follow," quoth young Lochinvar.

There was mounting 'mong Graemes of the Netherby clan;
Forsters, Fenwicks, and Musgraves, they rode and they ran:
There was racing and chasing on Cannobie Lee,
But the lost bride of Netherby ne'er did they see.
So daring in love, and so dauntless in war,
Have ye e'er heard of gallant like young Lochinvar?— ■

Love Me, Love My Dog

BY ISABELLA VALANCY CRAWFORD

He had a falcon on his wrist,
    A hound beside his knee:
A jewelled rapier at his thigh,
    Quoth he, "Which may she be?"
My chieftain cried, "Bear forth, my page,
    This ring to Lady Clare,

Thou'lt know her by her sunny eyes,
    And golden lengths of hair;"
But here are lovely damsels, three,
    In glitt'ring coif and veil;
And all have sunny locks and eyes—
    To which unfold the tale?"

Out spake the first, "O pretty page,
    Thou hast a wealthy lord:
I love to see the jewels rare
    Which deck thy slender sword!"
She smil'd, she wav'd her yellow locks,
    Rich damask glow'd her cheek.
He bent his supple knee, and thought—
    "She's not the maid I seek."
The second had a cheek of rose,
    A throat as white as milk;
A jewell'd tire upon her brow,
    A robe and veil of silk.

"O pretty page hold back the hound,
    Uncouth is he and bold:
His rough caress will tear my veil:
    My fringe of glitt'ring gold."
She frown'd, she pouted ruby lips:
    The page he did not speak:
He bent his curly head and thought
    "She's not the maid I seek."

The third, with cobweb locks of light,
    And cheeks like summer dawn,
Dropped on her knee beside the hound,
    Upon the shaven lawn.
She kiss'd his sinewy throat, she strok'd
    His bristly rings of hair:
"Ho," thought the page, "she loves his hound,
    So this is Lady Clare!" ∎

The Jeannie C.

BY STAN ROGERS

Come all ye lads draw near by me
    that I be not forsaken
This day was lost the Jeannie C.
    and my living has been taken.
I'll go to sea no more.

Now it's well you know what the fishing has been—
    it's been scarce and hard and cruel
But this day, by God, we sure caught cod,
    and we sang and we laughed like fools.
I'll go to sea no more.

I'll never know what it was we struck,
    but strike we did like thunder
John Price give a cry and pitched overside.
    Now it's forever he's gone under.
I'll go to sea no more.

A leak we've sprung, let there be no delay
    if the Jeannie C. we're saving
John Price is drown'd and slip'd away.
    So I'll patch the hole while you're bailing.
I'll go to sea no more.

But no leak I found from bow to hold.
    No rock it was that got her.
But what I found made me heart stop cold,
    for every seam poured water.
I'll go to sea no more.

My God, I cried as she went down.
    That boat was like no other
My father built her when I was nine,
    and named her for my mother.
I'll go to sea no more.

And sure I could have another made
    in the boat shop down in Dover
But I would not love the keel they laid
    like the one the waves roll over.
I'll go to sea no more.

So come all ye lads, draw near to me,
    that I be not forsaken
This day was lost the Jeannie C.,
    and my whole life has been taken.
I'll go to sea no more. ■

Investigating the Models

IDEA FILE

It may help you to know these terms as you read and discuss the ballads in this unit:

Stanza: a group of lines in a poem whose content and form distinguish them as a single unit

Rhyme scheme: the pattern of similar-sounding words used at the end of lines of verse

Refrain: lines repeated at intervals in a poem

1. A ballad tells a dramatic story in a simple, direct style. Briefly summarize the narratives presented in the three models.

2. Many traditional ballads begin with a climactic episode and then briefly sketch the setting, action, and people involved. Read all three ballads again and determine whether the poets have structured their narratives in this manner.

3. Typically, the narrator of a ballad tells the story tersely, without expressing his or her personal attitudes or feelings. Is this true of the models? Explain why or why not.

4. Ballads may be written in the first or third person. How is the point of view of the first two ballads different from that of "The Jeannie C."? What impact does the point of view chosen have on the telling of these stories?

5. The narrative of a ballad often depends largely on action and dialogue. To what extent is this true of the models? Explain.

6. Traditional ballads often employ clichéd phrases such as "blood-red wine" and "milk-white steed." Do the models include such expressions? Explain.

WRITING TIP

A **cliché** is a phrase that has been used so often that it appears trite. Sometimes writers use clichés intentionally to establish a sense of time and place, or to convey a particular impression of a character. However, because the use of a cliché often suggests a lack of originality on the part of the writer, it is generally better to avoid these phrases and invent fresh, original expressions.

7. Diction is the choice of words a writer or speaker makes to convey meaning. How does the diction in the first two ballads evoke the romantic ideal of chivalry common to medieval Europe?

8. Folk ballads are often characterized by informal diction to achieve a natural, conversational tone. Is this true of "The Jeannie C."? Explain.

9. Repetition is characteristic of many traditional ballads and may be used to emphasize a particular detail or impression, or to convey a tone. Identify examples of repetition in the models and comment on their effect.

10. The rhyme scheme of a typical ballad stanza is a quatrain: four lines in which the second and fourth lines rhyme (abcb). Is this true of the models? Explain.

Checkpoint: Ballad

 As a class, create a checklist of common features of ballads, based on the models and your own experience. You can use the checklist to help you create your own ballad.

Writer's Workshop

1. Brainstorm several events—happy, sad, or even funny—that have appeared in local, national, or international news and have caught your attention. From these, choose one you feel is worthy of being immortalized in a ballad.

2. Consider the "5 W's + H" questions and summarize in point form the details you recall about this event. Decide if you have enough information to proceed. If not, for further details, refer to newspapers, library vertical files, the Internet, and any other resources available to you.

Learning Goal

• **write a ballad**

3. Choose a point of view from which to recount the event. Will you speak directly to your reader, or will you use the voice of a person actually involved in the event?

4. Consider how you might organize the information about your event. Will you begin with a climactic episode and then briefly sketch the setting, action, and people involved, or does another method of organization suggest itself? Using whatever plan seems appropriate, outline the content of your ballad.

5. Write a draft of your ballad, making certain to rhyme the second and fourth lines of each stanza.

6. Decide whether a refrain will help underscore the impression of the event you wish to convey and/or the people involved. If so, write this refrain and decide where it might be used to best advantage.

☑ 7. Revise your ballad using the list you created at Checkpoint.

TECHNO-TIP

If you type your work on a computer, try experimenting with the fonts you have available to find one that suits the tone and subject matter of your ballad. For example, many computers have fonts that recreate handwriting or old English lettering.

𝕿𝖍𝖎𝖘 𝖎𝖘 𝕲𝖔𝖚𝖉𝖞 𝕿𝖊𝖝𝖙.

This is Monoline Script.

This is Nuptial Script.

ORAL LANGUAGE EXTENSION

Designed for singing or oral presentation, early ballads were an important means of passing along stories from group to group and from generation to generation. In fact, in the eighteenth century, ballads dealing with sensational subject matter were printed on large, double-columned sheets of paper that included a suggested tune and were sold for a penny. These "penny ballads" served the function of our modern tabloids. Many early ballads—and modern ones such as "The Jeannie C."—are available on CD.

Working in a group of four or five, choose either "Love Me, Love My Dog" or "Lochinvar" (or your teacher may assign you another ballad) and read it aloud several times, listening to the rhythmical pattern of the lines. Then, choose a well-known song whose melody you feel would be suitable for the ballad. (Besides current tunes, consider traditional music, especially songs for young children that follow a simple rhythmical pattern.) Practise performing the ballad, making use of musical instruments and costumes if you feel this will add to your presentation, and then perform it for the class.

Grammar

There are eight main word classes, or **parts of speech**. The four most important are nouns, verbs, adjectives, and adverbs.

A **noun** is a word that names a person, place, thing, quality, or idea.

Lochinvar   Scotland   sonnet   love

1. Make a chart with the following headings: People, Places, Things, and Qualities and Ideas. Find the nouns in the three models and list them under the appropriate headings. Which column has the fewest entries? Which has the most?

Learning Goal

- **identify and use parts of speech correctly: nouns, verbs, adjectives, and adverbs**

A **verb** is a word that shows action (**action verb**) or a state of being (**linking verb**). Sometimes a verb may be made up of more than one word: a main verb and one or more **helping** (or **auxiliary**) **verbs**.

He **swam** the Eske river where ford there *was* none.

   action   *state of being*

This day was lost the Jeannie C. and my living *has been* **taken**.

                                         helping verb   **main verb**

2. Find at least three other lines in the models that contain action verbs, three that contain linking verbs, and three that contain helping verbs.

Adjectives and **adverbs** are modifiers, words that give information about other elements in a sentence.

An **adjective** describes or tells about a noun or pronoun while an **adverb** describes a verb, an adjective, or another adverb. When describing verbs, adverbs tell *how, when,* or *where.*

Adjectives: "Thou'lt know her by her **sunny** eyes, /
And **golden** lengths of hair;"

Adverbs: So **boldly** he enter'd the Netherby Hall,
(modifies *enter'd*)

"There are maidens in Scotland **more** lovely by far,"
(modifies *lovely*)

3. Find three lines in the models that contain modifiers. Tell whether the modifiers are adjectives or adverbs, and identify the words they modify.

Many words can act as different parts of speech depending on the way they are used in a sentence.

I *love* to see the jewels rare.   (*love* is a verb)

My *love* I do intend to share.   (*love* is a noun)

4. Identify the part of speech of each of the boldface words. Then write another sentence using the same word as a different part of speech. Identify the new part of speech.

a) My chieftain cried, "Bear forth, my page, / This **ring** to Lady Clare."
b) But here are lovely damsels, three, / In glitt'ring coif and **veil**.
c) He **bent** his supple knee, and thought— / "She's not the maid I seek."
d) "His rough **caress** will tear my veil."
e) Through all the wide **Border** his steed was the best.
f) "And now am I come, with this lost love of mine, / To lead but one
       measure, drink one cup of wine."
g) The bride had consented, the gallant came **late**.
h) "I **long** woo'd your daughter, my suit you denied";—
i) Come all ye lads, **draw** near by me / that I be not forsaken.

MEDIA LINK

Events in a story are not always presented in the order in
which they occur. Some stories begin with the events in the
middle of the story and then go back in time to fill in the
necessary plot details. This technique is called "flashback."
Occasionally the reader or viewer is allowed a glimpse of the
future in a "flashforward." Film conventions such as dissolves,
soft-focus effects, or fades indicate that a time change is
coming up. Name some films you have seen that use flashback
or flashforward and discuss the reasons these techniques may
have been used.

In small groups, create a storyboard for one of the ballads you
have written, for one of the models, or for another ballad you
know. Mark on the storyboard the most visually exciting
moment in the story and rearrange your storyboard to start at
this point. What film conventions will you use to show that the
events after this new introduction are flashbacks? Could you
possibly use a flashforward? Why or why not?

Mechanics & Design

Because writers use commas more than any other form of punctuation, it is
important to recognize their many uses. Here are some of the most
important uses of the comma.

Use	Example
Between items in a series	Scott, Crawford, and Rogers wrote their ballads in very different times.
To replace the word *and* between two or more adjectives	The first two poems look back to a romantic, unrealistic world of chivalry and high adventure.
After an introductory group of several words	On the other hand, Stan Rogers tells a sad but realistic tale about the life of a fisherman.
To set off words that interrupt a flow of thought	"The Jeannie C.," though written in the late twentieth century, is typical of a lot of older ballads that tell about tragedies and mishaps.
To separate two complete sentences joined by *and, but, or, nor, so,* or *yet*	He staid not for brake, and he stopp'd not for stone.
To separate words or expressions that refer to the same person or thing	Isabella Valancy Crawford, now considered an important nineteenth-century Canadian poet, was virtually unknown during her lifetime.
To separate a subordinate clause from the main clause that follows it	While Stan Rogers and Sir Walter Scott lived in different times and places, they were both concerned with preserving the history and heritage of their respective countries through their writing.

1. Because Sir Walter Scott wrote in the late eighteenth and early nineteenth centuries, his use of punctuation is quite different from that found in contemporary writing. Find at least two commas in "Lochinvar" that you feel are unnecessary. Explain why you feel the commas are not needed.

Learning Goal

• use commas correctly

2. There are other rules for using commas that have not been discussed above. Working with a partner, write at least two other rules and make up sentences illustrating each. Compare your findings with other groups and make a note of any rules you may have overlooked.

WRITING TIP

Sometimes, people use *too many* commas. Do **not** use commas

- to separate a verb from its subject or object
- before or after a list
- to separate a string of adjectives (except to replace the word *and*)
- to separate an adjective from the noun it modifies

3. Referring to the writing tip above, work with a partner to identify 10 unnecessary commas in the following passage. Then share your work with another group to see if you agree.

Sir Walter Scott, one of the leading, literary figures of the romantic period, was born in Edinburgh, Scotland, on August 15, 1771. The son of educated, middle-class, parents, Scott was seriously ill as a child and, confined to his bed, he became an avid, reader. He was particularly fond of Scottish legends, and heroic ballads, and these latter played a major role, in his writing. In fact, his three-volume *Minstrels of the Scottish Border* is a collection of ballads from Scottish oral tradition. Many of his poems, including "Lady of the Lake," are among the most popular romantic ballads, ever written. In 1810, he was offered the poet laureateship of England, but he declined this honour. As he, continued to write poetry, Scott focused more, and more on character, and eventually turned to prose, writing several, popular novels including *Waverley, Ivanhoe,* and *Rob Roy.*

Usage & Style

Metre is the rhythmical pattern of stressed and unstressed syllables used in poetry.

Of course, not all poetry follows a metrical pattern. In **free verse**, for example, the poet tries to capture the flow of natural speech. With its close ties to music, however, it is not surprising that the ballad is often associated with a strong metre.

Learning Goal

• **investigate the use of metre in poetry**

The **foot** is the basic metrical unit of poetry consisting of a set pattern of stressed and unstressed syllables. Note the pattern of stressed and unstressed syllables that Isabella Valancy Crawford followed in writing "Love Me, Love My Dog":

Hĕ hád │ ă fál │ cŏn ′on │ h̆is wŕist,

Ă hoúnd │ bĕsíde │ h̆is kńee:

The most common metrical patterns used in poetry are identified below. Note the position of stressed syllables in relation to those that are unstressed.

Foot	Example
iambic	ŭn │ fóld
trochaic	slén │ dĕr
spondaic *	nó móre
anapestic	Lŏch │ ĭn │ vár
dactylic	sín │ ĕw │ y̆

* The spondaic foot cannot be the basic metre of a poem because it neither rises nor falls. Since all language has accented and unaccented syllables, the spondaic foot appears in poetry as a variation of other rhythmical patterns.

1. Which metrical foot does Crawford use in her ballad?

The metre of a poem depends on the number of feet a line of verse contains. These terms describe the number of feet in a line:

monometer:	one	**pentameter:**	five
dimeter:	two	**hexameter:**	six
trimeter:	three	**heptameter:**	seven
tetrameter:	four	**octameter:**	eight

Therefore, the metre of a poem is described in terms of the type and number of feet per line. For example, much of Shakespeare's writing and poetry can be described as iambic pentameter.

The typical ballad stanza includes alternating lines of **tetrameter** and **trimeter** verse, meaning that the first and third lines usually contain four accented syllables, while the second and fourth lines contain three.

2. Read "Love Me, Love My Dog" aloud and listen for the tetrameter and trimeter verse patterns of Crawford's ballad. Then, copy eight lines of the ballad and mark the feet as well as the stressed and unstressed syllables in each line.

3. Choose either "Lochinvar" or "The Jeannie C." and, working with a partner, select a stanza from the ballad. Take turns reading the lines aloud, listening for the pattern of stressed and unstressed syllables. Write the lines with the stresses marked, and identify the metre of the ballad.

WRITING TIP

Poets often use contractions such as *ne'er* (never) to change the emphasis of syllables. Poets also rearrange the usual order of words to achieve a specific pattern of stressed and unstressed syllables. Read the following passage aloud:

But here are three lovely damsels

Now read aloud the arrangement that appears in "Love Me, Love My Dog," noting the difference in the rhythm of the words:

But here are lovely damsels, three

When writing poetry, try using contractions and rearranging your words in various ways to achieve a particular rhythm or rhyme scheme.

4. Find at least three examples in the models where the poets have arranged words in an unusual order to conform to a rhyme pattern or metre. Rewrite them in a more familiar order and try rereading the poem with the new arrangement. What happens to the metre? Now try writing another line that the poet could have used, using the proper metre. Share your revision with a classmate.

5. Read your ballad aloud and determine whether you have followed a regular pattern of stressed and unstressed syllables. If not, try using contractions, adding and omitting words, and rearranging their order.

Word Study & Spelling

WORD STUDY & SPELLING

Learning Goal

- use a dictionary to find the etymology of a word

A dictionary entry gives far more information than the correct spelling and meaning of a word. Along with these important features, a dictionary may also provide details about the word's pronunciation, hyphenation, part of speech, related words, and etymology. **Etymology** is the study of the origin of words; an etymological entry, therefore, tells you where a word comes from and what its original meaning may have been. Note the etymology of the word *damask*, which Isabella Valancy Crawford uses to mean "of a red colour."

She smil'd, she wav'd her yellow locks,

Rich *damask* glow'd her cheek.

---

damask, *dam' ask, n.* figured stuff, originally of silk, now usually of linen, the figure being woven, not printed : Damascus steel or its surface pattern. —*adj.* of a red colour, like that of a damask rose.—*n.* **damascene** (*dam' a sen*), (*cap.*) a native of Damascus: a Damascus sword : inlay of metal (esp. gold) on steel.—*v.t.* to decorate metal (esp. steel) by inlaying or encrusting : to ornament with the wavy appearance of Damascus steel—also **damascene**, **damaskeen**.—*ns.* **dam'ask-plum**, the damson; **dam'ask-rose**, a species of pink rose. [From *Damascus*, in Syria, where damask was originally made.]

Most dictionaries use abbreviations to show the origins of words. The following are only a few of these abbreviations:

Brit.	British	**L**	Latin
Cdn.	Canadian	**ME**	Middle English
Du.	Dutch	**OE**	Old English (before 1100)
F	French	**OF**	Old French (before 1400)
G	German	**Pg.**	Portuguese
Gk.	Greek	**Scand.**	Scandinavian
Ital.	Italian	**Sp.**	Spanish

1. Use a dictionary to find the etymology of the following words from the models:

   a) rapier   b) ring   c) tale   d) forsaken
   e) uncouth   f) fringe   g) scaur   h) lawn
   i) kiss   j) knight   k) dastard   l) woo
   m) coif   n) tire   o) keel

2. The origins of the words *craven* and *quaff* are obscure, meaning that no one is certain where they came from. Working with a partner, invent etymological entries for these words. Share these with the class to determine whose entry is the most logical, whose is the most creative, whose is the most humorous, etc.

WORD ORIGINS

"O, come ye in peace here, or come ye in war ..."

The word **ye** is derived from the Old English word *ge* and is an archaic plural form of the word *you*. **Archaic** words are words that are no longer commonly spoken; however, authors—especially those who write historical fiction—may use them to create a sense of a previous time. Find the meanings of the following archaic words used in the models, and then write sentences using their modern equivalents.

quoth   thou   spake   staid   brake

Looking Back

Before handing in your final edited draft, have a classmate check your ballad, paying particular attention to the following:

- ✓ Has the poet used commas appropriately?

- ✓ Has the poet maintained a particular metre and rhyme scheme?

- ✓ Has the poet used appropriate language and vocabulary?

- ✓ Are all words spelled correctly?

Unit 2 Short Story

What is a short story?

A short story is a work of prose fiction that presents a main character involved in a single episode that begins, develops, and ends in a limited space. In sharing this character's experience, in particular the manner in which the character responds to the conflict central to the event, the short-story writer conveys an understanding about life and living known as the story's theme. In his story "Bearing Up," author Matt Hughes portrays the anxiety of a young man who must confront his greatest fear.

Learning Goals

- write a short story
- use parts of speech correctly: pronouns, prepositions, conjunctions, and interjections
- punctuate and capitalize dialogue correctly
- identify the point of view in a narrative
- use a dictionary to identify the pronunciation of a word

Bearing Up

BY MATT HUGHES

HE WOULD KICK AND YELL HIS WAY OUT OF DREAMS WHERE the bear was after him, his chest cold and sweat-slick, breath bellowing. When he was little, the noise brought Mom or Dad to check on him, tuck him back in, kiss the bad stuff away.

At fifteen, he didn't want his parents coming to his rescue—well, maybe he wanted it a little, but it would have bent his self-image. So it was enough if Mom called out, "Are you okay, Mike?" from across the hall, and he would call back, "Yeah, I'm okay."

He would hear them mumbling about him, but in the morning, nobody made a big deal about it.

He'd been having the bear dream for as long as he could recall, although it didn't start out as a bear. Back when he was a kid, it had been dinosaurs: dagger-toothed tyrannosaurs hopping through the patio doors, hunting him across the family room at the old house in Ottawa.

Another time, a golden-eyed tiger glided after him into the garage, and once, when he was really little, the Cookie Monster had shadowed him around the day care, all goggle-eyed and blue-shaggy, peering at him from behind the activity centre.

But, by the time he was into his teens, it was the bear. It would come for him every five or six months; not that he could count on it to keep to a schedule, so sometimes it could be twice in the same week. The settings would vary, but never the sequence of events.

He'd be doing something ordinary—getting off a bus, walking up his front steps—when he would catch a flicker of movement from the corner of his eye. He'd turn, and there'd be a glimpse of something dark sliding around a corner or dipping down behind a wall.

The glimpse always shot him through with a bolt of white terror. He would back up, turn around, edge off in another direction. But if he fled the house, it would be lurking in the yard. Get back on the bus, and it would come snuffling at the automatic door. Try to outrun it, and he would feel its breath bursting hot on the back of his neck.

At the end he would be trapped, hedged in, the bear stalking closer and closer. That was the worst part: it seemed to *enlarge* itself toward him, like a dark balloon swelling across his field of vision, or as if he were a lost spacewalker falling toward a vast dark planet.

And then, the instant before it touched him, when he was sprung tight as a musical saw, there'd come a high-pitched whine, loud enough to make his teeth buzz, and he would burst out of the dream, sweating and gasping, his muscles weak as blue milk.

*   *   *

He'd once asked the school counsellor if she knew anything about dreams.

"Well, of course, I'm influenced by Jung," said Mrs. Skinner, interrupting her perpetual search for order in the jumble on her desk, which was crammed into a former supplies closet beside the washrooms. Mike stood, because the visitor's chair was buried in books in which adults explained exactly what you had to do to be a successful teenager.

"Okay," Mike said.

She located a form printed on blue paper, lifted her eyeglasses to squint at it, then tucked it into a yellow file folder. "That means I view the psyche as being fundamentally fragmented," she continued.

"Okay," he said again, edging toward the door.

She closed the yellow file, then re-opened it. She took out the blue paper, peered at it again, then slipped it into a red folder, and looked up at Mike.

"How do I put this?" she asked herself. "Jung's idea was that each of us is a collection of different people inside our heads—like your personality is made up of different pieces that mesh together, well, more or less. When they don't mesh properly, that's trouble."

"Trouble like scary dreams, like where something's chasing you?"

"Uh huh," she said, picking up a green form, and frowning at it as if willing it to change colour. "A monster in a dream might be some part of you that frightens you, some fear that your unconscious wants you to deal with, maybe, and so one part of you is trying to get in touch, to get you to look at the problem. But you don't want to so you run from it, but you can't get away."

"So what do I do?" Mike asked.

"Stop running. After all, anything or anybody you meet in a dream is only another part of you, so what's to be afraid of?" She peered up at him through filmed lenses. "Is there something you want to talk about?"

He had a feeling that if he started talking about the bear with Mrs. Skinner, he'd find himself wandering into parts of the forest he wasn't ready to deal with yet. Things would come up. Things like leaving all his friends behind, like being lonely, like not fitting in. Like being scared and not knowing why.

This was the small town of Comox, at the end of a little stub of land that hung off the east coast of Vancouver Island into Georgia Strait. It was home to a few thousand people, many of them attached to the air force base at the landward end of the peninsula.

Three squadrons operated out of CFB Comox. One flew the big, grey submarine-hunting Auroras that wheeled over town on four throbbing turbo-props, their fuselages so jam-packed with electronic detection gear that the crew could spot a Coke can half-submerged in the Pacific from a mile high. Or so he'd heard kids at school saying.

Another squadron flew forty-year-old T-33 jet trainers, the same machines that every serving pilot in the Canadian Forces learned to fly in, the fast-movers that zoomed up from the base and out over the harbour, with torpedo-shaped pods at the ends of their stubby wings that made each one look like a flying *X*.

Whatever he might be doing, Mike stopped and looked up when the planes went over. Especially one bright morning when the air force aerobatics team appeared over Comox, for two weeks of practice. He couldn't believe how the local folks just kept puttering around in their gardens, not looking up as 10 red and white Snowbirds hurtled over their roofs, practising how to spiral up and loop down in tight turns, wing-tip to wing-tip, so fast and so just right.

Mike's father was neither a jet-jockey nor a sub-hunter. He had been posted to the third group operating out of CFB Comox, the historic 442 Search and Rescue squadron. He was an air force SARtech—a specialist, he liked to say, "in getting people out of situations where if they had any sense they wouldn't have got themselves into them in the first place."

SARtechs went out in the slow-flying De Havilland Buffalo—big brother to the tough little Twin Otters that the bush pilots used to open the Canadian north—or in the lumbering, two-rotor Labrador helicopters. If a fisherman abandoned a burning boat, the Lab would hover in the air so that Dad could jump into the cold sea, put a harness around the man before hypothermia killed him, and wait in the water while the victim was winched to safety, and they lowered the cable again to retrieve the SARtech.

It was dangerous work. Once, a Lab was picking stranded rock-climbers off a mountain. The shivering civilians had been lifted aboard, and the last rescuer was coming up the cable when an engine suddenly shuddered and died. With the Labrador at maximum payload, one rotor couldn't hold the helicopter in the air. It fell, crushing the life from the SARtech dangling beneath it.

Mike's father said there was no point thinking about it. Somebody had to go when people needed help; if it was risky, then it was risky, but somebody still had to go.

"It's not being a hero," Dad said. "It's just a job that's got to be done. It's *my* job."

"You didn't have to be a SARtech, though," Mike said. "You volunteered. You used to be a cook."

Dad shrugged. "Don't worry about it. Nothing's going to happen."

"But don't you get scared sometimes?"

"You don't let that get in the way." His father hunted around in his mind for a moment; he wasn't good with words. "You have to walk through the being scared part. 'Cause on the other side of scared is this other place where everything opens up, you feel really great, and ... and you're just *there*."

* * *

Mike's chore was the after-dinner dishes. He was methodically scrubbing fried rice off a Teflon-coated skillet whose powers of nonstickiness had long since been scratched away, and not thinking about anything much when he said, "Mom, do you worry when Dad goes out on a mission?"

His mother put three plates on the counter by the sink and looked through the archway into the living room, where Dad was watching the sports report on TV.

"I used to," she admitted, "but your father's very good at what he does." Then she sighed. "Besides, there's no point worrying. He loves it. He's not going to stop doing it. It's a big part of who he is."

"Pretty dangerous, though."

"Doesn't matter. It's what he does. What you and I have to do is live with it." She put a hand on Mike's arm. "Are you afraid he might get hurt ... or something?"

"Nah," Mike said. "I was just wondering how you felt."

* * *

On an afternoon late in September, a wind blew up—not a big wind, but big enough to whittle white points onto the grey-green chop of Georgia Strait. And that was too big for the comfort of four couples who had crowded into an undersized skiff to go hand-trolling for coho salmon three miles out from the boat launch at Point Holmes.

The boat owner, a welder who worked at Field's sawmill, decided it would be wise to head for shore. But when he pulled the lanyard on the outboard, it started, sputtered, and died. He did all the things he knew to do: checked the spark plug, checked the fuel line, checked the gas tank—and found it empty. He'd forgotten to fill up before launching.

By the time the skipper had identified the problem, the wind was brisking up, causing the overloaded skiff to wallow in steepening waves, shipping water over the gunwales.

He looked at the white faces of the three men and four women who had come out with him, without life jackets or even warm clothing, and said, "We're gonna row in. Break out the oars."

The oars were pulled from beneath the thwarts and run through the oarlocks, and the two strongest men tried to haul the boat shoreward. But the wind was offshore, and growing stronger as each long minute passed. Even with two men to an oar, the overloaded skiff barely made headway.

"We're in trouble," said the welder, watching the light fade behind thickening clouds, and reached for the emergency radio in the locker below his seat. Fortunately, he was more conscientious about the strength of the radio's batteries than the contents of the gas tank. When he tuned to the emergency channel, depressed the talk switch and said, "Mayday, mayday," CFB Comox came right back.

*   *   *

"I won't be home for supper," Dad said over the telephone. "There's some boaters in trouble." Five minutes later, they heard the Labrador racketing up from the base and heading out to sea.

An hour crawled by. Mike and his mother sat in the darkening kitchen, drinking coffee and trying not to look out the window. The clouds were low, eight shades of grey raggedly streaming on the wind that bent the tops of the fir trees out back. Cold rain tittered on the glass.

They turned on the lights and drank more coffee, talking about nothing. Mom started dinner and Mike cleared the table; then they realized that neither of them was hungry, so they brewed more coffee.

Near eight o'clock they heard the helicopter coming back and started dinner again. But a few minutes later the Labrador passed overhead again and headed back out.

By nine, with the sky black and the wind stage-whispering around the eaves, the Lab was still up. Mom called the dispatcher at the base. Mike saw her knuckles whiten on the handset, heard her brief question, watched her face go quiet. She hung up.

"There were eight of them in a little boat, out of gas," she said. "The Lab couldn't carry all of them and the crew, too. Your father volunteered to stay in the boat until they came back for him. When they got there, no boat. Probably swamped by a wave and sunk. They're looking."

*   *   *

At eleven o'clock, Comox's missing SARtech was the second story on the CBC late news. The TV showed file footage of Labradors taking off, and a coloured map of where the search was concentrating.

Mike watched the images and heard the reporter's accompanying voice-over: "Georgia Strait fills a deep and narrow trench between Vancouver Island and the rest of North America. Strong tidal currents sweep the bone-chilling water southeast, down past the Gulf Islands and on into the Strait of Juan de Fuca, then around the southern tip of the big island.

"Anything floating on the surface gets flushed out into the north Pacific and lost forever. Unprotected from the cold, in seas tossed high by stiff winds, a human being in the water can die in a few hours. Add a survival suit and expert knowledge, and life expectancy—and hope—increase. The search continues."

The camera cut back to the news reader, who began talking about a freeway pile-up in Coquitlam. Mike switched off the set.

"They'll find him, and he'll be all right," Mom said. Some of her friends had come over to help them wait. They talked cheerfully, in low voices. Mike nodded and said "yeah, sure," a lot, but he didn't hear most of it.

By midnight the sky was clearing, stars making holes in the clouds and poking through in twos and threes. CFB Comox had everything up—Labs, a Buffalo, an Aurora—and a Coast Guard ship was quartering the Strait below where Dad had last been seen.

Mike couldn't stay inside any more. He put on his jacket and slipped out the back door.

They lived on two cleared acres that backed up against a stand of second-growth timber in Comox's northeast corner. The valley's big spruce and cedar were long gone, cleared to make farmland and lumber back before the twentieth century was a toddler. The yard was unfenced, the lawn ending in a thicket of blackberry bushes that grew over a ditch between their property and the woods.

Mike sat on the back steps for a minute, but he could still hear the encouraging voices from the living room. The wind was dying, making a stillness under the trees, and he got up and crossed the lawn to where he could cut through a gap in the blackberry bushes. A few metres into the woods lay a waist-high, half-buried boulder forgotten by some careless glacier. It was a good solid place to be.

Mike walked around the rock, then leaned his forearms on the old granite so that he was looking back toward the house. The stone was cold and the wetness left by the rain seeped into his jacket sleeves. He listened: far to the east, a search plane's engines murmured at the edge of his hearing.

The last clouds tattered and moved off, letting the full moon silver the floor of the woods. The kitchen light shone yellow between the stark bars of the trunks. Then the plane's engines faded into the distance, and the only sound was a drop of rainwater working its way down through the branches.

In the perfect quiet, Mike caught a flicker of movement from the corner of his eye. He turned to look, but the best night vision is peripheral vision, and all he could see straight on was a darkness in the gap between the berry bushes.

And then the darkness shifted. He froze. He heard a heavy body rustling among the thorny blackberry runners, wet smacking noises, and a whuffling exhalation of breath.

People had told him about bears coming into town to gorge on blackberries. Naturally, he'd imagined meeting one. But somehow, his imagination had always supplied daylight.

Back slowly away, they'd said. But the moment he moved to ease his weight off the boulder, the berry-eating noises stopped. He distinctly heard the animal *sniff* twice, followed by a deep-throated *huff!* Then it came toward him.

Now it was just like the dream, a black mass growing steadily larger, looming between Mike and the lights of the house. And, as in the dream, he couldn't move.

The bear eased forward, slowly but without hesitation, until only the width of the boulder separated them. It rose up and leaned its forelegs against the stone; Mike heard the scrape of claws on granite. Then the animal stopped still, as if posing for a picture of two friends leaning toward each other over a small table.

Mike's skin moved of its own accord; his neck hairs prickled his collar. He was so completely filled by fear, it felt as if thunderless sheet lightning played across the muscles of his back and down into his thighs.

Then the lightning died and all he could sense was the unavoidable *reality* of the bear: the sight of its rough head silhouetted against the house lights; the oily-musty smell of its fur; the suffle of its breathing; the wet warmth of its breath on his face.

It's so real, he thought. *So completely real. But it feels just like a dream.*

It was silly. He knew it was silly, but he also knew he had to speak to the bear. He whispered, "Do you want to … tell me something?"

The bear cocked its head sideways and eased back a little, as if it were deciding how to answer this unusual question.

But Mike already had the answer. As if a tap had been opened, all of the fear suddenly drained out of him, and he was filled instead with a peculiar sensation of lightness—as if he might now just float away, up through the forest canopy, off between the stars, to some place where he was somebody else altogether, somebody who was so much *more*.

It could have been only seconds, or it could have been forever, that he and the bear faced each other across the boulder. Then the back door opened and his mother's voice called, "Mike! They found him! He's all right!"

And then, like magic, the bear was *gone*. He heard it scuttling through the trees. Mike laughed, because the feeling of lightness did not disappear with the bear.

The feeling stayed with him, even after his father came home, enfolded Mike and Mom in one giant hug, then ate a stack of buttermilk pancakes, and slept for sixteen hours straight.

The bear never came back, not to the woods, not to Mike's dreams. ■

Investigating the Model

1. At the heart of every story is a conflict, the problem or struggle that triggers the action. Conflicts may be *external*, between the main character and another character (or force). A character battling for survival in a violent snowstorm is an example of an external conflict. A second type of conflict is *internal*, in which the main character must reach a decision about something that is troubling her or him. Identify the conflict in the story "Bearing Up," and explain whether this conflict is external or internal.

2. A story's theme is usually closely tied to the *change* that occurs in the story. For example, the main character's *situation* may change, or the reader's *opinion* of the main character may change, or the main character may undergo a change in the way she or he views something. Identify what changes during the story "Bearing Up," and explain what the writer shows us about life and living through this change.

3. The title of a short story should intrigue the reader as well as identify— or hint at—an idea that is central to the story's action or theme. Do you think "Bearing Up" is a suitable title for the model? Why or why not? Suggest another title for the story and offer reasons for your choice.

4. The lead (opening section) of a short story should catch the reader's attention. It may also introduce various aspects of the story, including the main character (who the story is about), the nature of the conflict, the setting (where and when the story takes place), and the point of view of the narrator. Examine the first section of "Bearing Up." Analyze how it grabs the reader's attention, and explain what it tells about each of these aspects of the story.

5. One characteristic of all short stories is their limited number of characters. Even minor characters perform specific functions: they may advance the plot or provide the reader with information, or, in some cases, relieve tension. Identify each of the minor characters in "Bearing Up" and identify the functions they perform.

6. Even writers of fantasy, who invent imaginary or bizarre worlds for their characters, understand that the setting of a story is only an effective backdrop for the action if it includes enough detail to make it plausible. Choose three different settings in "Bearing Up," and identify specific details in each that help readers visualize the time and place.

7. Most short stories span a relatively brief time period. Is this true of Matt Hughes's story? How does Hughes include important details that happened much earlier than the main action of the story?

8. Short-story writers must be economical, carefully selecting the scenes they will include and often leaving their readers to imagine those they have omitted. Identify at least two scenes Matt Hughes could have included in "Bearing Up" but chose to leave out, and explain his reason for doing so.

9. Sometimes, a writer repeats details in a short story to emphasize ideas that are central to the story's theme. What details does Matt Hughes repeat, and how does their repetition further our understanding of the story?

Checkpoint: Short Story

✓ As a class, create a checklist of common features of short stories, based on the model and your own experience. You can use the checklist to help you create your own short story.

Writer's Workshop

Many stories grow out of images that move or surprise the viewer in some way. Canadian author Tim Wynne-Jones says that the idea for his award-winning novel *The Maestro* began with the image of a piano suspended from a crane. From that image, he created a moving story of a runaway teenager befriended by an eccentric musician whose piano is delivered by helicopter to his remote cabin. In much the same way, Matt Hughes has constructed his story "Bearing Up" around a central image:

> He would kick and yell his way out of dreams where the bear was after him, his chest cold and sweat-slick, breath bellowing.

This image of pursuit by a frightening creature is one nearly all children have encountered in their dreams. Not only does it grab the reader's attention at the beginning of the story, it also figures prominently in conveying Hughes's theme of facing one's fear.

1. Brainstorm a list of images that moved or surprised you in some way. Choose one you would like to explore further.

IDEA FILE

Look for images for your story

- on the street (for example, a homeless person wearing roller blades)

- in magazines or newspapers (for example, a child standing beside a crumpled airliner)

- in your own dreams

2. Start to construct a story around the image you have chosen. Try using the 5 W's + H (who, what, when, where, why, and how) questions to get you started. Record the answers that you feel are both interesting and plausible.

3. The plot of a short story revolves around a conflict of some sort. What conflict might be suggested by the image you have chosen? Will it be internal (within the character) or external (in the outside world)?

4. Take some time to understand your main character. Give her or him a name (feel free to change this later) and jot down details about her or his physical features, family members, friends, school, job, favourite things, dislikes, talents, hopes, dreams, and fears. Although you will not use every detail, this exercise will help you envision your character so that you can make her or him appear real for your reader.

5. When deciding how to resolve the conflict in your story, listen to the character you have created. Let the circumstances, along with what you know about her or his personality, guide you to a plausible resolution. Ask yourself, "What would so-and-so do (or feel) in this situation?"

6. Use a flow chart to write down the events of your story and to fine-tune the plot. Remember that the action should span a relatively brief time period. Ask yourself whether every scene builds toward the climax and prepares the reader for the resolution that follows. Cut those that you decide are unnecessary. (You might consider beginning with your central image and then weaving it into the rest of your story, as Matt Hughes has done.)

IDEA FILE

Writers often begin a story quite close to the end, or resolution, then move back in time to fill in any missing information. Writing this way allows you to start the story at an interesting point in time and gets the reader hooked right from the opening paragraph.

7. Share the plot of your story with a partner, who will listen carefully to identify anything that is unclear or difficult to believe and then offer suggestions for improvement. Following this, reverse roles and listen carefully as your partner shares her or his story with you.

8. Write a draft of your short story, remembering to begin as close to the end of the story as possible and working in necessary details as you write.

 9. Refer back to the list you created at Checkpoint, and revise and edit your short story until you are satisfied with its focus, content, and organization.

ORAL LANGUAGE EXTENSION

Working in a small group, select one of the five main scenes from "Bearing Up" (each group will choose a different scene). Prepare a radio drama of this portion of the story, combining narration with dialogue, sound effects, and—if appropriate—music to help establish the mood. Practise your performance several times before taping it. At a later time, listen to the tape and evaluate the success of your group's efforts, both technically and artistically. As the tapes are played in class, each group can receive and offer feedback.

Grammar

Although you can construct complete sentences using only nouns, verbs, adjectives, and adverbs, your writing would be tiresome to read if these were the only parts of speech you used. There are four other parts of speech that help to make sentences more varied and interesting. These parts of speech are **pronouns, prepositions, conjunctions,** and **interjections.**

> **Learning Goal**
>
> - **use parts of speech correctly: pronouns, prepositions, conjunctions, and interjections**

A **pronoun** takes the place of a noun.

He would hear **them** mumbling about **him,** but in the morning, **nobody** made a big deal about **it.**

Using pronouns allows the writer to avoid the needless repetition found in the following sentence:

Mike would hear *Mike's parents* mumbling about *Mike*, but in the morning, *neither Mike's parents* nor *Mike* made a big deal about *Mike's nightmare.*

There are several different types of pronouns. They include the following:

Personal pronouns	*I, me, mine, you, your, yours, he, him, his, she, her, hers, it, its, we, us, our, ours, they, them, their, theirs*
Indefinite pronouns	*all, another, any, anybody, anyone, anything, both, each, either, every, everybody, everyone, everything, few, little, many, much, neither, nobody, none, no one, nothing, one, other, several, some, somebody, someone, something*
Reflexive pronouns	*myself, yourself, himself, herself, itself, ourselves, yourselves, themselves*
Relative pronouns	*who, whom, whose, which, that*
Demonstrative pronouns	*this, that, these, those*
Interrogative pronouns	*what, which, who, whom, whose*

A **preposition** shows the relationship between two words in a sentence.

Usually, the word or phrase following a preposition (known as the object of the preposition) is a noun (phrase) or pronoun. In the example below, the prepositions are in **bold,** and their objects are in *italic.*

It was home **to** *a few thousand people,* many **of** *them* attached **to** *the air force base* **at** *the landward end* **of** *the peninsula.*

However, a preposition can also be followed by a verb to form the infinitive (*to be*), by an adjective (*from bad to worse*), or by an adverb (*from before*).

Some other frequently used prepositions include *with, by, from, in, on, under, over, across, along, before, after, between,* and *through*.

A **conjunction** connects words, phrases, or clauses.

Coordinating conjunctions join two or more words (*Mike* **and** *his mother* sat in the darkening kitchen), phrases (Sheet lightning played *across the muscles of his back* **and** *down into his thighs*), or complete sentences (*Mike nodded a lot,* **but** *he didn't hear most of it*). The four most common coordinating conjunctions are *and, but, nor,* and *or*.

Subordinating conjunctions join only clauses, and one of these clauses depends on the other. Subordinating conjunctions can appear either at the beginning or in the middle of a sentence.

When he tuned to the emergency channel, depressed the talk switch and said, "Mayday, mayday," CFB Comox came right back.

Your father volunteered to stay in the boat **until** they came back for him.

Other subordinating conjunctions include *as, although, because, before, since, unless, which,* and *while*.

An **interjection** indicates strong feeling or sudden emotion.

Examples of interjections are *hey, wow, huh,* and *gosh*.

1. Identify whether the boldface words are pronouns, prepositions, conjunctions, or interjections. Explain your choice in each case.

   a) **He** would kick and yell his way out of dreams where the bear was **after** him, his chest cold and sweat-slick, breath bellowing.

   b) **At** fifteen, he didn't want his parents coming to his rescue—**well**, maybe he wanted it a little, **but** it would have bent his self-image.

   c) He'd been having the bear dream **for** as long as he could recall, **although** it didn't start out as a bear.

   d) It would come for him every five or six months; not that he could count on it to keep to a schedule, **so** sometimes it could be twice **in** the same week.

e) **That** was the worst part: it seemed to enlarge **itself** toward him, like a dark balloon swelling across his field of vision, **or** as if he were a lost spacewalker falling toward a vast dark planet.

f) **Whatever** he might be doing, Mike stopped and looked up **when** the planes went over.

g) **If** a fisherman abandoned a burning boat, the Lab would hover in the air so that Dad could jump **into** the cold sea, put a harness around the man **before** hypothermia killed him, and wait in the water **while** the victim was winched to safety, **and** they lowered the cable again to retrieve the SARtech.

2. A word's part of speech depends on its use in a sentence. For example, many words can act as either prepositions or subordinating conjunctions. Identify the part of speech of each boldface word and explain your choice.

a) **Since** 5:30, CFB Comox had had several Labs, a Buffalo, and an Aurora searching for Mike's father.

b) **Since** he was no longer in the boat, there was less chance Mike's father would survive the storm.

c) The feeling of lightness stayed with Mike **after** the bear disappeared.

d) **After** his supper of pancakes, Mike's father slept for sixteen hours straight.

3. Choose another word that can act as either a preposition or a subordinating conjunction. Write two sentences, each using the word as a different part of speech.

4. Working with a partner, read the last five paragraphs of the story and list at least four pronouns, prepositions, and conjunctions the author has used.

Mechanics & Design

Dialogue is one of the most effective devices a writer can use to help readers visualize a story as it unfolds. First, dialogue offers variety. Instead of relying solely on narration to tell the story, the writer can use characters to reveal important information in their conversations. Dialogue can also help to advance the plot by providing opportunities for characters to come into conflict with each other. Two of the most useful functions of dialogue, however, are to reveal relationships among characters and to show readers what characters are like through spoken comments and expressions that are unique to them.

> **Learning Goal**
>
> - **punctuate and capitalize dialogue correctly**

1. Quote a passage of dialogue from "Bearing Up" that performs one or more of these functions, and explain the function(s) it serves.

2. When authors write dialogue, they want their characters' speech to sound natural and realistic. Read some of the dialogue from the model out loud. With a partner, discuss how the author has tried to create realistic speech. What do you notice about the length of spoken sentences and the author's choice of words? Give examples to show what you mean.

WRITING TIP

Too much dialogue in a story can be just as monotonous as too much narration. Try to find a balance between the two. When writing dialogue, read it aloud like a script to see if it sounds natural.

3. Look closely at the way Matt Hughes capitalized and punctuated the following passages of dialogue. Working with a partner, make a detailed list of punctuation guidelines for writing dialogue. Then, share your work with other groups. Add any guidelines you may have forgotten to your list.

    Mike would call back, "Yeah, I'm okay."

    "Well, of course, I'm influenced by Jung," said Mrs. Skinner.

    "So what do I do?" he asked.

    "It's not being a hero," Dad said. "It's just a job that's got to be done."

    "I used to," she admitted, "but your father's very good at what he does."

    Then the back door opened and his mother's voice called, "Mike! They found him! He's all right!"

4. Summarized talk does not require quotation marks, while quoted speech does. Look at the following sentences (which lack capital letters and punctuation) and decide which is summarized talk. Rewrite the other one so it follows the rules you outlined in activity 3.

   a) dad said there were some boaters in trouble and he would not be home for supper
   b) mom said when they went back to get your father the boat was gone

5. Note the use of the comma in the following passage of dialogue, and explain why the comma is necessary.

   "Are you okay, Mike?"

   If you have not covered this type of punctuation in your guidelines, add it now.

6. Explain the use of single quotation marks in the following passage. Include an item in your list of punctuation guidelines covering when to use single quotation marks.

   "Mr. Rodriguez," reads the official report, "expressed his gratitude for the efforts of the Comox Search and Rescue team. He commented, 'I especially want to thank the brave man who stayed behind in the boat.'"

7. Most of the time, quotation marks appear in pairs. However, this is not the case in the television reporter's description of the search. Find this passage in the story and explain how and why Hughes punctuated it differently. Include this explanation in your list of punctuation guidelines for dialogue.

8. Use your guidelines to capitalize and punctuate the following passages.

   a) i can't believe you didn't fill up the gas tank said ramone
   b) steve growled you could have checked it yourself
   c) don't you think carla interrupted that we have more important things to worry about than whose fault it is
   d) what about the oars asked diane can we use those
   e) it'll be hard rowing said ramone the wind is really picking up
   f) steve said that rowing was their only chance

9. Most of the examples in activity 8 contain a speaker tag (i.e., *Mike asked, Dad said*) that identifies who is speaking. Find a passage of dialogue in "Bearing Up" that does not include a speaker tag and explain why the author did not use one. Why should a writer avoid using speaker tags for all passages of dialogue? Besides speaker tags, what can a writer use to indicate who is speaking?

10. Read your short story and see if you have made use of opportunities to have characters speak aloud. If so, check that you have capitalized and punctuated your dialogue correctly. If not, see if there are passages where you can replace narration with dialogue.

MEDIA LINK

Like the lead of a short story, the lead of a movie (opening scenes) should catch the viewer's attention. It is likely to introduce the main character, the possible nature of the conflict, the setting (chronological, geographical, and/or psychological), and the point of view from which the story will be told.

Select one recently popular film and view the opening sequence at least three times, once without the sound. Does it clearly establish each of the above components? How does it catch your attention? You should comment on the elements of cinematography and soundtrack. Consider also the pace and the use of graphics. What expectations about the rest of the film are set up in this sequence?

Usage & Style

One of the most important decisions a writer must make when writing a piece is the choice of **point of view** because it shapes what the writer will share in that piece as well as how the reader will respond to it. Imagine, for example, hearing two accounts of a house fire, one offered by a news reporter and the other given by one of the occupants who barely escaped alive. While the first might include only details about how the fire started, the extent of the damage, and the condition of the survivors, the second would no doubt be filled with emotional descriptions of the event and its aftermath.

There are two main points of view: **first person,** in which the writer is a *participant* in the events being narrated, and **third person,** in which the writer reports the events that *others* are participating in. In fiction, however, there are varying degrees of third-person point of view.

- In the **omniscient** point of view, the narrator is all-knowing and, therefore, able to convey information about the actions, thoughts, and feelings of all the people involved.

- In the **limited omniscient** point of view, the narrator is able to convey the thoughts and feelings of only one person involved.

- Writing from the **objective** point of view, the narrator conveys only those things that she or he can see or hear.

WRITING TIP

Rarely will writers switch from one point of view to another, unless they want to achieve a particular effect. Unless you have a specific reason for changing perspective, be sure you maintain the same point of view throughout your narrative.

1. Working in a small group, make a chart like the one below. Complete your chart with the missing information.

Point of View	Advantages	Disadvantages
First person	This is the most intimate and involving point of view because the writer "hears" the story from a person directly involved in the experience. Also, the reader must carefully weigh what this character is saying to determine the reliability of her or his information.	The writer can only include information that this character would know and cannot include details about events that are happening elsewhere or do not include the narrator.
Omniscient		Because the writer can tell us what any character is thinking or feeling, the reader has little need to interpret the motives of the characters, which can lessen the opportunity for discovery and eliminate the element of surprise.
Limited omniscient		
Objective		The writer can only include details that can be seen or heard, not details about what characters are thinking and feeling, unless they speak about their thoughts and feelings.

2. Which of the three third-person points of view has Matt Hughes used to tell his story? How do you know?

3. Why do you suppose Hughes did not choose the first-person point of view to tell his story?

4. Consider the viewpoint you have used in your short story. Have you chosen the most appropriate point of view, and have you maintained this same viewpoint throughout?

Word Study & Spelling

Writers most often use dictionaries to find the correct spelling and meaning of a word. However, another valuable use is identifying a word's correct pronunciation.

> By the time the skipper had identified the problem, the wind was brisking up, causing the overloaded skiff to wallow in steepening waves, shipping water over the **gunwales**.

This word looks as if it should be pronounced *gun ´ - wails* because it contains two familiar-looking words (*gun* and *Wales*) whose pronunciations are well known. However, the following dictionary entry offers the correct pronunciation (along with an alternative spelling of the word).

> **gun•wale** also **gun•nel** (gŭn'əl) *n. Naut.* The upper edge of the side of a vessel. [So called because guns were on it.]

Learning Goal

- use a dictionary to identify the pronunciation of a word

Note how the pronunciation of a term is in parentheses and follows the word written in boldface. Dictionaries use special symbols, called diacritical marks, to indicate the phonetic spelling of a word, and the meanings of these symbols are provided in a key at the beginning of most dictionaries. Some of the most common diacritical marks are shown in the table on the following page.

ă	pat	r	roar
ā	pay	s	sauce
âr	care	sh	ship, dish
b	bib	t	tight, stopped
ch	church	th	thin
d	deed, milled	*th*	this
ĕ	pet	ŭ	cut
ē	bee	ûr	urge, term, firm
f	fife, phase, rough		word, heard
g	gag	v	valve
h	hat	w	with
hw	which	y	yes
ĭ	pit	z	zebra, xylem
ī	pie, by	zh	vision, pleasure, garage
îr	pier	ə	about, item, edible
j	judge		gallop, circus
k	kick, cat, pique	ər	butter
l	lid, needle* (nēd'l)		
m	mum		
n	no, sudden* (sŭd'n)		

Other Languages

ng	thing	A	*French* voilà
ŏ	pot, bother, father	ø	*French* deux
ō	toe	œ	*French* oeuf
ô	caught, paw		*German* schön
oi	noise	ü	*French* tu
o͝o	took		*German* über
o͞o	boot	KH	*German* ich
ôr	pour		*Scottish* loch
ou	cow, out, loud	N	*French* bon
p	pop	ny	*French* gagner
		R	*French* rouge

* In English the consonants *l* and *n* often constitute complete syllables by themselves.

1. Below are vocabulary words from the story "Bearing Up" written using diacritical marks. Use the key on page 59 to figure out their pronunciation, and then write them in standard form.

   a) drēm
   b) flōt
   c) rĕs′kyo͞o
   d) nŭk′əl
   e) dĭ-tĕk′shən
   f) sē′kwəns
   g) pə-rif′ər-əl
   h) tĕk-nĭsh′ən
   i) fyo͞o′sə-lŏzh′

2. Try writing the following words phonetically using the diacritical marks provided. When you have finished, share your attempts with a partner and explain why you wrote them this way. Then, check a dictionary to see if you are right.

   a) cedar
   b) straight
   c) squadron
   d) schedule
   e) electronic
   f) expectancy
   g) peculiar
   h) especially
   i) tyrannosaur
   j) conscientious

3. The last name of Carl Jung, the psychologist Mike's counsellor refers to, is often mispronounced. Try writing it phonetically, and then check with your teacher to see if you are correct.

4. Read your short story carefully to find and correct any spelling errors, especially in words that are spelled differently from the way they sound.

WORD ORIGINS

"That means I view the psyche as being fundamentally fragmented," she continued.

Psyche was the name of a beautiful maiden in Greek mythology with whom Eros (also known as Cupid) fell in love. The word **psyche** comes from a Greek word, meaning "breath, life." In modern usage, *psyche* refers to "the mind functioning as the centre of thought, emotion, and behaviour."

Working with a partner, research the Greek or Roman mythological figures from whom we have derived the following words and expressions. Explain the connection between each figure and the word or expression that is named after her or him.

**atlas   narcissism   echo   Herculean
Midas touch   Achilles' heel**

Looking Back

Before handing in your final edited draft, have a classmate check your short story, paying particular attention to the following:

- [✓] Has the author used dialogue effectively to create variety and to further the plot?

- [✓] Is the dialogue punctuated and capitalized correctly?

- [✓] Has the author chosen an interesting and appropriate narrative point of view and used it consistently?

- [✓] Are all words spelled correctly?

Unit ③ Film Adaptation

What is a film adaptation?

In a film adaptation, the writer translates another work, such as a short story or novel, into a screenplay. Unlike a stage play, which is often driven primarily by dialogue and action, film is a more visual medium, so the screenplay also makes use of images and technical elements, such as special camera angles and movements, to convey impressions and ideas. In the following excerpt from a recent film adaptation of William Shakespeare's *Romeo and Juliet*, the star-crossed lovers meet at a sumptuous costume ball held at the home of Juliet's parents, the Capulets, who are trying to interest Juliet in the governor's son, Dave Paris. Juliet is dressed as an angel.

Learning Goals

- write a film adaptation of a work
- use subjects and predicates correctly
- use objects and subject complements to complete the meaning of transitive and linking verbs
- apply conventions of screenplay format to a film adaptation of a work
- explain how authors use figurative language to achieve particular effects
- use a thesaurus to find concise synonyms and antonyms

Romeo and Juliet

(Excerpt)

BY CRAIG PEARCE AND BAZ LUHRMANN

INT. BALLROOM—NIGHT

Romeo is spying on the angel [Juliet] from around the
arches on the hall side of the dance floor.

CLOSE ON: Romeo whispers.

> ROMEO
> Did my heart love till now?
> Forswear it, sight.
> For I ne'er saw true beauty till this
>   night.

Romeo begins to circumnavigate the dance floor in an
attempt to get closer to Juliet.

CUT TO: Dave slow-dancing with Juliet. Romeo tracks with
them from behind the arches.

Juliet's eyes search the room for the boy.

CLOSE ON: Romeo.

CLOSE ON: Juliet.

Their eyes connect.

Juliet looks quickly back to Dave, who, oblivious, returns
his most devastating smile.

CUT TO: The songstress; her voice soars.

CUT TO: Juliet. Unable to look away from the boy, she
stares over Dave's shoulder.

CUT TO: Romeo, positioning himself behind an arch ever so
near her.

With the diva's spiralling final notes, the ballad concludes. The crowd cheers and screams its applause. An avalanche of balloons, tinsel, and confetti rains down from the roof. The light dims. Juliet has her back against the arch; her eyes search the darkness, but the boy is gone.

CLOSE ON: Juliet. Suddenly: A gasp; Juliet's eyes widen, shocked.

In the dark, a hand has shot out from the folds of cloth in the curtained archway and clasped hers. Juliet barely dares breathe.

She glances furtively to Dave Paris. He watches the stage.

Slowly, Juliet turns toward the hand; there through a break in the curtain she can see eye, cheek, and lips of the mystery boy. As the diva continues her curtain call, Romeo, ignoring the dangerous proximity of Dave Paris, manoeuvres his lips to almost touch Juliet's ear. He whispers as he brings her hands to his lips.

> ROMEO
> If I profane with my unworthiest hand
> This holy shrine, the gentle sin is this.
> My lips, two blushing pilgrims, ready stand
> To smooth that rough touch with a tender
>   kiss.

Juliet, pulling her hand away, slips around the column out of sight of Gloria [Juliet's mother] and Dave.

CUT TO:

INT. GRAND HALL—NIGHT

> JULIET
> Good pilgrim, you do wrong your hand too
>   much,
> Which mannerly devotion shows in this.
> For saints have hands that pilgrims' hands
>   do touch,

She offers her hand in a chaste handshake.

                    JULIET (cont.)
        And palm to palm is holy palmers' kiss.

Romeo, ignoring the polite gesture, edges his way closer,
attempting a kiss.

                        ROMEO
        Have not saints lips, and holy palmers too?

Juliet glides her lips out of range of his and moves off.

                        JULIET
            Ay, pilgrim, lips that they must use in
                prayer.

Juliet, turning in front of the elevator in the grand
hall, brings her hands together to mime a praying angel.

                        ROMEO
            O, then, dear saint, let lips do what hands
                do,

Gently parting her praying hands—

                        ROMEO (cont.)
            They pray: grant thou,

His lips closer and closer—

ROMEO (cont.)
Lest faith turn to despair.

They are so close they can feel each other's breath.

JULIET
(attempting reason through short breaths)
Saints do not move, though grant for
    prayer's sake.

ROMEO
Then move not while my prayer's effect I
    take.

CLOSE ON: Romeo's lips deliciously close to Juliet's. She does not deny him as ever so gently they ...

SUDDENLY: Juliet's eyes awaken with horror.

CUT TO: JULIET'S P.O.V. Gloria and Dave are hunting toward them through the crowd.

SUDDENLY: BING. The elevator doors open. Juliet, seizing the moment, pulls Romeo inside.

CUT TO:

INT. ELEVATOR—NIGHT

The doors close, shrouding them from Gloria and Dave. Romeo and Juliet kiss, swept up in the momentum of the rising elevator. A gentle reticence; Juliet shies away. Their hearts race; close, warm, breathless.

ROMEO (cont.)
Thus from my lips, by thine, my sin is
    purged.

JULIET
Then have my lips the sin that they have
    took.

ROMEO
Sin from my lips? O trespass sweetly urged!
Give me my sin again.

They fall toward each other to kiss again when ... BING,
the doors of the elevator open.

                                                CUT TO:

INT. GRAND HALL LANDING—NIGHT

JULIET'S P.O.V.: Gloria and Dave, having reached the top
of the stairs, are petrifyingly close.

Juliet dares not move; her eyes fix on the approaching
couple through the feathers of a passing peacock costume.

                                                CUT TO:

INT. ELEVATOR—NIGHT

CLOSE ON: Juliet's hand working the "close" button.

                                                CUT TO:

INT. GRAND HALL LANDING—NIGHT

The peacock has moved and Dave and Gloria stand, backs
turned, directly in front of the elevator.

TIGHT ON: Gloria turning toward Romeo and Juliet as the doors close in the nick of time.

CUT TO:

INT. ELEVATOR—NIGHT

Romeo and Juliet kiss deeply, long, entwined. All sense of time is lost in the dizzying, vertiginous spin of the falling elevator. Suddenly, it stops with a thud. Juliet breaks away, catching her breath.

> JULIET
> You kiss by the book.

Light bursts through the crack of the opening elevator doors behind them. Our focus moves from the lovers' longing look to the shocked features of the Nurse, now standing in the open elevator doorway.

CUT TO:

INT. GRAND HALL—NIGHT

> NURSE
> Madam, your mother craves a word with you.

She eyes Romeo severely.

                         NURSE (cont.)
          Come. Let's away.

She takes firm control of her charge.

Juliet furtively motions for the startled Romeo not to
follow as he trails them across the grand hall.

CUT TO: ROMEO'S P.O.V.: The Nurse and Juliet reach the
door, but instead of leaving, they turn and ascend the
staircase that arcs around to the mezzanine level. They
join a vexed Gloria Capulet, who clings to a patient Dave
Paris.

Inaudible words are exchanged. Juliet flicks her eyes
nervously to Romeo.

CUT TO: Romeo. He halts at the foot of the stairs, unsure.

CUT TO: Gloria. Catching Juliet's interest in the boy, she
indicates to her daughter to "come along."

CUT TO: Romeo; a dawning realization.

                         ROMEO
          (under his breath)
          Is she a Capulet?

CUT TO: Juliet. She stops halfway up the steps and turns
back.

CUT TO: Romeo, comprehending the reality of who she is.

CUT TO: Juliet. The Nurse whispers in her ear.

                         NURSE
          His name is Romeo, and a Montague,
          The only son of your great enemy.

HOLD ON: Juliet. Like a cloud passing across the sun, a
dark coldness descends upon her.

CUT TO: Mercutio. He throws himself upon the shell-shocked
Romeo.

```
                        MERCUTIO
            Away, begone, the sport is at its best.

     Mercutio shuttles Romeo toward the door.

                         ROMEO
              Ay, so I fear,

     A covert glance over his shoulder.

                         ROMEO (cont.)
              The more is my unrest.
```

Glossary

CUT TO:	Go to a new camera shot
INT.	Interior
EXT.	Exterior
CLOSE ON:	Close camera shot focusing on
P.O.V.	Point of view

Investigating the Model

1. The excerpt, which includes eight individual scenes, spans only one (Act I, scene v) in Shakespeare's original stage play. What makes it necessary for screenwriters to begin a new scene? What three pieces of information are necessary to identify each scene?

2. Compare the use of dialogue in this screenplay with the dialogue in Shakespeare's original play. Does dialogue figure as prominently in both types of script? Why or why not? What other differences do you notice in the way dialogue is used (e.g., how often characters speak, and how long the speeches are)? Discuss possible reasons for any differences you find.

3. Decisions about camera angles and movements are made by the director and then incorporated into the script by the screenwriter. Identify two different types of shots included in the excerpt, and explain the particular effect of each. Give examples to illustrate your ideas.

4. Note the numerous camera shots used in the final scene of the excerpt. What effect is achieved by the intercutting of several brief shots?

5. Visual imagery is particularly important in film. Identify at least one interesting visual image included in the excerpt and describe its intended effect on the viewer.

6. Because feature-length films are usually 90–120 minutes in length, screenwriters often omit parts or change the order of the original work their film is based on. For example, in the original party scene, Juliet's father prevents her cousin, Tybalt, from attacking Romeo, but the screenwriters chose to place this action earlier in their script. Read Act I, scene v of Shakespeare's *Romeo and Juliet* and identify what other parts the screenwriters have chosen to omit or change. Have Pearce and Luhrmann effectively reduced this scene to its most important elements? Why or why not?

Checkpoint: Film Adaptation

☑ As a class, create a checklist of common features of film adaptations, based on the model and your own experience. You can use the checklist to help you write your own film adaptation.

Writer's Workshop

1. Choose a work (e.g., a long narrative poem, short story, or novel) that interests you and meets your teacher's approval. (Your teacher may provide you with a list of works from which to choose.) Decide what you like most about that work—is it the main character? The conflict the character experiences? The plot? The theme?

2. Use the decision you reached in activity 1 to help you choose a pivotal scene that you would like to adapt to film. For example, if the element you most enjoyed was the main character, you might choose a scene where something important about that character is revealed, or a scene in which the character faces a turning point. Whichever scene you choose should have a definite beginning, middle, and end.

3. Read the passage again and, using a flow chart, storyboard, or other organizer, block out the scenes you will include. Remember, every time the location or time changes, a new scene is required. (This includes even subtle changes; for example, if a character in one scene was sitting inside a car and then steps outside the vehicle, you will need to begin a new scene to accommodate this change in location.) On your plot outline, briefly summarize the significant action that will occur in each scene.

Learning Goal

• **write a film adaptation of a work**

4. Unlike short-story writers or novelists who can include a character's thoughts and feelings in narration, screenwriters are limited to what the camera can record characters saying and doing. (Although it is possible to use voice-overs in which a character shares thoughts directly with the audience, screenwriters tend to avoid them because they lack realism.) Decide how you will include information that is contained in the narration. Can you convey this through dialogue or action?

5. Look for opportunities to use visual images to underscore atmosphere or convey understanding. (For example, a shot of a single tree on a hilltop could help to convey a character's feeling of isolation.) Brainstorm various images you could use, and choose one or more that will suit the context of the action and support the intent of your adaptation. Plan where in your script each image could be used to best advantage.

6. Once you are satisfied with the structure of your script, read the scene in the original work again and decide what your character(s) will say. Will you include dialogue as it is written in the work or will you revise it to suit the purpose of your adaptation? (Most exchanges of dialogue should be no more than two to three lines long.) Will you omit unnecessary exchanges of dialogue in the work? Will you invent others that you feel are required?

7. Write a draft of your adaptation, remembering to include brief directions for the action that will occur on screen.

 8. Read your adaptation aloud, focusing not only on the action you have sequenced but also on the sound of your characters' dialogue and the effectiveness of any technical devices you may have used. Revise your work using the list you made at Checkpoint.

ORAL LANGUAGE EXTENSION

Shakespeare's language is not always easy for the modern reader to understand, especially when read silently. But it is much easier to get the gist of what is being said when you see the play performed, or even hear the words spoken aloud. Working in a small group, choose another scene from *Romeo and Juliet* that interests you. You may wish to refer to a text that includes a synopsis of each of the scenes. Read it aloud together, each person assuming a specific role or roles. If possible, listen to a tape-recorded version of the scene as well. Look up any words or phrases you do not understand in a text annotation or dictionary. Discuss what happens in the scene, as well as its importance in the context of the play as a whole. Once you have a firm grasp of its meaning, prepare an oral reading of the scene for the rest of the class. Afterward, ask your audience for feedback on how successful you were in conveying the scene.

Grammar

Some of the most important parts that make up a sentence are the subject, the predicate, direct and indirect objects, and subject complements.

> The **subject** is the noun phrase that tells who or what the sentence is about.

The **simple subject** is the main noun (or pronoun) by itself; the complete subject includes all the words that describe or modify that noun or pronoun.

> The **predicate** is the verb phrase that either tells the action the subject is performing (e.g., *runs, laughs, eats*) or explains the condition or effect of the subject (e.g., *is, feels, seems*).

The **simple predicate** is the verb by itself; the complete predicate includes any words or phrases that modify the verb.

In the following examples, the simple subject is boldface and the simple predicate is italic.

Juliet's **eyes**	*search* the room for the boy.
complete subject	complete predicate showing action

Juliet	*has* her back against the arch.
complete subject	complete predicate explaining a condition of the subject

Learning Goal

• **use subjects and predicates correctly**

1. Identify the complete subject and complete predicate in each of the following sentences. Underline the simple subject and simple predicate. Then tell whether the predicate shows an action or explains a condition or effect.

   a) An avalanche of balloons, tinsel, and confetti rains down from the roof.
   b) A hand has shot out from the folds of cloth in the curtained archway.
   c) Romeo's lips were deliciously close to Juliet's.
   d) Juliet, pulling her hand away, slips around the column out of sight of Gloria and Dave.
   e) Gloria and Dave, having reached the top of the stairs, are petrifyingly close.

The action verb in a predicate can be either **transitive** or **intransitive**. A transitive verb needs a noun phrase, called a direct object, to complete its meaning.

> The **direct object** answers *whom* or *what* about a transitive verb.

Subject	<u>Transitive Verb</u>	*Direct Object*	
Juliet	<u>fixes</u>	*her eyes*	on the approaching couple.
Mercutio	<u>throws</u>	*himself*	upon the shell-shocked Romeo.

2. Being able to recognize transitive verbs and direct objects can help you understand Shakespeare's language, which is often written in a different word order from what you are used to. Each of the following quotations from *Romeo and Juliet* contains a direct object that does not come directly after the verb. Rewrite the passages, changing the order of the verb (underlined) and the object (italic) to make them sound more like modern English.

> **Learning Goal**
>
> • use objects and subject complements to complete the meaning of transitive and linking verbs

   a) Good pilgrim, you do wrong your hand too much,
Which *mannerly devotion* <u>shows</u> in this.
   b) Then move not while *my prayer's effect* I <u>take</u>.
   c) Then <u>have</u> my lips *the sin* that they have took.
   d) And *all my fortunes* at thy foot I'll <u>lay</u>,
And follow thee, my lord, throughout the world.

A transitive verb may also take an **indirect object**, which answers *to whom, for whom, to what,* or *for what* about a transitive verb.

Subject	<u>Transitive Verb</u>	*Indirect Object*	Direct Object
Dave Paris	<u>gives</u>	*Juliet*	his most devastating smile.
Juliet	<u>offers</u>	*Romeo*	her hand.

While an intransitive verb can be modified, it does not need a direct object to complete its meaning.

Subject	Intransitive Verb	Modifier
Their eyes	connect.	
The light	dims	*suddenly.*
She	stares	*over Dave's shoulder.*

Some action verbs can be transitive or intransitive, depending on the context in which they are used. For example, in the script direction *Romeo whispers,* the verb *whispers* is intransitive, but in the sentence *Romeo whispers Juliet's name,* the verb is transitive because its meaning is completed by the direct object *Juliet's name.*

Of course, not all verbs express action. Verbs that are not action verbs are called **linking verbs.** Linking verbs do not take direct or indirect objects. Instead, they link the subject to a subject complement in the predicate.

> The **subject complement** is a noun or adjective used after a linking verb that describes or renames the subject.

Subject	Linking Verb	Subject Complement
The boy	is	*a Montague.*
My lips	stand	*ready.*

3. Tell whether the verb in each of the following sentences is transitive, intransitive, or linking. Then label any direct objects (DO), indirect objects (IO), and subject complements (SC).

a) The boy is gone.
b) The songstress's voice soars above the crowd.
c) I ne'er saw true beauty till this night.
d) Juliet, turning in front of the elevator in the grand hall, brings her hands together to mime a praying angel.
e) All sense of time is lost in the dizzying, vertiginous spin of the falling elevator.
f) Like a cloud passing across the sun, a dark coldness descends upon her.

g) Romeo tracks with them from behind the arches.

h) Romeo manoeuvres his lips to touch Juliet's ear.

i) Juliet glides her lips out of range of his.

j) Light bursts through the crack of the opening elevator doors behind them.

MEDIA LINK

Our favourite movies often contain "magic moments" that we enjoy recalling. For many people, one such magical moment is the scene in Baz Luhrmann's *Romeo and Juliet* where the young lovers first catch a glimpse of one another through the aquarium. Watch this sequence several times to determine the elements that make it so memorable.

Brainstorm a list of magic moments from other movies and select one such moment to analyze in detail. Describe the scene in as much detail as you can. Consider the use of technical elements such as sound, music, lighting, composition of shots, movement, special effects, colour, camera angles, and editing. What exactly was the context of the scene? What was the quality of the acting? Did this scene have any relationship to your own life?

Mechanics & Design

Before a script can become a film, it must first be accepted by a producer. This is often the most difficult hurdle for a screenwriter to overcome. To improve the chances of their scripts being noticed, screenwriters follow specific conventions of screenplay format, some of which are listed on the following page.

Learning Goal

- apply conventions of screenplay format to a film adaptation of a work

- Leave lots of white space. In the fast-paced world of film, producers need to be able to read scripts quickly and won't bother wading through something that is hard to read.

- Keep descriptions of setting and action brief.

- Write your screenplay on a computer (if possible) in courier font. Leave 4-cm margins on either side.

- Identify the scene using block capitals (e.g., INT. ELEVATOR—NIGHT) in the left margin. Your descriptions of the action also begin at the left margin (e.g., "Romeo is spying on the angel from around the arches on the hall side of the dance floor.")

- Set off dialogue by indenting the words about 10 spaces from the left margin (tab 25), and 15 spaces from the right margin (around tab 60). Put the speaker's name directly above in block letters, starting around tab 45.

- Never break a character's lines at the bottom of a page. If there is not enough room for a character to begin and end a comment, start the speech at the top of the next page.

- When you begin a new scene, warn the reader by putting CUT TO: in the far right margin (around tab 65). This will help the director find the scene changes easily.

WRITING TIP

Generally, one page of script is approximately equal to one minute of screen time.

- Include a cover page with the following elements:
  - Centre the title and your name at the top of the page. Use capitals for the title.
  - If the script is an adaptation, give the source information (single spaced and centred) two lines below your name:

    Based on the play *Romeo and Juliet,* by William Shakespeare.
  - Write the name of the class, your teacher's name, and the date on separate lines (single spaced) in the bottom left-hand corner.

- Print your script using a good-quality printer. Computer-generated scripts not only look professional, they are also easier to revise than typewritten screenplays.

1. Use these guidelines to prepare a good copy of your adaptation. Pay close attention to neatness.

Usage & Style

One of the many reasons Shakespeare's work has stood the test of time so well is his almost unparalleled use of figurative language to evoke startling images and make unusual comparisons.

Figurative language is language that suggests more than it states.

In the following passage, Romeo compares Juliet's hand to a holy shrine, and his own lips to "two blushing pilgrims."

> If I profane with my unworthiest hand
> This holy shrine, the gentle sin is this.
> My lips, two blushing pilgrims, ready stand
> To smooth that rough touch with a tender kiss.

Figurative comparisons show relationships between things that are unlike in nature. Four types of comparisons often used by writers are simile, metaphor, personification, and symbolism.

Simile is a direct comparison using *like* or *as*.

1. Identify the simile that appears in the excerpt. Is this an effective comparison? Why or why not?

Metaphor is an implied comparison.

Learning Goal

- explain how authors use figurative language to achieve particular effects

When Romeo speaks of Juliet's hand as a "holy shrine," he conveys his adoration for her. When he calls his lips "two blushing pilgrims," he emphasizes not only their redness but also his eagerness to kiss her. Metaphor can be especially effective in painting vivid sensory impressions because it requires readers to participate in making the comparison by mentally associating one image with another. For example, the sentence "Light bursts through the crack of the opening elevator doors behind them" uses a single verb—*bursts*—to paint a mental picture of the suddenness with which the light enters the elevator.

2. Explain the metaphor in each of the following sentences taken from the excerpt, identifying the word or phrase that suggests the comparison.

   a) Their eyes connect.
   b) With the diva's spiralling final notes, the ballad concludes.
   c) In the dark, a hand has shot out from the folds of cloth in the curtained archway and clasped hers.
   d) Juliet, seizing the moment, pulls Romeo inside.
   e) They turn and ascend the staircase that arcs around to the mezzanine level.
   f) Juliet flicks her eyes nervously to Romeo.

3. Identify at least one other metaphor in the excerpt, and explain the comparison.

Some metaphors are used so often in our daily language that they lose their effectiveness and become **clichés.** Note the cliché (in italic) in the following camera shot:

> TIGHT ON: Gloria turning toward Romeo and Juliet as the doors close *in the nick of time.*

Although we often use them without thinking, it's best to avoid clichés whenever possible.

> **Personification** is a special comparison in which human qualities are given to something that is not human.

For example, when Juliet says, "Then have my lips the sin that they have took," Shakespeare has personified Juliet's lips, giving them the human capacity to take something.

4. Identify and explain at least one other example of personification in the excerpt.

> A **symbol** is an act or tangible object that represents more than itself.

Note, for example, the following description:

> Juliet dares not move; her eyes fix on the approaching couple through the feathers of a passing peacock costume.

The screenwriters—and Shakespeare, too—have used the masks and costumes as visual symbols of the social barriers that separate people (and groups) from one another, just as the senseless feuding between the Capulets and Montagues prevents them from discovering the common ground that Romeo and Juliet have come to share.

5. With a partner, discuss the symbolic value of each of the following images from the screenplay:
   a) the elevator
   b) Juliet's angel costume
   c) the light bursting through the crack in the elevator behind the kissing couple
   d) the archway

> An **oxymoron** is a figure of speech that places opposites together to create a particular effect, such as *fiery ice,* which conveys the burning sensation of intense cold.

6. Shakespeare was a master of wordplay who created numerous oxymorons such as those found in Act I, scene i, when Romeo shares with his cousin Benvolio how he longs for love. Identify at least seven examples of oxymorons in Romeo's speech.

> Here's much to do with hate, but more with love:
> Why, then, O brawling love! O loving hate!
> O anything, of nothing first create!
> O heavy lightness! serious vanity!
> Mis-shapen chaos of well-seeming forms!
> Feather of lead, bright smoke, cold fire, sick health!
> Still-waking sleep, that is not what it is!
> This love feel I, that feel no love in this.

7. Working with a partner, create oxymorons of your own by brainstorming several nouns and pairing them with adjectives that suggest their opposites. Share your most effective oxymorons with the class.

8. Read your own adaptation again and identify places where you could paint vivid sensory impressions by using the figurative language devices discussed here.

Word Study & Spelling

In the Mechanics & Design section of this unit, you learned that film producers want to read scripts quickly, so screenwriters must find ways of including necessary information as briefly as possible. One way screenwriters keep their descriptions of setting and action brief is to choose concise words that convey strong impressions. Note how the following action descriptions convey details using relatively few words:

Action Description	Details Conveyed
Romeo begins to **circumnavigate** the dance floor in an attempt to get closer to Juliet.	Romeo begins to **walk around the outside** of the dance floor in an attempt to get closer to Juliet.
The songstress's voice **soars**.	The songstress's voice **rises high above the crowd.**
CLOSE ON: Romeo's lips **deliciously** close to Juliet's.	CLOSE ON: Romeo's lips so close to Juliet's **that we can sense the powerful attraction he feels for her.**

1. Find the following action details as they appear in the excerpt and
    identify the concise words used by the screenwriters to convey strong
    impressions.

    a) Taking care not to be noticed, Romeo is looking at the angel [Juliet]
       from around the arches on the hall side of the dance floor.

    b) Juliet looks quickly back to Dave, who, unaware of her interest in
       Romeo, gives her a smile that emphasizes his handsomeness and
       charm.

    c) An enormous quantity of balloons, tinsel, and confetti falls in a
       continuous manner from the roof.

    d) Juliet, turning in front of the elevator in the grand hall, brings her
       hands together to give the impression that she is a praying angel.

One of the most useful tools a writer has for locating
concise words is the **thesaurus,** which is a collection of
synonyms and antonyms. Some thesauruses are arranged
alphabetically like a dictionary, while others provide
alphabetized lists of words in an index with numbers
indicating their locations within the text. Regardless of
how a thesaurus is arranged, writers know they should not

> *Learning Goal*
>
> • **use a thesaurus to
>   find concise
>   synonyms and
>   antonyms**

use a word that appears in a thesaurus entry unless they are sure of its
meaning. For example, the screenwriters of *Romeo and Juliet* might have
included the following description of Mercutio:

> Mercutio is a young person who often acts quickly without giving
> careful thought to the results of his actions.

One thesaurus lists the following synonyms for *careless:*

> thoughtless, negligent, reckless, rash, foolhardy, audacious, impetuous,
> imprudent, disorganized, chaotic, slovenly, messy

Note that the last four synonyms refer more to untidiness than lack of
thought, so it would be inaccurate to describe Mercutio as *a "slovenly"
youth.* A more precise adjective would be *rash* or *impetuous.*

2. Choose a concise synonym found in the model that will convey accurately and precisely the meaning of the words in boldface. (You may wish to rearrange words in a sentence to find the most suitable place for the synonym.) Use a thesaurus to help you identify possible choices.

   a) Romeo was unsure of his **nearness** to Juliet's mother.
   b) **The force of** Romeo's **weight** nearly resulted in his collision with the peacock-clad guest.
   c) **The reserved manner of** Juliet's **response** melted in the face of Romeo's passion.
   d) One guest found the balcony high above the ballroom to be a location **that gave her a feeling of dizziness.**
   e) Although aimed at helping the young lovers, the **secretive** actions of Friar Laurence later in the play helped lead to their destruction.

3. Use a thesaurus to find accurate synonyms for the boldface words found in the model. Be sure to use a dictionary to check the meanings of words you are not familiar with.

   a) **Forswear** it, sight.
   b) With the **diva's** spiralling final notes, the ballad concludes.
   c) Juliet glances **furtively** to Dave Paris.
   d) She offers her hand in a **chaste** handshake.
   e) They join the **vexed** Gloria Capulet, who clings to a patient Dave Paris.

4. Read your adaptation carefully to see if there are passages—especially descriptions of characters and actions—that could be written more vividly or concisely. Use a thesaurus to identify precise words and make sure you have used them correctly.

TECHNO-TIP

Many word-processing programs include a thesaurus, which you can access easily as you write.

WORD ORIGINS

You kiss by the book.

The word **book** comes from the German *buche,* meaning "beech," because the Germanic peoples first wrote on boards made from the beech tree. The expression *by the book,* which is now cliché, means to follow strict rules in the proper completion of a task. Therefore, Juliet's comment to Romeo can be interpreted two ways: she may be telling him that he kisses expertly, or she may be telling him that he kisses without passion, as though he learned it from a book.

Explain the meanings of the following expressions, and then identify and explain at least one other common expression that contains this word.

- **to be in someone's good (or bad) books**
- **to take a leaf out of someone's book**
- **to book a reservation**
- **to throw the book at someone**

Looking Back

Before handing in your final edited draft, have a classmate check your film adaptation, paying particular attention to the following:

☑ Is the script presented in the proper format?

☑ Does the cover page include the necessary information?

☑ Has the author used figurative language effectively?

☑ Are all words used (and spelled) correctly?

Reflect and Build on Your Learning

Reflecting on Narrative Writing Forms

1. Review the Learning Goals on page 17. Which goals do you think you have achieved most successfully? Which goals do you think will require you to do more work? For each goal that will require more work, list one specific action you will take to accomplish the goal.

2. Write a note to your teacher explaining the three most important things you learned about narrative writing during the study of this section.

3. Complete each of the following statements about the work you have done in the past three units on narration.

   • The unit I most enjoyed in this section was ... because ...
   • Two things I really had to work on in this section were ...
   • One thing I would like to know more about as a result of studying this section is ...
   • To be more successful in my learning during the next section, I will need to ...

Looking Over Narrative Writing Forms

1. Working with a small group, create a chart summarizing what you know about the features of ballads, short stories, and film adaptations. Include the following headings in your chart: Length, Plot, Use of Dialogue, Characterization, Point of View, Setting, and Theme. The class checklists you developed for each form will help you with this task. Once completed, compare your chart with those of other groups. How would you modify your chart based on what they have included in theirs?

Using Narrative Writing Forms

1. Outline three methods or techniques of narrative writing that can make a narrative more interesting.

2. A writer must choose the most appropriate form of writing to communicate her or his message. Explain why a writer might choose to use each of the following narrative forms to communicate a message. In other words, what are the particular advantages or uses of each form?

- friendly letter
- anecdote or humorous personal narrative
- legend
- autobiography or biography
- fable
- historical narrative
- myth
- short story
- script or film adaptation
- ballad

3. Working alone or in a small group, write a ballad based on either the story of *Romeo and Juliet* or the short story "Bearing Up." You may choose to use the metre and rhythm, and even some of the words, from "Lochinvar" as the basis for your ballad. For example:

O young Michael-o has moved out to the West,
Of all the brave SARtechs, his dad was the best;

4. Most narratives focus on a conflict of some sort. Recall a disagreement you had recently with a friend or family member, or imagine an argument two of the characters in the models of this section might have had. Write a brief dialogue for a scene in which the two characters argue because of their opposing points of view. You may choose to write your dialogue in the form of a script or as an excerpt from a short story. Be sure to provide your audience with necessary background information, such as where the argument takes place, and why the argument started in the first place.

5. a) Working in groups of three, discuss some interesting personal anecdotes that could form the basis of a short narrative. Then choose one person's experience and discuss it in more detail.

   b) Each person in the group should then write about this one experience as if it happened to her or him. No real names should be used in the story.

   c) Meet with another group of students in the class, and take turns reading your stories to the other group. The group listening to the stories will try to guess which of the three was written by the person the experience actually happened to.

BUILD ON YOUR LEARNING

Description

Writing descriptively is like painting with words. Just as painters carefully choose the shade of their colours and the intensity of their brushstrokes, writers of description carefully select their details and choose words that convey a single, dominant impression of their subject. Because few people see the same thing in exactly the same way, two writers might convey very different impressions of a single experience. Consider, for example, how a young child's description of the Brussels sprouts heaped on her plate might differ from that of her parents. Whether the subject is something tangible like Brussels sprouts or something intangible like an idea or a feeling, the process of choosing details and presenting them in a purposeful way is the same.

This section contains three forms of descriptive writing: sonnet, character description, and personal impression. Each piece paints a vivid impression of its subject, helping us to experience some part of the world through the eyes of another.

Features of Description

- Descriptions focus on creating a single dominant impression of a person, place, event, feeling, or idea.
- Writers of description choose words, images, and details that appeal to more than one sense and that reinforce the dominant impression they want to give their readers.
- Descriptive writing often uses figurative language techniques, such as simile and metaphor.
- Descriptions may be organized in various ways: spatially, chronologically, thematically, or in whatever way best suits the topic and purpose.

Learning Goals

- use a range of sources to gather information and explore ideas for your written work

- identify and use literary and informational forms appropriately in writing a sonnet, a character description, and a personal impression

- use a variety of organizational techniques to present ideas and information logically and coherently

- revise your written work independently and collaboratively to improve clarity, coherence, and style

- edit and proofread to produce final drafts using correct grammar, mechanics, usage, and spelling

- use knowledge of vocabulary and language conventions to write competently and effectively

- develop listening, speaking, and media literacy skills

- read a variety of literary and informational forms, such as sonnets, character descriptions, and personal impressions

- identify and understand the elements and style of a variety of literary and informational forms

Unit ④ Sonnet

What is a sonnet?

The sonnet—whose name is derived from the Italian word *sonetto,* meaning "little song"—is a 14-line lyric poem that follows a specific metre and rhyme scheme. Originally, sonnets dealt primarily with love and were accompanied by mandolin or lute music. In more recent times, the sonnet form has been used to explore a variety of subjects—even golf. Of the three sonnets given here, the first is from the nineteenth century, while the second and third are more modern.

Learning Goals

- write a sonnet
- use phrases and clauses correctly
- adapt punctuation and capitalization for poetry
- understand how authors use stylistic devices to achieve particular effects
- spell plurals, possessives, and contractions correctly

Sonnet xiv
(From *Sonnets From the Portuguese*)*

BY ELIZABETH BARRETT BROWNING

If thou must love me, let it be for nought
Except for love's sake only. Do not say
"I love her for her smile—her look—her way
Of speaking gently,—for a trick of thought
That falls in well with mine, and certes brought
A sense of pleasant ease on such a day"—
For these things in themselves, Belovèd, may
Be changed, or change for thee,—and love, so wrought,
May be unwrought so. Neither love me for
Thine own dear pity's wiping my cheeks dry,—
A creature might forget to weep, who bore
Thy comfort long, and lose thy love thereby!
But love me for love's sake, that evermore
Thou mayst love on, through love's eternity. ■

* Elizabeth Barrett Browning wrote "Sonnet xiv" (from *Sonnets From the Portuguese*) for her husband, Robert Browning, who called her "the Portuguese" because of her dark complexion. *Sonnets From the Portuguese* is considered by many to be the best collection of love poems ever written.

Oh Mother, Mother, Where Is Happiness?

BY GWENDOLYN BROOKS

Oh mother, mother, where is happiness?
They took my lover's tallness off to war,
Left me lamenting. Now I cannot guess
What I can use an empty heart-cup for.
He won't be coming back here any more.
Some day the war will end, but, oh, I knew
When he went walking grandly out that door
That my sweet love would have to be untrue.
Would have to be untrue. Would have to court
Coquettish death, whose impudent and strange
Possessive arms and beauty (of a sort)
Can make a hard man hesitate—and change.
And he will be the one to stammer, "Yes."
Oh mother, mother, where is happiness? ■

Golf

BY ALDEN NOWLAN

My friends believe in golf, address the ball,
however bent, to an appointed place.
Newtonians, convinced no orb can fall
out of the numbered course of time and space.

But I, from clumsiness or pity, drive
balls out of bounds and into woods and traps,
my knees and wrists vindictive in their love
for dark and tangled places not on maps.

"Golf's not your game," they say. But I persist.
"Next one goes straight ..." I promise. Oh, they're fooled
right cunningly by my secretive wrist
that treacherously lets the world go wild.

Let them attack the green. As for myself,
I pitch into the darkness, like a wolf. ■

Investigating the Models

IDEA FILE

It may help you to know the following terms as you read and discuss the sonnets in this unit:

Couplet: two successive lines of poetry that are similar in both metre and rhyme

Quatrain: a four-line stanza

Sestet: a six-line stanza

Octave: an eight-line stanza

1. There are two main sonnet patterns, distinguished mostly by their rhyme scheme. Browning's "Sonnet xiv" follows the Italian (or Petrarchan) rhyme scheme:

   abba abba cdcdcd

   Brooks's and Nowlan's sonnets, on the other hand, are English (or Shakespearean) in form. Identify the rhyme scheme of an English sonnet, based on the two examples given here. How does this pattern differ from the Italian?

2. Whereas narrative poetry tells a story, lyric poetry presents a personal and emotional impression of a subject. Identify the subject of each sonnet and the emotion that is central to its presentation.

3. The intensity of emotion in a poem depends largely on the point of view chosen by the poet. Each of the models is written from the most intimate of viewpoints, the first person, in which the narrator is someone directly involved in the situation being recounted. Identify and describe the persona of each narrator, and explain how the choice of persona influences the emotion that is conveyed.

IDEA FILE

In poetry, **persona** is the first-person narrator of a narrative poem or the voice we listen to in a lyric poem, and it is through this persona that the poet may project her or his own thoughts and words.

4. In the Italian sonnet, the octave (the first eight lines) usually presents a problem or situation, and the sestet (the last six) provides a resolution. Explain whether Browning presents her subject in this manner.

5. Each quatrain in an English sonnet typically develops a different aspect of the subject, while the final couplet sums up the poet's feelings toward her or his subject. Have Brooks and Nowlan structured their sonnets in this way? Explain.

6. The rhythmical pattern of sonnets can be described as **iambic pentameter,** meaning that there are five feet to a line, each foot consisting of two syllables, the first unstressed and the second stressed. (See Unit 1 for more on metre.) To hear and visualize this pattern, read all three poems aloud. Then copy the first line of each poem, break the words into syllables, group the syllables into feet, and mark the syllables that are stressed.

7. When attempting very structured writing forms like the sonnet, writers may use irregular pronunciations, unusual word order, archaic language, and even invented words to sustain a particular rhyme scheme or metre. Knowing when to use "poetic licence" of this sort is part of the art of writing good poetry. Listening carefully to the sound of the language, read each sonnet aloud and identify at least three instances where poetic licence has been applied. In each case, discuss whether you think the poet was justified in her or his use of poetic licence.

8. The rigid structure of a sonnet imposes strict limitations on a poet. Why do you suppose the authors of the models chose to present their ideas in sonnet form rather than using less exacting forms?

Checkpoint: Sonnet

✓ Create a checklist of common features of sonnets, based on the models and your own experience. You can use the checklist to help you create your own sonnet.

Writer's Workshop

Learning Goal

• **write a sonnet**

1. Brainstorm a list of people and things you love. Don't be concerned about their importance— sonnets about cats or computers can be just as relevant to modern readers as those about relationships between two people.

2. From your list, choose a subject that evokes an especially strong emotional response and explore your feelings about it. Decide whether it would fit best into an Italian or English sonnet pattern. In other words, does it lend itself more to a problem-solution approach or to an exploration of different aspects of the topic?

3. Choose a viewpoint from which to present your subject. Will you speak directly to your reader, or will you use a persona? What do you want the reader to know about the person speaking? How will you convey this understanding?

4. Consider which approach you will use to present your subject. If you plan to use the Italian sonnet form, identify what specific problem you will present in the first eight lines and what solution will emerge in the final six lines. If you want to write an English sonnet, describe which aspects of the topic you will explore in the first three stanzas and how you will sum up your feelings in the last two lines. For the moment, you can ignore issues of metre and rhyme scheme. Concentrate, instead, on sketching the content of your poem, including as many details as possible about your subject.

TECHNO-TIP

If you are using a computer, save your rough draft in a separate file so you can refer back to it if you get stuck. As you revise, save versions of your sonnet every so often in separate files marked sonnet1, sonnet2, etc. This way, you can go back to earlier drafts to retrieve words and expressions that you like. Remember that once you save your changes, your original cannot easily be retrieved. (You might want to set your computer's alarm to remind you to start a new file every five or ten minutes.)

5. The poet Robert Frost once commented that writing poetry without rhyme is like playing tennis without a net. Although conforming to a rhyme scheme can be a challenge for even the most accomplished writer, it can help focus your writing, just as the net offers the tennis player tangible evidence of the success or failure of a shot. As you draft your sonnet using the details you recorded in activity 4, avoid using the

first rhyming word that comes to mind. Try generating three or four different rhyming words before choosing the one that is most appropriate for a particular line. Record the others in a word bank since you may wish to use them later in your poem.

6. Once you have established the content and rhyme scheme of your poem, concentrate on metre. Read your lines aloud, listening for the number and position of stressed and unstressed syllables. There should be 10 syllables in each line, beginning with an unstressed syllable and alternating with a stressed one throughout. Try tapping your pencil or nodding your head as you read to establish the rhythm of your sonnet, adding or deleting words where necessary to maintain iambic pentameter throughout.

 7. Refer back to the list you created at Checkpoint, and revise and edit your sonnet until you are satisfied with it.

ORAL LANGUAGE EXTENSION

The task of interpreting poetry can be much less intimidating when you work as part of a group. With three or four classmates, select a poem and have a group member read it aloud while the others read it silently. Identify any unfamiliar words and determine their meaning. Then have another group member read the poem aloud, and take turns giving your initial response to it, referring to the specific details that generated this response. Do not comment on, question, or challenge a response until all group members have had a turn.

Once each person has spoken, you are free to discuss each other's ideas (in a respectful manner), always referring to details in the poem to support or to challenge an idea. If the discussion falters, have a group member read the poem aloud again. Feel free to read the poem many times during the discussion. Once the group has arrived at a satisfactory interpretation, have one student read the poem aloud a final time, and each person independently write her or his own explanation.

Grammar

A **clause** is a group of words that contains both a verb and its subject. A **phrase,** on the other hand, lacks one (or both) of these.

Noun phrase:	the war (lacking a verb)
Verb phrase:	will end (lacking a subject)
Clause:	the war will end (has subject and verb)

Phrases can act as nouns, verbs, adjectives, adverbs, and, occasionally, other parts of speech.

1. State whether each italicized word group is a phrase or a clause. If it is a phrase, tell what part of speech it functions as in the sentence.

   a) I cannot guess what *I can use* an empty heart-cup for.
   b) No orb *can fall* out of the numbered course of time and space.
   c) My secretive wrist *quite treacherously* lets the world go wild.
   d) My knees and wrists love *dark and tangled* places not on maps.
   e) I promise *the next one goes straight.*
   f) I, from *clumsiness or pity,* drive balls into woods and traps.
   g) He won't be coming back here *any more.*

A **main** (or independent) **clause** makes a complete thought and can stand alone as a sentence. A **subordinate** (or dependent) **clause** cannot stand alone as a sentence.

If thou must love me, *let it be for nought.*
     subordinate clause   *main clause*

Subordinate clauses begin with **subordinating conjunctions** such as *although, because, before, since, unless, until, while, when, as, if, as if, who, which, that, after,* and *though.*

And, or, nor, for, but, so, and *yet* are **coordinating conjunctions,** which are used to join two main clauses.

Subordinate clauses function as nouns, adjectives, or adverbs.

Subordinate noun clause:
Now I cannot guess / **What I can use an empty heart-cup for.**

Subordinate adjective clause:
Oh, they're fooled right cunningly by my secretive wrist
that treacherously lets the world go wild.

Subordinate adverb clause:
I knew / **When he went grandly out that door /**
That my sweet love would have to be untrue.

WRITING TIP

Often, you can tighten up your writing by changing a
subordinate clause into a phrase:

Subordinate clause: But I, **because I am clumsy or pity them,**
drive balls out of bounds and into woods and traps.

Phrase: But I, *from clumsiness or pity,* drive balls out of
bounds and into woods and traps.

2. Find all the subordinate clauses in your own sonnet and identify the
    function of each. Look for ways to reword the subordinate clause as a
    phrase, and decide which version works best in your sonnet.

MEDIA LINK

The original sonnets dealt primarily with love and were often
accompanied by music. To some degree, they reflected the
social reality of the times and contemporary relationships
between the sexes. What would be the equivalent of the
sonnet as love song today?

Create a slide-sound show to present your own sonnet to the
class. The images you choose should have a definite structure,
although they do not necessarily need to tell a story. Do not
attempt to do a literal interpretation. Begin with a clear
definition of the concept of your sonnet, prepare a storyboard,
shoot the images, select and sequence them, and, finally, time
your slide presentation with the reading of your sonnet.

Mechanics & Design

Everything in a poem should contribute to the overall emotional response the poet wishes to evoke. Punctuation and capital letters—as well as their absence—are important tools for achieving this purpose.

1. A capital letter is required for nouns used in direct address. Why do you suppose Gwendolyn Brooks chose not to capitalize *mother* in the following direct address?

   Oh mother, mother, where is happiness?

2. Dashes enable writers to insert parenthetical expressions and to indicate pauses by interrupting the flow of a passage. Both Elizabeth Barrett Browning and Gwendolyn Brooks make use of dashes in their sonnets. Explain their function, giving examples to illustrate.

3. Gwendolyn Brooks could have inserted the phrase *of a sort* between dashes but, instead, chose to include it in parentheses. What effect is achieved by their use? Explain.

4. A line break in a poem may signify a brief pause to the reader. A comma added to the end of a line break may extend that pause, thereby heightening the importance of a statement or image. Are commas used for this purpose in the three models? How do you know? Give examples to support your ideas.

5. In poetry, periods often appear at the end of lines to indicate the end of a complete thought and a pause before beginning the next. All three models include periods that do not appear at the ends of lines. Why did the authors end thoughts in the middle of lines? What effect is achieved by doing so? Explain.

6. Neither Brooks nor Browning includes spaces between lines. Why do you suppose Nowlan chose to present "Golf" as four distinct stanzas?

7. Read your own sonnet aloud and look for places where you can use punctuation, capitalization, or spaces to improve the poem or make it sound better when read aloud.

Usage & Style

Learning Goal

- understand how authors use stylistic devices to achieve particular effects

Because most poetry is meant to be read aloud, poets make use of language that appeals to the sense of sound. The most obvious example of this interest in sound is rhyme, but poets can use other devices that emphasize sound to achieve certain effects in their work.

> **Onomatopoeia** is the use of words that imitate sounds.

Onomatopoeic words like *clang* and *crash* can add drama to writing, while those such as *murmur* and *rustle* can help convey a peaceful mood.

1. Working with a partner, list at least five onomatopoeic words that might have been used by Alden Nowlan when describing someone playing golf.

> **Alliteration** is the repeated use of words that begin with similar sounds.

Repeated soft sounds like "l" or "m" can create a feeling of tranquillity (e.g., *lovers' lullaby*), while repeated hard sounds like "k" or "t" can emphasize action and excitement (e.g., *the puma pounced*).

2. Identify two examples of alliteration found in the models, and explain the effect created by each.

> **Assonance** is the repetition of similar or identical vowel sounds in a sequence of words.

Thine own dear pity's wiping my cheeks dry,—

> **Consonance** is the repetition of the same consonant sounds followed by different vowel sounds.

... that treacherously lets the world go wild.

Dissonance is the use of a deliberately harsh or disagreeable combination of sounds.

> Would have to **c**ourt
> **Coq**uettish death ...

3. Describe the effects achieved by assonance and dissonance in Gwendolyn Brooks's sonnet.

4. Find other examples of assonance, consonance, and dissonance in the models, and describe the effect of each.

5. Read your own sonnet aloud, and identify places where you could strengthen your writing by using language that appeals to sound.

Word Study & Spelling

Earlier in this unit, you learned that sound is an important element of poetry. However, many words create spelling problems for writers because they sound alike, and those with apostrophes can be particularly challenging.

> Thine own dear **pity's** wiping my cheeks dry,—
>
> Oh, **they're** fooled / right cunningly by my secretive wrist

Learning Goal

- spell plurals, possessives, and contractions correctly

1. a) What words are often confused with *they're?* Use each word correctly in a sentence.
   b) Create memory tricks that will help you recall when to use each. Compete with your classmates to invent the most memorable devices.

When you are not sure whether to use an apostrophe, remember the following rules:

- **Possessive pronouns** (e.g., *yours, hers, its, theirs, ours, whose*) do not require apostrophes.

- Words like *it's, there's,* and *who's* are **contractions.** They use an apostrophe to show that letters have been omitted.

- Nouns need an apostrophe only if they show possession (e.g., *pity's, Alden's*).

2. Find and correct any errors in the use of apostrophes in the following passage.

> The Italian sonnet reached it's highest form with the writings of the Italian poet Petrarch. Published after 1327, Petrarchs *Canzoniere*—which is Italian for "Songbook"—included 317 sonnets written to Laura, a Frenchwoman who's name he immortalized in his poems. Sir Thomas Wyatt and Henry Howard, the Earl of Surrey, are the people most often credited with introducing the sonnet form into England. Sir Philip Sidneys sonnet sequence titled *Astrophel and Stella* (1591) later established the Italian form in England. Because the English language was not as rich in rhyme's as the Italian language, writer's such as William Shakespeare and Edmund Spenser adapted the sonnet form to produce the English sonnet, also known as the Shakespearean sonnet. While early sonnets dealt primarily with love, sixteenth-century writers such as John Donne and John Milton used the sonnet form to explore other subjects including religion, politics, and personal matter's. The sonnet's popularity in the English language declined until the end of the eighteenth century when romantic poet's such as Wordsworth, Coleridge, Keats, and Shelley breathed new life into the form.

WRITING TIP

Before you include an apostrophe, look twice to be sure it is needed; most writers include too many apostrophes rather than too few.

3. Check your sonnet carefully to see if you have used apostrophes correctly, especially in words that show possession.

WORD ORIGINS

"Oh, they're fooled
right **cunningly** by my secretive wrist
that treacherously lets the world go wild."

The word **cunning** has changed its meaning over time. It comes from the Old English word *cunnan*, meaning "to know." In its original use, the word meant "skilful" or "ingenious." When we hear a person described as cunning today, however, we think of that person as one who uses trickery to achieve her or his ends.

Many words change their meaning or acquire new meanings over time. Working with a partner, identify a new meaning that has been added to each of the following commonly used words since the advent of computers.

surf   web   cookie   bit   monitor   mouse

Looking Back

Before handing in your final edited draft, have a classmate check your sonnet, paying particular attention to the following:

- ✓ Does the poem follow the correct form of a sonnet?

- ✓ Does the poem use grammatical constructions (e.g., subordinate clauses or phrases) effectively to maintain a consistent rhyme scheme and metre?

- ✓ Does the use of punctuation, line breaks, and stanzas add to or reinforce the meaning of the poem?

- ✓ Does the poem use sound devices such as onomatopoeia, alliteration, assonance, consonance, or dissonance effectively?

- ✓ Are all words, especially plurals, possessives, and contractions, spelled correctly?

Unit 5 Character Description

What is a character description?

A character description is a section of a novel, short story, or nonfiction piece that paints a portrait by choosing details—such as physical attributes, setting, dialogue, images, and actions—that convey a clear impression of the subject's personality and appearance. Both of the character descriptions that follow come from novels: the first describes the character Sara in the novel *The Underpainter* by Jane Urquhart. In the second, French writer Gustave Flaubert paints a vivid picture of Emma Bovary, the main character in his classic novel, *Madame Bovary,* set in nineteenth-century France.

Learning Goals

- write a character description
- use participles, gerunds, and infinitives correctly
- use commas, dashes, and parentheses correctly to set off nonrestrictive elements in a sentence
- use a variety of stylistic devices to "show" rather than "tell" in a piece of writing
- use proofreading symbols to identify and correct writing errors

From *The Underpainter*

BY JANE URQUHART

THE FIRST TIME I SAW SARA SHE WAS holding a large broom, sweeping, her body twisting around the object as if she were dancing with it. Later I drew the broom with great care, great precision, right down to the last bristle. I drew even the inconsequential rose on the label that was wrapped around the base of the handle. Sara's back was to me—I hadn't yet seen her face—and the curve of her spine was visible through her cotton uniform. She was sweeping the verandah of the hotel that had once housed businessmen and speculators from American cities, but that now catered to tourists who wanted the view from Lake Superior's north shore. She worked, in season, at the hotel and lived year-round in the small log house that her father had left her.

The house she has now left to me.

Had she not been working at the hotel I might never have seen her at all, though perhaps we would have passed each other on the track they called, and likely still call, The Avenue, when the lake, the vast inland sea, would have had all of my attention. Or she might have been walking behind me as I strolled toward the end of the settlement—a crescent moon of mostly uninhabited miners' houses around a subtle bay—and would have slipped inside her door, disappeared, before I turned around.

As it was, I was sitting in one of the wooden rockers on the verandah, drawing the offshore mine situated on the island for which the townsite was named. It was 1920, the first and last year of my father's connection with that fundamentally extinct operation, just before he took himself and

what was left of his money permanently back to the States. I was drawing the mine for my father, the last resident American speculator in the hotel, though I would rather have been concentrating on the rocks, the trees, even the hotel itself. But he had asked this one favour of me and I had agreed.

Through the cotton of her uniform I could see her strong, slim back, her shoulder blades shifting as she moved the broom. As her head was held in a slightly tilted position, I could see the long tendon on the side of her neck and one vein there, pulsing. She appeared to be trying to cover every square inch of wooden floorboards with the bristles of her broom, but there must have been a narrative running somewhere in the back of her mind, a narrative that did not, as yet, involve me. What was she thinking during those last few moments of innocent labour before I disturbed her life?

I could see the slight curve of muscle in her upper arm, could imagine the sharp edge of a graphite pencil capturing the motion, the gesture. Freezing it.

And yet, watching her, her unselfconscious grace, I wanted to interrupt the task, to add my own presence to the image. I wanted to hear her voice, and I wanted to hear it speaking to me.

"Would you like me to move?" I asked, already rising from the rocker. I wanted her to turn around, to face me.

She stopped sweeping then, pivoted, pushed a strand of hair back from her forehead and regarded me with surprise, as if she hadn't known that anyone was there at all. Her eyes were on me now. I could see her prominent cheekbones, her expressive mouth.

"Oh, no, sir," she said, "you can stay right where you are for as long as you like." ∎

From *Madame Bovary*

BY GUSTAVE FLAUBERT

EMMA WOULD SIT THERE IN HER dressing gown, its wide collar flung open over a pleated shift with three gold buttons. The gown was belted with a tasselled cord, and her dainty garnet-red slippers were adorned at the instep with a cluster of wide ribbons. She had bought herself a blotter, a writing case, an inkstand, and envelopes, even though she had no one to write to. She would poke about, dusting off the shelves, looking at herself in the mirror. Sometimes she picked up a book and then, starting to daydream between the lines, let it fall back on her knees. She longed to travel or to go back to the convent. She longed both to die and to live in Paris.

Charles, in rain or snow, rode along the rough country roads. He ate omelettes in farmhouse kitchens, reached into damp beds, caught lukewarm spurts of blood on his cheek, listened to death rattles, examined the contents of basins, pushed aside much dirty linen; but every evening he came home to a blazing fire, a well-prepared dinner, comfortable furniture, and a beautifully dressed, charming wife, with such a fresh, subtle fragrance about her that he never quite knew whether it was perfume, or whether her skin perhaps scented her clothes.

She delighted him by countless little refinements; sometimes it was a new way of making paper ruffs for the candlesticks, a different flounce on her skirt, or a fancy name for a very ordinary dish which the maid had spoiled, but which Charles relished, to the last morsel. She saw ladies in Rouen wearing a cluster of charms on their watch chains; she bought herself some. She shopped about to find a pair of tall, blue glass vases for her mantelpiece and, not long afterwards, decided that she needed an ivory sewing box with a silver-gilt thimble. The less Charles understood these niceties, the more he was seduced by them. They added in some mysterious way to the pleasure of his senses and the comforts of his home. They were like gold dust sprinkled along the narrow road of his life.

He looked well and felt well. His reputation was now firmly established. The country people liked him because he was not proud. He … never entered the local café, and besides, his whole way of life inspired

confidence. He was particularly successful in treating influenza and chest diseases. Very much afraid of killing a patient, Charles usually prescribed only mild sedatives, with an occasional emetic, footbath, or leeches. It was not that surgery frightened him; he bled people as freely as horses, and was known to have a "devil of a grip" when extracting teeth.

Recently, "to keep himself up to date," he had subscribed to *La Ruche médicale*, a new professional journal for which he had received a prospectus. He would read a bit of it after dinner, but the warmth from the fire, combined with the process of digestion, would make him fall asleep within five minutes. There he sat, under the lamp, his chin on his hands and his hair shaggy as a mane. Emma would look at him and shrug her shoulders. Why couldn't she at least have married one of those silent, scholarly men who work late at night with their books, until at last, when rheumatism sets in at the age of sixty, they can display a decoration in the form of a cross on their ill-cut black coats? She would have liked the name of Bovary, her name, to become famous, prominent in the windows of bookshops, mentioned in newspapers, known to all of France. But Charles had no ambition! A doctor from Yvetot, with whom he had recently consulted, had humiliated him at a patient's very bedside, before the assembled relatives. When Charles told her the story that evening, Emma burst into a fury at the other doctor. Charles was touched. He kissed her on the forehead with tears in his eyes. But it was shame that made her angry; she felt like hitting him. Finally she rushed into the hall, opened the window and took a breath of fresh air to calm herself.

"What a pathetic man!" she murmured, biting her lip. "Pathetic."

She was beginning to feel irritated with him in other ways. His manners grew coarser with age: he whittled the corks of empty wine bottles during dessert; after eating he cleaned his teeth with his tongue; he made gurgling noises when he swallowed his soup and, as he put on weight, his eyes, small to begin with, seemed to be pushed back into his head by his puffy cheeks.

Sometimes Emma tucked the red edge of his sweater under his vest, arranged his tie, or threw away the faded gloves which he liked to wear. Her efforts were not, as he believed, for his sake, but for hers, out of pride, or exasperation. At other times she would talk to him about things she had read, a passage from a novel, a new play, or a bit of gossip about high society from the paper. Charles, after all, was someone, a ready ear, an obliging listener. She even confided in her greyhound! Sometimes she even felt like talking to the logs in the fireplace and the pendulum of the clock.

Deep in her heart, however, she was waiting for something to happen. Like a shipwrecked sailor she kept desperate watch over the lonely horizon of her life, hoping that in the distance some white sail might appear out of the mist. She did not know what stroke of luck, what wind might bring it to her, or toward what shore it might bear her. Would it be a sloop or a triple-decked vessel, laden with anguish or full to the gunwales with joy? But every morning when she woke up, her hopes rose for the day. She listened for each sound, leapt out of bed, was astonished when nothing happened; then at sunset, sadder than ever, she began to long for tomorrow. ■

Investigating the Models

1. The writer's viewpoint determines the information she or he will include in a description. Explain how this is reflected in the details that Urquhart's first-person narrator notices about Sara, compared to the details about Emma offered by Flaubert's third-person omniscient narrator.

2. Although Sara is the subject of Urquhart's character description, the reader learns a great deal about the narrator as well. What information does the narrator offer about himself? How does Urquhart include this information without distracting the reader from the primary focus of the description?

3. An effective way to convey an impression of a character on the page is through physical description. To what extent is physical description important in the characterizations of Sara and Emma? What impressions are conveyed through these physical details?

4. Our possessions and the surroundings in which we live can be a reflection of our personalities. What do the details about Sara's and Emma's possessions and surroundings reveal about them? Refer to specific details in the models to illustrate your ideas.

5. The things people do often convey information about what they are like as human beings. What action has Urquhart chosen for Sara to perform? What does this action reveal about this character?

6. Because it is human nature to form opinions of people based on the way they react to others and to events around them, writers often include such details to convey a particular understanding of their characters. What impression does Flaubert convey of Emma through her reactions to Charles and her marriage? Identify the specific details that give rise to this impression.

7. The things people say as well as how they say them—for instance, correct or incorrect usage, language that is appropriate or inappropriate for a particular situation, language that is specific to a time or place, and so on—reveal much about them. To what extent is this true of Sara and Emma?

8. Often, a writer will make use of a visual image to convey an understanding of a character. Discuss how Urquhart's image of the broom and Flaubert's image of "the lonely horizon" contribute to our understanding of Sara and Emma.

9. Details that surprise the reader are often the most effective in conveying an impression of a character. Note the contrasts that Flaubert includes in the opening paragraph of the excerpt from *Madame Bovary*. In what way do they contribute to our understanding of Emma?

10. Although both character descriptions are excerpts from novels, they are presented in such a way that they seem complete. Choose one and explain how its structure contributes to this effect.

Checkpoint: Character Description

✓ As a class, create a checklist of common features of character descriptions, based on the models and your own experience. You can use the checklist to help you create your own character description.

Writer's Workshop

1. The focus of your character description will be yourself as seen through the eyes of someone who knows you. List people—excluding family members and close friends—with whom you come in contact on a regular basis. From your list, identify the person whose viewpoint you are most interested in exploring.

IDEA FILE

Consider people you see

- in school (classmates, teachers, administrators, maintenance workers, cafeteria staff, bus drivers, hall monitors, etc.)
- at extracurricular activities (teammates, coaches, faculty advisers, parent volunteers, etc.)
- at work (supervisors, co-workers, regular customers, etc.)
- during free time (neighbours, parents of friends, bank tellers, store clerks, salespeople, waiters, etc.)

2. Based on your past involvement with the individual you identified in activity 1, consider the dominant impression you think she or he has formed of you. Does this person see you as warm or reserved? Outgoing or shy? Serious or fun-loving? Cautious or impetuous? Energetic or lethargic? Open or secretive? Kind or cruel? (Remember, concentrate on the way this person sees you rather than the way you see yourself.)

Learning Goal

- **write a character description**

3. Make a chart with the following headings: Physical Features, Clothing/Possessions, Actions, Reactions, Comments, and Contrasts. Bearing in mind the dominant impression you identified in activity 2, brainstorm details about yourself that helped convey this impression. List as many as you can under the appropriate headings.

WRITING TIP

One way to convey a strong impression of a character is to invent a metaphor that will help your reader visualize a particular trait. In describing yourself, you might choose an attribute that you feel is especially characteristic of your personality or behaviour, and then illustrate it using a concrete thing (inanimate or living) with which a reader will associate this attribute. (For example, someone who is very methodical in the way she or he approaches every task might be compared to a worker bee or an assembly-line robot.) Concentrate on using specific nouns and verbs to draw the comparison.

4. Decide which point of view is best suited to your description. Will your narrator speak in the first person, as does the narrator of *The Underpainter,* or will your narrator be an omniscient third-person observer like the narrator of *Madame Bovary,* who not only provides information about Emma's appearance and actions but also shares what she is thinking and feeling?

5. If you are writing in the first person, what does the reader need to know about the person speaking? (You may wish to alter or invent some of this information to avoid embarrassing anyone.) If you have chosen the third person, how will you convey to the reader the perspective from which your description is offered?

WRITING TIP

Irony occurs when a character or reader believes (or expects) one thing, but something entirely different is the case. For example, the account of the Bovarys' marriage is ironic because, after learning of Charles's happiness with Emma, the reader discovers that Emma is intensely dissatisfied with her life—and with him.

"When Charles told her the story that evening, Emma burst into a fury at the other doctor. Charles was touched. He kissed her on the forehead with tears in his eyes. But it was shame that made her angry; she felt like hitting him."

Details that surprise a reader are often the most compelling or evocative. Consider including contrasting viewpoints in your own character description, emphasizing the difference between what your readers (i.e., your teacher and classmates) know about you and how your narrator describes you.

6. Choose a setting for your description and establish the background for the encounter. Will details about the setting and situation help establish the context quickly? How will you incorporate this information into your description without distracting the reader from the primary focus of your piece?

7. Since your description is not part of a longer piece of writing, such as a novel or short story, try to think of a structure that will enable it to stand alone. One suggestion is to begin with a physical impression, continue with details that provide a context for this impression, and then end with an observation that will give your writing a sense of completion.

8. Write a draft of your character description, bearing in mind that your main purpose is to convince your reader to share the narrator's attitude toward her or his subject.

 9. Refer back to the list you created at Checkpoint, and revise and edit your character description until you are satisfied with its focus, content, and organization.

ORAL LANGUAGE EXTENSION

Once you have completed your character description, form a group with three or four classmates and share your character descriptions with one another. Decide which piece of writing lends itself best to dramatization and, working as a group, adapt the description to a short play. Besides creating roles for each person in the group (e.g., acting or managing props), you will have to find ways to convey, through dialogue and action, the same impression presented in the written description. Remember to make good use of tone, facial expressions, and gestures.

Grammar

Some verb forms do not function as verbs. When a verb form functions as another part of speech, it is called a **verbal**. The three main types of verbals are participles, gerunds, and infinitives.

A **participle** is a verb form that can act as a verb only when it is accompanied by a helping verb (e.g., *be, have*). A participle on its own can also function as an adjective.

There are two types of participles:
* The **present participle** is the form of the verb that ends in *-ing* (e.g., *sweeping, going, gurgling*).
* The **past participle** is the form of the verb used after *have*. It usually ends in *-ed*, *-en*, or *-t* (e.g., *catered, seen, sent*).

> *Learning Goal*
> * use participles, gerunds, and infinitives correctly

A **gerund** is an *-ing* verb form that functions as a noun.

In other words, a gerund is a present participle that acts as a noun rather than an adjective.

> She stopped *sweeping* then. (direct object of the verb *stopped*)
>
> *Treating* influenza was Charles's specialty. (subject of the verb *was*)

1. Decide whether the following boldface words are acting as participles or gerunds.
   a) The first time the narrator saw Sara she was **holding** a large broom.
   b) **Sweeping** was usually done when guests were out of the hotel.
   c) She was **sweeping** the verandah, unaware that anyone was there.
   d) The narrator was **drawing** the mine on the island.
   e) He planned to give the **drawing** to his father as a gift.
   f) Every **holding** operated by the mining speculators was to be closed.

The **infinitive** is the basic form of the verb used with *to*.

> to run   to sing   to dive

Infinitives can function as adjectives, adverbs, or nouns.

Adjective:	Recently, **to keep** himself up to date, he had subscribed to *La Ruche médicale*. (modifies *he*)
Adverb:	She shopped about **to find** a pair of tall, blue glass vases for her mantelpiece. (modifies *shopped*)
Noun:	She longed **to travel**. (direct object of *longed*)

2. Tell whether the following boldface infinitives are acting as nouns, adjectives, or adverbs. Give a reason for each answer.
   a) Emma wanted **to die**.
   b) I was making the sketch **to please** my father.

c) **To entertain** herself, Emma went shopping.

d) I liked **to stroll** along the shore.

e) Charles hurried **to get home** to Emma.

WRITING TIP

Beware! If you mistakenly use a verbal as a verb, you will end up with an unintentional sentence fragment. Remember that verb forms that end in *-ing* and *-en* require a helping verb when used as a verb.

Fragment: Emma *sitting* at the table.

Sentence: Emma *was sitting* at the table.

3. Read your character description and look for verb forms that end in *-en* and *-ing*. Make sure those used as predicates have helping verbs.

MEDIA LINK

Like the characters in a novel, short story, or nonfiction piece, characters in a television or film drama exist in an imaginary world. They are created by the combined skills of the scriptwriter, set designer, actor, costume department, and make-up staff. We may know quite a lot about the characters before we enter the cinema or switch on the television—from their names, from reviews, from advertisements, from talk shows, or because we are already familiar with the story or series. We may also have expectations of the stars involved in playing the lead roles.

Choose one of your favourite characters from a television drama or from a movie. Analyze the ways in which you got to know and understand the character. Consider your own foreknowledge, the symbolism of the character's name, her or his appearance, symbolic objects associated with the character, speech patterns, gestures, actions, and, of course, the opinions and actions of others. Use your findings to analyze how characterization in a film or television drama differs from that of a novel, short story, or piece of nonfiction writing. Present your findings in an oral report to the class.

Mechanics & Design

When writing description, you will often find that you need to include explanatory details to provide a context for the reader. Note how each of the following passages begins with an idea that is expanded in a subsequent sentence.

> **Main idea:** It was 1920.
>
> **Explanatory detail:** That was the first and last year of my father's connection with that fundamentally extinct operation.

> **Main idea:** I was drawing the mine for my father.
>
> **Explanatory detail:** He was the last resident American speculator in the hotel.

One way to include this kind of information without making your writing sound choppy is to add descriptive phrases or clauses within a sentence, as Urquhart did in her original versions of these sentences:

> It was 1920, the first and last year of my father's connection with that fundamentally extinct operation ...

> I was drawing the mine for my father, the last resident American speculator in the hotel ...

When inserting details in this manner, it is important to punctuate them correctly. The use of commas, dashes, or parentheses can actually change the whole meaning of the sentence in some cases.

> *Never* use punctuation to separate **restrictive phrases** or **clauses** from the rest of a sentence.

Learning Goal

- use commas, dashes, and parentheses correctly to set off nonrestrictive elements in a sentence

A phrase or clause is restrictive if removing it changes the meaning of the sentence.

> Sara lived year-round in the small log house *that her father had left her.* (We need this information to understand which house she lived in.)

Why couldn't she at least have married one of those silent, scholarly men *who work late at night with their books?* (We need this information to know what men she is talking about.)

> *Always* separate **nonrestrictive phrases** or **clauses** from the rest of a sentence using commas, dashes, or parentheses.

Nonrestrictive phrases or clauses give additional information, but the sentence can stand alone without them.

She would have liked the name of Bovary, **her name,** to become famous.

He had subscribed to *La Ruche médicale*, **a new professional journal for which he had received a prospectus.**

WRITING TIP

Use commas to set off most nonrestrictive phrases and clauses. Use dashes and parentheses when you really want to slow down a sentence and make a reader take note of details. However, use parentheses sparingly as they can make a nonrestrictive element seem like an afterthought.

Note how Urquhart uses dashes around the nonrestrictive passage in the following sentence to emphasize how the miners' houses differ from the rest of the settlement:

Or she might have been walking behind me as I strolled toward the end of the settlement—a crescent moon of mostly uninhabited miners' houses around a subtle bay—and would have slipped inside her door ...

1. Identify the phrase or clause in each of the following sentences that provides additional information, and decide whether it is restrictive or nonrestrictive. Add any necessary punctuation.

   a) The broom that Sara was using bore the image of a rose.
   b) Charles's eyes small to begin with seemed to be pushed back into his head.

    c) Emma saw ladies in Rouen who wore clusters of charms on their watch chains.

    d) Dr. Meurot with whom Charles had recently consulted humiliated him at a patient's bedside.

    e) Another doctor who was present agreed with Charles's diagnosis.

2. Read your character description and make sure you have punctuated restrictive and nonrestrictive phrases and clauses correctly.

Usage & Style

"Show, don't tell" is a good practice for many kinds of writing, but it is especially appropriate when writing about people. Writing that "tells" merely summarizes an impression or event, while writing that "shows" paints a picture of that impression or event in the reader's mind.

Writing that "shows"

- uses the active rather than the passive voice
- lets the character's words, appearance, and actions speak for themselves
- is economical (uses specific nouns and verbs rather than relying on modifiers)
- includes reactions (thoughts and feelings) of the people involved wherever possible
- includes dialogue rather than summarized talk
- includes details of time and place
- makes use of comparisons and contrasts
- is filled with figurative language

> **Writing that "tells":** Sara was a bit of a dreamer, but she had a certain something that drew my attention right away. When I first saw her, she was sweeping.
>
> **Writing that "shows":** The first time I saw Sara she was holding a large broom, sweeping, her body twisting around the object as if she were dancing with it.

Learning Goal

- use a variety of stylistic devices to "show" rather than "tell" in a piece of writing

1. Find the corresponding passage that "shows" the impression or event each of the following sentences "tells." Read each passage aloud and identify the kinds of details the author has included to make her or his writing "show" rather than "tell." Record one detail from each model that you found particularly vivid.

From *The Underpainter:*

a) I would rather have been concentrating on my surroundings.
b) I could see the way Sara's body moved under her uniform.
c) Sara was sweeping diligently.
d) She stopped sweeping and looked at me.
e) Sara told me I could stay where I was.

From *Madame Bovary:*

f) Emma would sit there dressed in fine clothes.
g) The things Emma did pleased Charles.
h) Charles was a competent doctor.
i) Emma became upset when she learned about Charles's humiliation.
j) Emma was dissatisfied with her life.

2. Read your character description carefully, looking for passages where you may have "told" (summarized impressions or events) rather than "shown." Rewrite these passages using the kinds of details you noted in activity 1.

Word Study & Spelling

Learning Goal

- use proofreading symbols to identify and correct writing errors

Proofreading is an essential part of the writing process because correctness conveys that you value what you have written and you respect the time your readers have taken to read it. Proofreading is very different from other kinds of reading. When you proofread, you focus less on the content of the piece and more on the correctness of the language used.

The following tips will help you proofread more effectively:

- If possible, allow two or three days to pass before proofreading a piece of writing. The more time that passes, the more likely you will find errors in your writing.

- Keep a personal list of errors you know you make frequently, and check your list before proofreading to remind yourself of common problems to watch for in your writing.

- Read slowly, making sure you see each word and sentence separately. Try reading the piece out loud, or in reverse order, beginning with the last sentence, then reading the next-to-last sentence, and so on.

- Proofread more than once, looking for a different kind of error each time. For example, proofread once for grammar, another time for punctuation, and still another time for spelling. You will probably notice other mistakes as you read.

- Be especially careful with the spelling of people's names. Try checking at least two different sources for these spellings.

- Even if you write on a computer, always proofread a hard copy because it is easy to miss mistakes on a computer screen.

TECHNO-TIP

Although computer grammar checks and spell checks are helpful, many programs do not recognize incorrect usage. Also, some will identify colloquial spellings and certain sentence structures as incorrect even when they are not. If you use these computer checks, make sure an error actually exists before you accept each suggestion. Also, do not depend on these features to identify all your errors.

Once you have proofread your piece and corrected all the errors you can find, ask someone else to proofread it for you. She or he can use proofreading symbols such as the ones on the following page to identify writing errors.

Proofreading Symbols

Λ	insert a letter or word	I wanted to her voce ... (insert "hear" and "i")
$\mathcal{G}$	delete a letter or word	Emma would sit there in in her dressging gown ...
$\P$	begin a new paragraph	¶ Charles, in rain or snow, rode along the rough country roads.
$\equiv$	change to a capital letter	She longed both to die and to live in paris.
$/$	change to lower case	... when the Lake, the vast inland sea ...
$\sim$	transpose	"Would you like me to move?"
$\odot$	insert a period	He looked well and felt well.
$\wedge$	insert a comma	The less Charles understood these niceties the more he was seduced by them.
$\vee$	insert an apostrophe	Why couldnt she at least have married one of those silent, scholarly men ...
$\#$	insert a space	I could see the slight curve of muscle in her upper arm ...
.....	leave it as is	And yet, watching her, her unselfconscious grace ...

1. Recopy 10 sentences from the models, but include a grammar, spelling, punctuation, or other error in each one. Exchange your list with a partner, and check her or his sentences against the original. When you find an error, use the appropriate proofreading symbol to mark it.

2. Following the tips in this section, proofread your character description and use the appropriate proofreading symbols to identify any writing errors you find. Correct these errors and make a final polished draft.

WORD ORIGINS

"Recently, 'to keep himself up to date,' he had subscribed to *La Ruche médicale*, a new professional journal for which he had received a prospectus."

The word **prospectus** is Latin and means "a printed statement describing and advertising something, such as programs offered by a college, or funds, stocks, etc. of interest to investors."

Many Latin expressions are in current use, especially those relating to legal matters. Which of the following expressions do you recognize? Use a dictionary that contains Latin words and phrases to find their meanings.

pro bono   verbatim   proviso   caveat emptor

flagrante delicto   modus operandi

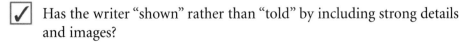

Looking Back

Before handing in your final edited draft, have a classmate check your character description, paying particular attention to the following:

✓ Has the writer used verbals with helping verbs when necessary?

✓ Has the writer "shown" rather than "told" by including strong details and images?

✓ Has the writer punctuated nonrestrictive phrases and clauses correctly?

✓ Has the piece been carefully proofread, and are all words spelled correctly?

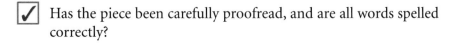

Unit **6** Personal Impression

What is a personal impression?

A personal impression is a description in which the writer strives to convey in words his or her perception of an event. Unlike informative description, which uses factual details to convey a precise understanding of what happened, a personal impression uses images that appeal to the reader's emotions and create an overall mood. In the following letter to his son, astronaut Jerry Linenger describes the experience of walking in space.

Learning Goals

- write a personal impression of an event
- use verb tenses correctly
- use end punctuation appropriately
- use sentence fragments to create particular effects
- use knowledge of spelling strategies to correct spelling errors

It's All Downhill From Here

BY JERRY LINENGER

Dear John,

Whenever someone has eaten some unusual meat—rabbit, deer, dog, frog, whatever—the question "What did it taste like?" is asked. People usually say chicken, but they know that it really did not taste just like chicken, but rather exactly like rabbit, deer, dog, or frog. Try this one yourself. What does beef taste like? Your reply? Pork? Bacon? Chicken? All answers are not quite right, right? Beef tastes like beef, period. What is a spacewalk like? Like a spacewalk. But let me give you the "sorta like chicken" answer, so that you at least have a feel for it.

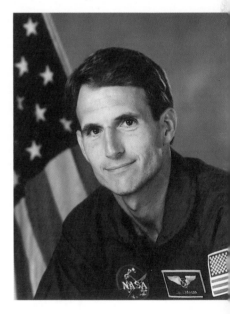

    Imagine this. You are in scuba gear. Your vision is restricted by the size of your underwater mask. Your fins, wetsuit, and gloves make you clumsy and heavy. The water is frigid; in fact, it is thickly frozen overhead with only one entry-exit hole drilled. Your life depends on your gear functioning properly the entire time. The further away you venture, the further away the escape hole in the ice, and the less you can tolerate any failure whatsoever.

    There is no bottom. Up and down are confused. Your path is not straight, but rather around obstacles on a constantly convex, falling away, prime surface. As you round one obstacle, the next appears, and soon enough it is difficult to determine from where you came.

    You are not in water, but on a cliff. Crawling, slithering, gripping, reaching. You are not falling from the cliff; instead, the whole cliff is falling and you are on it. You convince yourself that it is okay for the cliff and yourself on the cliff to be falling because when you look out you see no bottom. You just fall and fall and fall.

The sun sets swiftly. Blackness. Not merely dark, but absolute black. You see nothing. Nothing. You grip to the handhold ever more tightly. You convince yourself that it is okay to be falling, alone, nowhere, in the blackness. You loosen your grip.

Your eyes adjust, and you can make out forms. Another human being silhouetted against the heavens. When it first got dark, you were feet-first falling. Five minutes later, as the cliff itself rotates, you feel as if you have reached the crest of the roller coaster and are now barrelling down steeply—steeply to the point that you feel you will flip headfirst out of your seat—toward Earth. You come out of your seat, and are falling spread-eagled. Now head first. You want to flip back upright. You can't.

You decide it is okay to be diving headfirst into nothing.

You need to work with your hands. You let go. You depend on the two tethers you placed on handholds to hold. You rotate, twist, and float—all randomly and uncontrolled—still the cliff is falling and rotating. You know you are falling with it; you tell yourself surely you are falling with it because you just attached your tethers; yet it is difficult to discount the sensation that you are moving away, alone, detached. You feel as if you are at the end of a fishing pole, which gets longer and longer and thinner and thinner at the end, and you, the fish, are hooked to its flimsy end. It sways back and forth; you, being attached, sway back and forth. The pole no longer looks rigid and straight, but rather like a skinny S-curve. You are hanging to the thinnest limb of the tallest tree in the wind. The tree is falling. You convince yourself that it is a strong oak, that the limb will stay attached and not fracture, and that the forest bottom is far away.

In the midst of all of this, you carry out your work calmly, methodically. You snap a picture or two and, below, notice the Strait of Gibraltar narrowly opening to the Mediterranean.

That is how it felt, best as I can describe it. What did I do actually?

Exited the airlock and climbed out onto a horizontal ladder. With my partner, I transferred a dresser-sized optical properties monitor (OPM) along the convex surface of the space station module, past protruding, sharp-edged solar sensors, solar panels, and other equipment, to a long telescoping pole. We then attached the OPM and myself to the end of the pole. My partner, using a three-foot-diameter ring that encircled the pole,

slid along the pole to its base, which was located on a different module of the station. The hand crank controls for moving and extending the pole were located here.

The OPM and I were then swung away on the tip of the pole, telescoped out further, and then translated—very precisely and with many changes of direction in order not to collide with solar panels—to the end of a third, even more distant, module.

Upon arrival, I attached the pole to its new location, and we rejoined at my end and installed the OPM. A third cosmonaut, inside the space station, confirmed that our cable connections were good by looking at some sensors inside. We returned by the same means to the original module, where we detached two large (1.5 m^2) cosmic dust/space debris collector panels for return, attached a radiation dosimeter, and re-entered the airlock with the panels.

Closed the outer hatch. Repressurized the airlock. Opened the inner hatch. Yanked ourselves out of our spacesuits. Opened the second inner hatch. Ate dinner. Did some required post-spacewalk work in the airlock. Went to bed. Slept soundly, contentedly—all tasks accomplished flawlessly (in the words of the ground controllers, with no argument from me).

Good night, John. I hope that you aren't awakened by a nightmare where you are falling, falling. Shuttle will be coming soon—it is all downhill from here.

Love,
Dad ■

Investigating the Model

1. Linenger could have begun his piece as follows: "What is a spacewalk like? Imagine this. You are in scuba gear … " What purpose does his discussion of the taste of meat serve? Which opening do you prefer— the original or the more direct opening given here? Why?

2. One of the most effective ways to describe something that is unfamiliar to others is to compare it to something the reader will recognize and understand. What comparisons does the writer use to describe the experience of spacewalking? Which do you feel is most effective? Why?

3. In drawing a comparison, writers must include sufficient details to make the similarities clear to readers, often appealing to a number of senses appropriate to the situation. Which senses do the details in the model appeal to? Why?

4. Writers of description may arrange their details in a variety of ways: spatially, chronologically, in order of importance, and so on. What order has Linenger followed in presenting the details of his personal impression? Was this order appropriate for his subject? Explain.

5. An important aspect of a personal impression is the emotion it conveys. What emotion does the model evoke in the reader, and what images contribute to this emotion?

6. Personal impressions make use of figurative language to paint vivid, interesting pictures for the reader. Give examples of at least three figurative devices used in the model.

7. The tone and language used in a personal impression are often different from those used in an objective account. Read the final third of the letter beginning at "That is how it felt, best as I can describe it" and compare the language used in this portion of the description with that used in the rest of the letter.

   a) What particular techniques does the writer use to make the contrast? What characterizes the language and tone of the first half of the letter?

   b) Why do you think the author included the objective account at the end? Do you think it is appropriate? Why or why not?

8. Writers seldom use the second-person ("you") point of view because it can easily become tiresome to read. Does the writer use it successfully in the model? Does his shift from the second-person to the first-person point of view seem appropriate? Why or why not?

9. The conclusion of a personal impression should give the writing a sense of completion. Writers may achieve this by

   - telling what effect the event or encounter had on the person
   - explaining the significance of the event
   - returning to an image or theme mentioned earlier in the piece

   Evaluate the effect of the conclusion of the model. What method does it use to complete the piece? Is it effective? Explain why or why not. Suggest another way the author might have chosen to end the description.

Checkpoint: Personal Impression

 As a class, create a checklist of common features of personal impressions, based on the model and your own experience. You can use the checklist to help you create your own personal impression.

Writer's Workshop

1. First-time events can make good subjects for description because they often have special significance for the person involved. Brainstorm several of your own first-time events, and put check marks beside those you remember most clearly.

IDEA FILE

 Do you remember the first time you ...
   - attended high school?
   - dived off the high board?
   - scored a goal?
   - spoke in public?
   - flew in an airplane?
   - rode a roller coaster?
   - attended a concert?
   - drove a car?
   - got lost?
   - sat in an emergency room?
   - attended a funeral?

2. Choose the event that evokes in you the strongest emotional response and briefly identify your overall impression of this event. This will be the focus of your description.

3. Working as quickly as possible, record all the details you recall about the event, drawing on as many senses as possible. Do not concern yourself with their order—just jot them down as quickly as you can.

4. Put check marks beside the details that most clearly reflect your overall impression of the event. For example, if your focus is the fear you felt when riding a roller coaster, you will probably omit the boredom you experienced while waiting in line for your turn. On the other hand, you may wish to include details about this wait if they help convey the mounting trepidation you felt as your turn approached.

5. Imagine that the person who will read your description has never experienced the event you are describing. Can you compare it to something that will enable her or him to visualize it clearly? Identify similarities that will heighten the comparison. Do they reflect the overall impression you wish to convey?

6. Choose an order for your details. You may find you need to organize different parts of your writing in different ways. The three types of organization that are most likely to be useful in your personal impression are as follows:

   • **Order of impression** (the order in which details caught your attention) helps readers see things through your eyes, or experience something as you experienced it.
   • **Spatial order** (from near to far, left to right, top to bottom, etc.) helps readers visualize a particular location.
   • **Chronological order** (the order in which the events happened) helps readers understand the sequence of events.

7. Write two or three different leads for your piece. Choose the best lead and then write a draft of your personal impression, remembering to use figurative language to create strong images.

WRITING TIP

When writing your lead, you could

- begin with an action that sets events in motion
- focus on a specific detail and then draw back to reveal the big picture
- use dialogue to draw attention to a particular quality of the experience

 8. Revise your work using the list you created at Checkpoint.

ORAL LANGUAGE EXTENSION

Form a small group with two or three classmates and, with your teacher's permission, go to a different part of the school (e.g., hallway, gymnasium, library, computer lab, office, cafeteria, etc.). For 10 minutes, silently observe everything that happens there. Do not record notes and do not rely only on sight—simply concentrate on the scene, and use as many senses as possible to focus on every detail of the experience. Then return to the classroom and share orally what you observed (each group member adding to, rather than repeating, the information being shared), as classmates jot down your observations. (Groups may wish to compete to see which one can relate the most details observed.)

Grammar

Most of Jerry Linenger's description of his spacewalk is written in the present tense. Writers often use the present tense to generate excitement and tension because it makes readers feel as though they are right there, watching or participating in the event.

Learning Goal

- **use verb tenses correctly**

You *are* in scuba gear ... Your fins, wetsuit, and gloves *make* you clumsy and heavy.

Note that although Linenger used the present tense to describe the experience of walking in space, he used the past tense when listing the activities he performed during his spacewalk.

> Upon arrival, I *attached* the pole to its new location, and we *rejoined* at my end and *installed* the OPM.

Although writers often switch verb tenses for particular purposes, make sure you do not use two verb tenses by mistake. Choose a tense that is appropriate for your purpose and use it consistently throughout your piece of writing.

> There are three **simple verb tenses:** present, past, and future.

Simple present:	(I, you, we, they) *walk*; (he, she, it) *walks*
Simple past:	(I, you, he, she, it, we, they) *walked*
Simple future:	(I, you, he, she, it, we, they) *will walk*

However, some time relations are more complex and are indicated by the perfect tense.

> The **perfect tenses** are used to describe actions that are completed at some time in the past, present, or future.

> He *had wanted* to be an astronaut ever since he saw Neil Armstrong walk on the moon. (Wanting to be an astronaut occurred in relation to the moonwalk.)

To form the perfect tense, use a form of *have* with the past participle.

Present perfect:	(I, you, we, they) *have walked*; (he, she, it) *has walked*
Past perfect:	(I, you, he, she, it, we, they) *had walked*
Future perfect:	(I, you, he, she, it, we, they) *will have walked*

> **Progressive forms** are used to indicate continuing actions.

Progressive forms of present and perfect tenses are constructed by using a form of *be* plus the present participle.

Present progressive:	*is/are walking*	
Past progressive:	*was/were walking*	
Future progressive:	*will be walking*	

Present perfect progressive:	*has/have been walking*
Past perfect progressive:	*had been walking*
Future perfect progressive:	*will have been walking*

1. Underline each verb or verb phrase in the following sentences and identify its tense.
   a) Whenever someone has eaten some unusual meat, people ask what it tasted like.
   b) By the time the shuttle arrives to take me home, I will have been up here for over three months.
   c) You are now barrelling down steeply on your imaginary roller coaster.
   d) The ground controllers told us we had accomplished all of our tasks flawlessly.
   e) You have been hanging to the thinnest limb of the tallest tree in the wind.

2. In each of the following sentences, replace the verb in parentheses with a perfect or progressive form that seems appropriate. Explain your choice.
   a) When the astronaut finishes this mission, he (walk) over 3000 km in space.
   b) The space station (rotate) one complete turn by the time the spacewalk ended.
   c) Without knowing it, the astronaut (sing) nonstop into his microphone as he worked.
   d) Linenger (write) several letters to his son that can be viewed on NASA's web site.
   e) NASA (receive) several images from the space station when the transmission was cut off.

3. The passage on the following page is supposed to be written in the present tense, but it contains some past-tense verbs. Rewrite the passage using the correct tense throughout.

The astronaut slides cautiously along the solar panels, taking care not to catch the material of his spacesuit on its sharp surfaces. One clumsy move meant the difference between life and death in the black vacuum that surrounds him. He gestures to his partner, who waves her gloved hand in reply. They know exactly what they had to do, and with less than an hour to accomplish the task, they have no time to waste. The first astronaut reached for the damaged panel and loosens the mounting bolts holding it securely to the outer frame of the space station. As he detaches it, the second astronaut moved the replacement panel into position. Their movements are a silent ballet, like that of synchronized swimmers in an endless ocean of emptiness.

4. Read your own personal impression, and check to see that you have chosen an appropriate tense and used it consistently throughout. If you changed the tense, did you do it for a good reason?

MEDIA LINK

News photographs help shape our perception of an event. They may appeal to our emotions and help create an overall mood. Bring three different daily newspapers published on the same day to class. Examine the front pages and note the photographs on each. Consider the choice of subject, the details of the photo, the camera angle, the distance from the subject, and the caption. Which photograph attracts your interest most strongly? Why? What message is created by the photo?

Photographers or editors may change a photograph after it has been shot by cropping it at the printing stage. This practice can radically alter the intended meaning of a photograph. Using two L-shaped frames, experiment with your newspaper photographs. Which photographs look better when they are cropped differently? How might the meaning of the image be altered by removing some of the elements from the original frame and by changing the caption? Share your findings with the class.

Mechanics & Design

There are four basic types of sentences: declarative, imperative, interrogative, and exclamatory. Note the forms of punctuation used after each.

Learning Goal

- use end punctuation appropriately

Type	Purpose	Example
Declarative	makes a statement	You are in scuba gear.
Imperative	issues a command or request	Try this one yourself.
Interrogative	asks a question	What does beef taste like?
Exclamatory	expresses strong feeling	The tree is falling!

Although everyone knows that a period is used to end most sentences, problems often occur when a writer must decide between using a period and a question mark, or a period and an exclamation point. Note, for example, the difference in punctuation between the following direct and indirect questions.

Direct question: What did it taste like?

Indirect question: Linenger asked what it tasted like.

Some direct questions are not meant to be answered because the answer is obvious. These are called **rhetorical questions,** and writers use them to emphasize a point, as Linenger does in the following:

All answers are not quite right, right?

Although they do not require answers, rhetorical questions do require question marks.

WRITING TIP

Writers often use a series of questions as a way of drawing the reader toward a particular understanding.

"What does beef taste like? Your reply? Pork? Bacon? Chicken? … Beef tastes like beef, period. What is a spacewalk like? Like a spacewalk."

Note that the model contains no exclamation points, even though the description of the spacewalk includes many sentences that evoke strong feeling in the reader.

> Five minutes later, as the cliff itself rotates, you feel as if you have reached the crest of the roller coaster and are now barrelling down steeply—steeply to the point that you feel you will flip headfirst out of your seat—toward Earth. You come out of your seat, and are falling spread-eagled. Now head first. You want to flip back upright. You can't.

Too many exclamation points can make writing appear trite. Instead of overloading his writing with punctuation, the writer of the model includes detail after detail to generate the excitement associated with walking in space.

1. Copy the following sentences and add appropriate end punctuation. Give reasons for your choices.
    a) Linenger's partner asked if he could reach the hand crank controls
    b) That panel is about to explode
    c) What is the purpose of the optical properties monitor
    d) The pole no longer looks rigid and straight, but rather like a skinny S-curve, and you suddenly believe the slightest tug could send you hurtling off into endless space
    e) The ground controllers asked if the astronauts required more time
    f) An astronaut's survival depends on what factors

2. Read your own personal impression and check to see that you have used end punctuation appropriately.

Usage & Style

A **sentence fragment** is a group of words that looks like a sentence but expresses an incomplete thought.

Sentence fragments may lack a subject, a verb, or both, as in the example "Crawling, slithering, gripping, reaching." Note, however, that the subject is sometimes implied but not written in imperative (or command) sentences such as the following:

[You] Sleep tight.

[You] Don't worry.

Even though the subject is not stated, these types of sentences are not considered fragments.

On the other hand, sentences that begin with a coordinating conjunction (*and, but, or*) are technically fragments even if they contain a subject and a predicate because the conjunction is not linked to anything, so the thought is incomplete.

While they are common in everyday speech, fragments should be used in writing only to create a particular effect. For example, writers frequently use sentence fragments in dialogue to convey a sense of realism, but fragments are useful in achieving a number of other effects, too. Note, for example, how the writer uses fragments in the following passage to establish the informal tone of his piece:

What is a spacewalk like? *Like a spacewalk. But let me give you the "sorta like chicken" answer* ...

In the following passages, the author uses fragments to reinforce the mood of the description, underscoring the dangers of spacewalking.

You are not in water, but on a cliff. *Crawling, slithering, gripping, reaching.*

The sun sets swiftly. *Blackness. Not merely dark, but absolute black.*

A short fragment used at the end of several long sentences can emphasize a particular detail or impression.

Five minutes later, as the cliff itself rotates, you feel as if you have reached the crest of the roller coaster and are now barrelling down steeply—steeply to the point that you feel you will flip headfirst out of your seat—toward Earth. You come out of your seat, and are falling spread-eagled. *Now head first.*

A couple of short sentence fragments written together can generate excitement by quickening the pace of a piece. However, a long string of fragments can have the opposite effect, emphasizing the repetitive quality of an experience. Linenger uses this technique in the following passage to convey the routine nature of life in space.

> Closed the outer hatch. Repressurized the airlock. Opened the inner hatch. Yanked ourselves out of our spacesuits. Opened the second inner hatch. Ate dinner. Did some required post-spacewalk work in the airlock. Went to bed. Slept soundly, contentedly—all tasks accomplished flawlessly (in the words of the ground controllers, with no argument from me).

WRITING TIP

One strategy for identifying unintentional fragments in long pieces is to read the piece backwards, beginning at the last sentence, then reading the next-to-last sentence, and so on.

1. Unintentional sentence fragments make writing appear careless and lessen the overall impact of a piece, so it is important to be able to identify and correct them. Identify whether the following groups of words are sentences (S) or sentence fragments (F). Rewrite the sentence fragments to make them sentences.

   a) When it first got dark during the spacewalk.
   b) Imagine this.
   c) Five minutes later, as the cliff itself rotates.
   d) You feel as if you are at the end of a fishing pole.
   e) In the midst of all of the work the astronauts had to do.
   f) Exited the airlock and climbed out onto a horizontal ladder.
   g) A third cosmonaut who was inside the orbiting space station.

2. Read your personal impression aloud to see if there are places where sentence fragments can be used to achieve a desired effect. Also, check to make sure you have not overused sentence fragments, which can make your writing sound stilted and awkward.

TECHNO-TIP

Some word-processing programs that have built-in grammar checkers will flag every sentence fragment as an error. These tools can help you notice unintentional fragments in your writing, but you need to decide for yourself, fragment by fragment, which ones you want to keep and which you should correct.

Word Study & Spelling

One quality of effective description is that it appeals to a variety of senses. One characteristic of effective spellers is their use of the senses to help them recall the spellings of words. You can use both sight and sound strategies to help you become a more proficient speller.

Learning Goal

- **use knowledge of spelling strategies to correct spelling errors**

Sound Strategies

- Say words aloud, pronouncing them correctly so you hear the letters clearly.
- Say longer words slowly, sounding out each syllable separately.
- Break compound words into separate parts and say each part distinctly.
- Exaggerate sounds that are difficult to hear when you say the word normally.
- Think of words that sound the same and have similar spelling patterns.
- Invent rhymes for important spelling rules and say them aloud.
- Use mnemonic devices like puns, word associations, and rhymes.

Visual Strategies

- Look closely at the word, visualizing its spelling in your mind.
- Write the word and highlight letters you find difficult to remember.
- Look at the shape of the word and draw its outline; then fill in the letters.

1. **a)** Read the words in the following list, all of which are taken from the model. With a partner, take turns reading the words aloud while the other partner writes them down. Note which of the words you had trouble spelling, and use any of the memory tricks listed on the previous page to help you remember the correct spellings. Then take the test again. Did you improve?

- restricted
- obstacles
- venture
- tolerate
- methodically
- Mediterranean
- optical
- protruding
- solar
- encircled
- module

- telescoped
- precisely
- original
- sensors
- detached
- debris
- collector
- repressurized
- accomplished
- contentedly

    b) Prepare a master list of mnemonic devices (puns, rhymes, word associations, etc.) for the words on the list. If you think any of these devices will help you remember the words better, write them in your notebook. In two weeks' time, have a contest to see who can spell the most words correctly.

2. Create a dictionary of words you have trouble spelling. Every time you notice a spelling mistake in your work, decide whether this is a word you will use again. If so, add it to your dictionary and, beside it, make a note of a strategy that will help you remember its spelling.

3. Read your personal impression and lightly mark any word that does not look right. Try writing the word several ways, and then check a dictionary to be certain. Be sure to add to your personal dictionary all the words you are likely to use again.

WORD ORIGINS

"Another human being silhouetted against the heavens."

The word **silhouette,** which means "the outline of a form," is named after Etienne de Silhouette, who was the French minister of finance in 1759. Although noted for spending money sparingly, he proposed to tax the French nobility heavily and, as a result, his name was applied mockingly to anything cheap. Over the years, his name became associated with the outline rather than the substance of things.

With a partner, consult dictionaries, encyclopedias, and history books to find the meanings of the following words, all of which relate to politicians:

Trudeaumania   **gerrymander**

Bennett buggy   **Reaganomics**

Looking Back

Before handing in your final edited draft, have a classmate check your personal impression, paying particular attention to the following:

✓ Are verb tenses used correctly and consistently?

✓ Are any question marks and exclamation points used appropriately?

✓ Are any sentence fragments used purposefully and effectively?

✓ Are all words spelled correctly?

Reflect and Build on Your Learning

Reflecting on Descriptive Writing Forms

1. Review the Learning Goals on page 89. Which goals do you think you have achieved most successfully? Which goals do you think will require you to do more work? For each goal that will require more work, list one specific action you will take to accomplish the goal.

2. Write a note to your parent or guardian explaining the three most important things you learned about descriptive writing during the study of this section.

3. Complete each of the following statements about the work you have done in the past three units on description.
   - The most interesting part of the descriptive writing section for me was ...
   - If I were to change a piece of writing I did in this section, it would be ... because ...
   - In the future, when I am writing description, I will need to be careful to ...
   - I would rate my work in this section as (choose one): weak, fair, okay, good, great.

Looking Over Descriptive Writing Forms

1. Working with a small group, create a chart summarizing what you know about the features of sonnets, character descriptions, and personal impressions. Include the following headings in your chart: Purpose, Audience, Dominant Impression, Sensory Details, Figurative Language, and Organization. The class checklists you developed for each form will help you with this task. Compare your chart with those of other groups. How would you modify your chart based on what they have included in theirs?

Using Descriptive Writing Forms

1. Outline three methods you would use in writing a sonnet, character description, or personal impression to make your descriptions come alive.

2. A writer must choose the most appropriate form of writing to communicate her or his message. When would you choose to use each of the following descriptive forms of writing? Provide one specific example to demonstrate when you might use each form either inside or outside of school.

   - character description
   - setting description
   - comparison
   - travelogue

   - event description
   - personal impression
   - profile
   - poem

3. Choose a character from a novel you have read in school this year. Write a first-person description in which you meet the character, and give your personal impression of her or him. Use elements such as the setting; the actions, clothing, and physical appearance of the character; and direct dialogue to reveal your impressions.

4. Collect different issues of magazines such as *People,* and clip images of celebrities or models dressed in fancy or exotic clothing. Choose one image that appeals to you, and write a fashion commentary on her or his clothing. Deliver your commentary to a group of classmates. Before you begin, you may wish to meet with a group of classmates to discuss the type of language and the kinds of descriptions used in fashion shows, or to view a fashion show and listen to the descriptions given by the commentator.

5. a) Find a photograph of a person, place, or thing that appeals to you. The photograph may be from your own family albums, or from a magazine or newspaper. Write a brief factual description of the picture, describing only what is actually there.
   b) Write another description that describes the feelings and impressions the image evokes in you.
   c) Note the difference in the language you chose for each kind of description, and list some specific methods you used in order to make your description personal and compelling.

Exposition

Expository writing, the sharing of factual information, is focused on what readers need to know. It is writing that tells who, what, when, where, why, and how. Expository writing presents information in such a way that the reader can understand the concepts being presented and easily find the information that is relevant to her or his needs. Clarity, conciseness, and coherence are especially important in this kind of writing.

This section contains three forms of expository writing: feature article, research report, and leaflet. Although these forms are very different from one another, each presents factual information in a format that is useful and understandable to the reader.

Features of Exposition

- Exposition involves presenting facts to a specific audience.
- Expository writing is arranged to make information as accessible and understandable to the reader as possible.
- Expository writers often define unfamiliar or technical terms by comparing them with something more familiar to the reader.
- The writer's personal opinion and value judgments are usually not part of expository writing.

Learning Goals

- use a range of sources to gather information and explore ideas for your written work

- identify and use informational forms appropriately in writing a feature article, a research report, and a leaflet

- use organizational techniques to present ideas and supporting details

- revise your work independently and collaboratively to improve accuracy, clarity, coherence, and style

- edit and proofread to produce final drafts using correct grammar, mechanics, usage, and spelling

- use knowledge of vocabulary and language conventions to write competently and effectively

- develop listening, speaking, and media literacy skills

- read a variety of nonfiction such as feature articles, research reports, and leaflets

- identify and understand the elements and style of a variety of nonfiction

Unit ⑦ Feature Article

What is a feature article?

A feature article is a popular type of news story found in newspapers and magazines that provides information of human interest. Feature articles deal with real events (people and places), issues, and trends. They differ from hard news stories in that they may reflect the point of view of the writer; however, their main purpose is to inform and entertain. The newspaper feature article reprinted here discusses a new trend in computer technology: scanning.

Learning Goals

- write a feature article
- identify prepositional, participial, gerund, and infinitive phrases
- learn the design features of a feature article
- apply the concepts of unity and coherence
- use homophones correctly

EYE SPY

Biometrics: Your Body as Password

BY JOHN M. MORAN

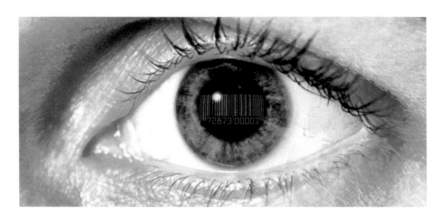

By now, you are buried in passwords.

There's one for your PC, one for your ATM [automated teller machine] card, one for your long-distance calling card, one for your voice mail, one for your Internet-access account. And that's before you even start talking about all the passwords you use on the Internet for everything from buying books, to checking e-mail, to trading stocks.

On and on and on it goes. A seemingly endless stream of secret codes designed to tell the multiplying machines in your life that you are you.

But not only are these myriad passwords difficult to remember and annoying to use, they're not really all that secure. Indeed, entire software programs have been created to help crack the most common passwords.

Now comes an approach to computer security that may one day eliminate the need for passwords, keys, or identification cards. It's called biometrics, and it relies on precise measurements of your body or your movements to identify you.

Like what? Fingerprints, voice prints, iris prints (from the coloured circle in your eye), facial features, and even the way you sign your name—all can be used to distinguish you from everyone else.

"In the security realm, it's called 'I and A' for identification and authentication," said IBM program manager John Baghot. "It's either based on something you have, like a credit card or a key, or things you know, like a password.

"The thing that's kind of exciting about biometrics is that it creates a whole new category: things about a person."

Once limited to ultra-secure government and industrial sites—both in the movies and in real life—biometric security devices have reached mainstream use. Part of the reason is a rapid advance in the quality of biometric technologies, as well as a tumble in prices. For example, fingerprint scanners once costing thousands of dollars can now be had for less than $100.

At the same time, the rising use of computers and other electronic devices means we need to identify ourselves more often. And with the wildfire growth of the Internet, we increasingly need to verify our identity over the network for electronic commerce.

In short, biometrics do double duty as substitutes for passwords and as a kind of digital signature for doing business in cyberspace.

"It's taken a long time to mature, but you're starting to see the momentum in the marketplace to make this stuff happen," said Ed Murrer, director of business development for Veridicom, which makes biometric security products. "I think you'll start to see some real deployment of this in the near future."

Perhaps the earliest adoption of biometrics in the consumer market is the use of fingerprint scanners to substitute for PC passwords. Typically, such scanners are attached to the PC or embedded in the computer keyboard. Users then touch one or more fingers to the scanner, which reads their fingerprints and compares it to fingerprints already on file. If it matches, the computer provides access to the user.

"Biometrics, because it measures a part of your physical being, provides a secure and convenient way of identifying yourself," said Nancy Van Natta, a vice-president for Digital Persona, which makes "U.are.U," a fingerprint scanner. Simply put, you can't forget your fingerprint and you're equally unlikely to lose it or leave it at home by accident.

One reason fingerprint scanning seems to have an early lead among biometrics is that, after decades of law enforcement work, the technology needed to scan and identify fingerprints is well understood.

But there are plenty of challengers to the fingerprint identifier. One is the handwritten signature.

An image of a fingerprint sensed by the world's first microchip capable of identifying fingerprints is shown on a monitor at Nippon Telephone and Telegraph Corp. laboratories in Atsugi, west of Tokyo. The 2.25-cm^2 chip with 0.5 mm thickness, shown underneath the finger, can identify a fingerprint in half a second with accuracy of 99 percent or more.

Steve Borza at DEW Engineering, vice-president of America Biometric Corporation, shows new fingerprint scanning technology.

Kirk LeCompte, marketing director for PenOp of New York, said a digital signature, which people write on a computer pad with a stylus, is far more secure than the traditional ink-on-paper signature. That's because PenOp's technology not only records the look of the signature, but also picks up many other features, such as the speed at which the signature is completed, the angle of the pen, and the pressure of the pen. So even if someone traced a signature perfectly in an attempt at forgery, the PenOp scanner could tell that it had been written by someone other than the original signer.

A somewhat more exotic biometric technology is iris scanning, which uses a camera to read the unique pattern in the coloured ring of the human eye.

"The uses for iris recognition pretty much span anything where someone needs to be identified," said Kelly Gates of IriScan Inc. in Marlton, New Jersey. "It's quick, it's reliable. It's easy to use. When you consider cost, risk reduction, and privacy protection, it turns out to be quite affordable."

For now at least, iris scanning tends to be used mainly in business and security applications. But it is starting to be used for bank ATMs, where the advantage over personal identification numbers is clear. If someone steals or guesses your PIN [personal identification number], he or she can take money from your account. But no one can swipe the iris from your eye.

Yet another biometric technology is voice scanning, which uses a PC micro-phone and software to create a unique voice print.

"From a cost standpoint, voice is probably the least expensive because it uses a standard sound card and microphones are relatively inexpensive," said Clinton Fuller, an executive for SAFlink of Tampa, Florida. "So for $5 to $10, you can get a microphone that's adequate, and you can use the sound card that's in the machine."

Among those convinced of the potential of biometrics is PC maker Compaq.

"I think it's clearly the coming thing," said Compaq spokesman Jim Cortese. "The miniaturization and the reduction in cost of the devices are really the news here."

In the end, experts say, no single biometric approach will solve all problems in all situations. In fact, in some cases, multiple biometrics may be used. At an ATM, for example, an iris scan might be used to identify a particular account holder and a digital signature might also be needed to make payments or fund transfers.

"If we are going to a world in which we can log on to computers anywhere and log on to our data anywhere, we have to have a way of identifying ourselves," said Digital Persona's Van Natta. "And biometrics is the leading way of identifying ourselves." ■

Investigating the Model

1. Feature articles provide depth and meaning to an event, issue, or trend, by clarifying and interpreting its importance. Identify the event, issue, or trend explained in the model. Give two examples where the author has clarified or interpreted the importance of it.

2. Feature articles, like all newspaper and magazine articles, begin with a headline that grabs the reader's attention and tells something about the article's subject. Discuss the headline of the article. Is it effective? What is the significance of "Eye Spy"? Can you suggest an alternative headline?

3. In addition to the headline, writers of feature articles try to "hook" readers by writing an interesting lead or opening paragraph(s). Identify the lead in the model and comment on its effectiveness.

4. Unlike hard news stories, the writer of a feature article usually looks at the topic from a particular angle, or point of view. Often, the angle involves human interest—reference to individuals and their feelings and experiences. How has the author of the model tried to include a human interest angle in his story about scanners?

5. The level of formality used in a feature article usually conforms to the style of the newspaper or magazine that it appears in. Consider the level of formality of the model. Would you describe it as formal or informal? Give at least three examples that support your analysis.

6. As expository writing, feature articles are based on facts (who, what, when, where, why, and how). However, they often contain opinions as well. Read through the model and list five facts and one opinion. How has the author of the model incorporated opinions into the article?

7. Identify at least three main points in the model, and explain how the writer has supported each point. What other ways might he have chosen? Why do you think he chose the kind of supporting detail that he did?

8. How effective do you find the illustrations and photographs that accompany the model? What other aspects of the article do you think could have been illustrated?

Checkpoint: Feature Article

 As a class, create a checklist of common features of feature articles, based on the model and your own experience. You can use the checklist to help you write your own feature article.

Writer's Workshop

1. Choose a topic that will interest both you and your audience. Since your topic should be related to an event, issue, or trend, scan newspapers and magazines—both feature articles and hard news stories—for possible topics. As you scan these sources, try to think about how you could bring out the human interest aspect of the topic. For this writing assignment, your audience will be students of your own age.

Learning Goal

• **write a feature article**

IDEA FILE

You might choose to write about
   • some unusual aspect of a person's life
   • how a person gained special recognition
   • interesting celebrations
   • a new invention
   • an historical event
   • a trend you have noticed around the school

2. Narrow your topic by writing a single sentence to explain the specific focus of your article. This sentence may or may not appear in your article; however, it will help you focus your ideas and thoughts. For example, the author of "Eye Spy" might have written, "Biometrics will soon replace existing passwords and will improve both convenience and security."

3. Gather as much information on your topic as possible. This information may come from your own knowledge, interviews, or printed and electronic resources. When you do interviews, schedule them after you have gathered information so that you can develop thoughtful questions.

4. Feature articles use different types of organization (chronological order, order of importance, spatial order, order of impression). Decide how the information in your article can best be presented. You may choose to arrange your information by feature, as the writer of the model has done; or, you may decide that your topic lends itself more to a different approach.

5. Write several possible leads for your article.

6. Draft the body of your article. In the body, make sure that you address the focus sentence you wrote. Include plenty of details and entertaining or informative quotes.

7. Think of a catchy headline that will attract readers and give them some idea of what the article is about.

 8. Before writing a final draft, revise your feature article using the checklist you created at Checkpoint.

ORAL LANGUAGE EXTENSION

Prepare a brief presentation—no longer than five minutes—summarizing your feature article. Present your summary to the class or a small group using only your notes for support. Follow these steps in preparing your speech:

- Prepare an introduction to your speech in which you give the title of your feature article and an explanation of why you chose this topic.

- Include a sentence or two that describes the main idea of your article.

- Explain each of the main points made in your article. Illustrate each one briefly.

- Write down in point form what interested or surprised you most about the topic.

- Write a sentence that sums up your thoughts on the topic or restates your first sentence.

Grammar

A phrase is a group of words that lacks a subject or a verb (or both) but functions as a unit within a sentence. There are several types of phrases: **prepositional, participial, gerund,** and **infinitive.**

> A **prepositional phrase** begins with a preposition and ends with a noun or pronoun.

Prepositional phrases are among the most commonly used phrases. They usually act as adjectives or adverbs.

Adjective phrases: Iris scanning uses a camera to read the unique pattern *in the coloured ring of the human eye.*

Adverb phrases: *By now,* you are buried *in passwords.*

1. Find at least four prepositional phrases in the model.

2. Identify the prepositional phrases in the sentences below, and label them as adjective phrases (ADJ) or adverb phrases (ADV).

    a) Make sure during ATM transactions that no one sees your PIN.
    b) Every person in this family has three different passwords.
    c) The iris scanner with the built-in camera is quick, reliable, and easy to use.
    d) In the future, passwords may be unnecessary.
    e) None of these approaches will solve all our security problems.
    f) Giving out your credit card number without proper security is risky.

> *Learning Goal*
>
> • identify prepositional, participial, gerund, and infinitive phrases

> A participle becomes a **participial phrase** when modifiers are added.

Participial phrases, like participles, function only as adjectives.

The technology *needed by consumers* to scan and identify fingerprints is well understood.

The camera, *scanning your face,* reads the unique pattern in the eye.

3. Identify the participial phrases in the following sentences, as well as the noun each modifies.

   a) The scanner recording the signature belongs to PenOp.
   b) Frightened by technology, some people will not welcome the new machines.
   c) The company scrapped the rapidly aging scanner for a new one.
   d) Tired and disgruntled, the employee worked for a long time to find the customer's code.
   e) The fingerprint being scanned can be compared to prints already on file.
   f) Some people, dazed and confused by the number of passwords they have to remember, are looking for another solution.

> A **gerund phrase** is a group of words that contains a gerund and words that modify the gerund.

Like gerunds, a gerund phrase functions as a noun and can act as a subject, a direct object, an object of a preposition, or a subject complement.

Subject:	*Scanning fingerprints* requires users to touch one or more fingers to the scanner.
Direct object:	Businesses use *high-tech scanning* to maintain security.
Object of preposition:	They developed a foolproof method of identification by *scanning signatures*.
Subject complement:	The newest biometric technology is *scanning irises*.

4. Identify the gerund phrases in the sentences below, and indicate whether the phrase is a subject, a direct object, an object of a preposition, or a subject complement.

   a) I am tired of remembering all these codes.
   b) Reading fingerprints is easy for scanners to do.
   c) Our business prefers iris scanning as a security measure.
   d) The hardest thing about the new scanning technologies is paying for them!

An **infinitive phrase** consists of the infinitive with its modifiers.

Like an infinitive, an infinitive phrase can be used as a noun, an adjective, or an adverb.

Noun: *To install a voice scanner* is relatively easy and inexpensive.

Adjective: We have different passwords *to remember for various functions.*

Adverb: Entire software programs have been created *to help crack the most common passwords.*

5. Identify the infinitive phrase in each of the following sentences. Identify whether the phrase is used as a noun, an adjective, or an adverb.

a) To record a signature is easy.
b) The new scanners are simple to use.
c) They have new scanning techniques to learn.
d) The bank teller is the person to ask about a password.
e) To study biometrics at university is his goal.
f) To finish first, biometric developers must keep their prices down.

WRITING TIP

Use a variety of phrases to make your sentences flow smoothly and to avoid repetition.

Repetitive: One reason *fingerprint scanning* seems to have an early lead among biometrics is that the technology for *scanning and identifying fingerprints* is well understood.

Smoother: One reason *fingerprint scanning* seems to have an early lead among biometrics is that the technology needed *to scan and identify fingerprints* is well understood.

6. Look through your feature article to review your use of phrases. Pay particular attention to places where you could substitute a phrase for a subordinate clause, or where you could use different types of phrases to make your writing less repetitive.

Mechanics & Design

Learning Goal

- **learn the design features of a feature article**

What makes you decide to read a feature in a newspaper? Designers know that layout has a lot to do with getting the attention of readers. Here are a few of the techniques used by newspaper and magazine designers to catch your eye and make an article reader-friendly.

- **Font**   Most newspapers use Times Roman because it is traditional and easy to read, and allows them to fit a lot of information onto a page. However, magazines often choose a typeface that reflects their particular image: from serious, sedate, and intellectual to young, vibrant, and "hip." The size of the type also helps to convey to the reader the image the publication wants to present.

  Small type, with little space between lines, may indicate that the content is serious, intellectual, or technical.

  Larger type is easier to read and appeals to a broader audience.

- **Headline**   The size of the headline is an indication of the importance of the topic. In newspapers, the more important an article is, the closer it is to the front page.

- **Deck**   This is the smaller headline that often appears above or below the main headline of a news story. In the model, the deck is "Biometrics: Your Body as Password." Writers use the deck to add information that couldn't be included in the headline for the sake of brevity, or to introduce another angle on the issue that may appeal to readers.

- **Lead**   The first paragraph of a newspaper or magazine feature is meant to hook the reader into wanting to read more. Often, magazines print the first few paragraphs in larger type beside the headline, to make the lead more noticeable.

- **Columns** The body of most feature articles in newspapers and magazines is set in columns. Columns are easier to read, and they allow the publication to fit more words on a page. The paragraphs in a news feature are often very short—many are only one sentence long. This technique not only makes the information easier to digest, it makes it easier for editors to cut the article down, if necessary, to fit the available space.

- **Photographs or illustrations** Most features are illustrated in some way. Notice how the model contains both photographs and the graphic illustration of a thumb print, with the text wrapped around.

- **Captions** A photograph is often accompanied by a caption that identifies people and explains what is happening in the picture.

- **Subheads** Often, longer feature articles are broken up by subheadings. A common practice is to use a passage or quotation from the body of the text, set in large type, as a kind of subhead. If the passage is interesting, readers will be enticed to read on.

- **White space** Designers try to incorporate some white space into the layout of a feature article. White space (e.g., in margins, around pictures or charts, and between columns or lines of text) makes the writing easier to read.

1. Working in groups of three, examine the model and assess its design using the list of features on pages 156 and 157. Discuss how each of the features identified contributes to the overall effect of the article and the information contained in it. Suggest ways to improve the design or layout of the article.

2. Look through newspapers and magazines to find effective examples of each of the design features identified in this section. Bring your examples to class and share them with a small group of your classmates. Discuss why you think your examples are effective.

3. Use the information you learned about the design of feature articles to format your own feature article. If you have access to a computer, experiment with fonts, two-column type, graphics, and white space. If you do not have access to a computer, type or write out your article neatly and mount it on a large piece of Bristol board. Add a headline and a deck, and include captioned photographs or illustrations.

TECHNO-TIP

Many word-processing programs will allow you to create two- or three-column text, insert headlines, and wrap text around pictures. Desktop publishing programs give you even more options, including templates for different layouts, which you can modify as you wish.

MEDIA LINK

Photojournalism is a type of journalism that tells stories through photographs. These photographs are sometimes supplemented with text. Photojournalists try to take pictures that capture the essence of people's feelings during a particular event. The viewer of the photographs must "read" the photos, and think about what they are saying. Much of the material in *LIFE* magazine is created by photojournalists.

In small groups, examine an example of an effective photograph from a magazine such as *LIFE*. Identify the technical elements that make the photograph so powerful. State in one clear sentence the meaning of the photograph. Present your findings to the class.

Using a camera, take several pictures that could be used to support your feature story. Choose the photos you like best, and then arrange them on a large piece of paper or board in an order that best supports your story.

Usage & Style

Learning Goal

• apply the concepts of unity and coherence

When you write your feature article, you should aim for a finished piece that is unified and coherent.

Unity means oneness. A piece of writing that has unity contains only ideas that are relevant to the main idea of the piece. Everything, including the text, titles, subtitles, quotations, and visual aids, should work together to support the main idea. If a piece of writing is not unified, the reader becomes confused, unable to see how the ideas connect to one another.

Coherence means "hanging together." A coherent piece of writing has ideas arranged in a natural, sensible order that the reader can understand easily. As well, ideas flow together smoothly. Each sentence flows into the next; each paragraph flows into the next.

One way to make the unity and coherence of your work more obvious is to use transitional expressions to connect sentences and paragraphs. Transitions can

- show order (Finally, …)
- show time (In the past, …)
- show importance (A major factor …)
- show cause and effect (For this reason, …)
- show a comparison (Likewise …)
- show a contrast (One difference …)
- show location (Across …)
- emphasize or reinforce (Furthermore, …)
- clarify (For this reason …)
- summarize (In conclusion, …)

1. In each of the following sentences and paragraphs taken from the model, identify the transition and explain what it shows or does.

   a) For now at least, iris scanning tends to be used mainly in business and security applications.

   b) At the same time, the rising use of computers and other electronic devices means we need to identify ourselves more often.

   c) But not only are these myriad passwords difficult to remember and annoying to use, they're really not all that secure.

   d) Yet another biometric technology is voice scanning, which uses a PC microphone and software to create a unique voice print.

   e) Part of the reason is a rapid advance in the quality of biometric technologies, as well as a tumble in prices.

2. Find five other examples of transitions in the model. Identify each transition and explain what it shows or does.

3. Two other methods of improving the coherence of your ideas are to repeat a key word you have already used earlier in the same paragraph or in a previous paragraph, or to use a pronoun to replace the word. Find one example of each of these devices in the model.

4. Evaluate your feature article for unity and coherence. Use the suggestions presented in this section to help you revise your work.

Word Study & Spelling

Learning Goal

• use homophones correctly

The list below contains some familiar words that are frequently misspelled. One of the reasons these words cause difficulty is that they get confused with their homophones—other words that sound just like them, but are spelled differently.

• bye	• knew	• right
• for	• know	• so
• heard	• might	• some
• here	• our	• their
• hole	• one	• threw
• it's	• piece	• too

1. Write the homophone(s) for each word in the list above. Then write sentences to clarify the meaning of each word.

Example: *one/won*   There is more than **one** biometric approach to use.

The company **won** the race to invent iris scanning.

Here are a few different strategies that may help you distinguish the correct homophone.

• Associate the word with others that have similar spelling patterns (e.g., *right, fight, slight*).
• Use a mnemonic trick (e.g., remember how to spell *some* by saying, "*So* some will come to *me*."

- Spell out contractions (e.g., the word *there's* can be replaced with *there is*, but *theirs* cannot: *there's* [*there is*] more cake in the fridge, but it is *theirs*).
- Use a pronunciation cue (e.g., we usually extend the sound of the "y" in *bye*, but not in *by*).

2. In the model, find five words that have homophones. For each homophone pair, identify which of the strategies in this section would work best to help you remember how to spell the word.

WORD ORIGINS

Biometrics is derived from the Greek word *bios* meaning "life." Biometrics has to do with the statistical study of things relating to, caused by, or affecting life or living organisms.

Look up the meaning for each of the following words, which are also derived from the root *bios*.

biology	**biography**	**biomechanics**
bionic	**biopsy**	**biosphere**

Looking Back

Before handing in your final edited draft, have a classmate check your feature article, paying particular attention to the following:

☑ Has the writer avoided repetition by using different kinds of phrases?

☑ Is the article effectively designed?

☑ Is the article unified and coherent?

☑ Are all words, especially words with homophones, spelled correctly?

Unit (8) Research Report

What is a research report?

A research report presents research findings from outside sources rather than from a person's own knowledge or experience. The purpose of research reports is to help the reader understand more about a particular topic by presenting or summarizing factual information (not the writer's own opinions). Research reports are required in most subjects across the curriculum as well as in business. The report in this unit was written by a Grade 10 student.

Learning Goals

- write a research report
- avoid the use of misplaced and dangling modifiers
- use in-text citations and a bibliography to identify borrowed material
- use active and passive voice appropriately
- spell scientific terms correctly

The Use and Abuse of Antibiotics

BY BRONWEN MCCURDY

Introduction

In the fourteenth century, a disease that came to be known as the Plague wiped out a third of the population of Europe. Doctors were helpless to treat the disease because they had no knowledge of how it was spread or what caused it. The resulting devastation changed the history of the world.

We now know that the Plague was caused by a bacterium carried by rats, who then infected the human population. Nowadays, plague victims can be successfully treated with antibiotics—the same kind of drugs that are used to treat all sorts of once-fatal afflictions, including tuberculosis and rheumatic fever. For 50 years, since the discovery of the first antibiotic, penicillin, we have enjoyed a holiday from these diseases. And we have come to rely on antibiotics to cure everything from acne to pneumonia.

But there are signs that the holiday may be about to end. In 1994, a case of the bubonic plague diagnosed in a young boy in Madagascar refused to respond to the usual treatment. And this case is just the tip of the iceberg; more and more frequently, stories of "superbugs" that do not respond to even the strongest drugs are reported in the news. Hospitals now routinely isolate patients who are transferred from another hospital to check for these virulent germs.

What is happening? Why don't our miracle drugs work as well as they used to? This report will examine how and why bacteria are becoming resistant to antibiotics.

Background

Bacteria are one of the most abundant and simplest forms of life on earth. They are single-celled, microscopic organisms that grow on or inside living things and can reproduce very quickly. Under ideal conditions some bacteria can produce a new generation almost every 20 minutes (Wait). Bacteria play an important role in human digestion and help to maintain the environment by destroying toxic elements. However, they can also cause disease.

One hundred years ago, nothing could be done about bacterial infections. Then, in 1928, Alexander Fleming discovered penicillin, the "miracle drug," which was one of the first effective tools for fighting bacterial infection. Others soon followed. Microbiologist Selman Waksman coined the term *antibiotics* to describe these natural substances that stop the growth of other micro-organisms (Levy 31).

Antibiotics affect bacteria in many different ways. Some attack bacterial cells directly; others produce chemicals that are toxic to the bacteria or stop the cells from dividing and reproducing; while still others boost the body's natural defences. In short, antibiotics help the body to fight bacterial infections (Sherwin).

Antibiotics and Resistance

Unfortunately, bacteria can fight back. Bacterial resistance was first noted by Alexander Fleming himself. He warned that the misuse of penicillin could lead to mutant forms of bacteria that were resistant to the drug. Resistance began to show itself soon after penicillin was introduced into clinical medicine. At first, the problem was found mostly in hospitals, but as time went on it became more widespread.

> Today, everywhere, we see the results of the widespread massive use of antibiotics. Under antibiotic selective pressure, resistant strains have emerged "victorious" in the world of microbial competition. In certain parts of the world, antibiotic resistant strands of common bacteria have edged out those susceptible to antibiotics (Levy 75).

Bacteria can become resistant to antibiotics in several ways. On the one hand, bacteria are capable of adapting to changes in the environment that threaten their survival, such as the presence of antibiotics. Each new generation of a bacterium may inherit some resistance from the generation before.

The second method by which bacteria develop antibiotic resistance is by "talking" to other bacterial species. Even if one species has no immunity to an antibiotic (or has never encountered it) it can pick up that resistance from contact with another species of bacteria, just as scientists working in different parts of the world share information and resources to fight disease.

Causes of the Problem

The problem of resistance is partly due to the inappropriate use of antibiotics by doctors and patients. When penicillin was first put on the market, it was used in many over-the-counter preparations, including "salves, throat lozenges, nasal ointments, and even cosmetic creams" (cited from Cowen and Segelman in Levy 50). People began to believe that the applications of the drug were limitless.

By 1955, most countries had restricted the use of penicillin to prescription only, but the damage had already been done. People now believed that there was "a pill for every ill" and insisted on getting antibiotics for all their illnesses, whether or not they were bacterial. Many people still believe in the antibiotic myth, and doctors often give in to demands for antibiotics, even when prescribing them will make no difference to the outcomes. As the saying goes, "An untreated cold goes on for seven days; a treated cold lasts a week" (Levy 106). The overuse of antibiotics by doctors and patients is a major factor in the emergence of the "superbugs."

In many developing countries, the use of antibiotics is not restricted; they are still available over the counter, without a prescription. One result is that people often take the drugs unnecessarily or use the wrong one. Furthermore, even when antibiotics are appropriate, people may not take enough to completely eliminate the infection. A single infection involves millions of bacteria, and some of them are more easily treated than others. A full course of antibiotics kills most of the bacteria and the final surviving few are eliminated by the body's immune system. However, a partial treatment will kill only the weakest bugs, leaving too many of the resilient ones for the immune system to destroy. The surviving bacteria become even stronger since they no longer have to compete with those that have been destroyed and they may multiply and reinfect the body. This new population of bacteria is better adapted to surviving the antibiotic, and the drug is less likely to work the next time. Thus, uninformed use of antibiotics contributes to the spread of antibiotic-resistant bacteria and disease.

Another cause of resistance is the overuse of antibiotics in agriculture, where they are routinely fed to livestock. Farmers do this for two reasons. First, they are used to cure diseases in animals. Second, they are added to livestock feed to make the animals grow bigger. Antibiotic-resistant bacteria develop in animals' digestive systems and are then excreted. This process introduces the bacteria into the ecosystem, where they can relocate in other hosts and pass along the resistance to other bacteria. Another problem with feeding animals antibiotics is that the food they produce also contains resistant bacteria. Thus, when humans eat the food, the bacteria enter their system.

Conclusion

Antibiotics have been the major treatment for curing and preventing infectious diseases for the last 50 years. However, because of drug-resistant bacteria, people are now dying from illnesses that were easily treated 20 years ago. Although scientists are looking for new antibiotics, these are only a temporary cure until they can find a more lasting solution. Otherwise, the cycle will continue until we find ourselves back where we started, with no antibiotics to treat the many bacterial infections that attack living things. As antibiotics lose their effectiveness, society is becoming aware of the damage caused by improper use of these miracle drugs.

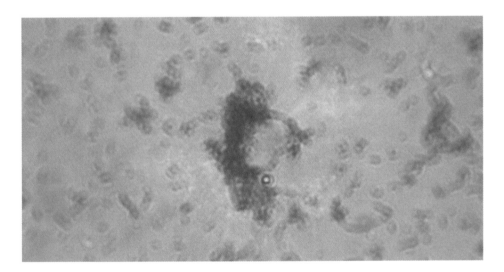

Bibliography

Cowen, D. L. and A. B. Segelman. <u>Antibiotics in Historical Perspective</u>.
Rahway, NJ: Merck Sharp and Dohme International, 1981.

Levy, Stuart B. <u>The Antibiotic Paradox: How Miracle Drugs Are Destroying
the Miracle</u>. New York: Plenum Press, 1992.

Sherwin, Chris. "Bacterial Resistance to Antibiotics: How Antibiotics Work."
(1997). 27 Nov. 1999 <http://www.cs.hmc.edu/tim/bio52/project_1/
1_HowTheyWork/index.html>.

Wait, Jeni. "Bacterial Resistance to Antibiotics: How Bacteria Develop
Resistance." (1997). 27 Oct. 1999 <http://www.cs.hmc.edu/tim/bio52/
project_1/2_Resistance/index.html>. ■

Investigating the Model

1. The purpose of a research report is to present or summarize factual
   information and experts' opinions in a clear, concise manner. Identify
   two important facts or experts' opinions in the model that you were
   previously unaware of. Comment on the author's effectiveness in
   presenting this information clearly and concisely.

2. The introduction of a research report should catch the reader's interest
   and explain what the report is about in a clearly written thesis
   statement. Comment on how well the introduction of the model
   achieves these two purposes. Who do you think the author intended as
   her audience?

3. Writers of research reports must gather information from a number of
   sources and arrange their findings (facts, examples, and ideas) under
   subtopics in the body of the report. List one fact, example, or idea the
   author has included under each heading in her report.

4. Reports are usually written in the third person and in the present tense.
   Is the model written this way? Prove your answer by citing some
   examples. When is the use of the past tense justified? Provide an
   example from the model.

5. Most paragraphs used in research reports begin with a topic sentence followed by details that support the topic sentence. Select two paragraphs from the model that clearly demonstrate this type of paragraph organization. Identify the topic sentence and the supporting details in each paragraph.

6. A research report documents both the primary and secondary sources of information used by the author. This documentation occurs both within the report (as footnotes or in-text citations) and at the end of the report (in a bibliography). Identify one idea in the model that came from another source and identify the source.

7. A research report contains a conclusion that either summarizes important points in the report or restates the main idea. Find the conclusion in the model and identify what it does.

Checkpoint: Research Report

 8. As a class, create a checklist of common features of research reports, based on the model and your own experience.

Writer's Workshop

Learning Goal

- **write a research report**

The more time you spend getting a clear picture of where you're going with your research report and how to get there, the less time you'll need for the actual writing. Therefore, plan to spend considerable time on steps 1 to 4 below.

1. The purpose of your report is to inform. Your audience is anyone fifteen years of age or older. With this in mind, choose a topic for your research report. Try to find a subject that is of real interest to you. (After all, you are going to spend considerable time working on it!) Make sure the topic is neither too broad nor too narrow and that there is enough information available on the subject from both primary and secondary sources.

IDEA FILE

Here are some ideas to get you thinking about a topic. Consider writing about

- the history of ...
- a person you admire
- an occupation that interests you
- an invention or an inventor
- a disease that affects someone you know
- a topic related to space exploration
- a place you would like to know more about
- the life of your favourite author

2. Make a chart with the following headings: What Do I Already Know? What Do I Want To Know? Fill in the two columns. The second column should be a list of questions you need to find answers to. Browse through books, magazines, newspapers, encyclopedias, CD-ROMs, and the Internet, or watch a film or television program to get a general idea of what the topic is about. Identify further questions that could be added to your chart. Also, ask some members of your intended audience to identify some questions they would like answered about the topic.

3. Look through the questions on your chart, and then write a focus statement or question that highlights what your report is mainly going to be about; for example, *The point of my research is to inform other students and adults about the use and abuse of antibiotics.* Notice that this statement also includes the purpose (to inform) and audience (students) for the report. Your focus statement or question will not appear in your final report but will serve as a guide as you do your research.

4. Based on the questions in your chart, make a list of possible subtopics to include in your research report. Then transfer each subtopic to a separate file card. File cards allow you to arrange and rearrange your information as you work. Designate some cards (perhaps a different colour) for recording bibliographical information.

5. Arrange your cards in a temporary order, from most important to least important. This order will allow you to cut some subtopics if the list is too long and to insert other subtopics if you find new information during your research.

6. Search resources for information that supports the focus statement of your research project and relates to one of the subtopics. Make sure the information is accurate, up to date, and interesting. Record important words, phrases, and quotations on the appropriate file card in your own words. If you are going to use a source's exact words, make sure you put quotation marks around them and credit the author. Record the proper bibliographical information (see Mechanics & Design section) on a separate file card.

TECHNO-TIP

When gathering information on the web, you need to make sure that the information is accurate. Here are some questions you can ask yourself to help evaluate the credibility of a web site.

- In which domain is the site listed? Educational sites (edu), government sites (gov), and organizational sites (org) usually contain more authoritative information.

- Who is the author? What authority or special knowledge does the author have?

- Is a bibliography included? Are there links to other reliable sources?

- Is the site factual, or does the site show bias or slant?

- How long ago was the information produced? When was the site last revised?

- Is the discussion of the topic comprehensive? Are supporting materials (e.g., graphs, charts) given? Are there links to other resources on the topic?

7. When you think you have enough information, ask yourself the following questions:

   • Have I adequately addressed the topic of my report?
   • Have I consulted an adequate number and variety of resources to ensure that I have different people's views on the topic?
   • Do I have enough information under each subtopic?
   • Is each point listed under each subtopic relevant?
   • Is the order of my cards appropriate?

8. Write your first draft, including an introduction, body, and conclusion. Remember to begin a new paragraph for each subtopic and to include a topic sentence in each paragraph.

 9. Refer back to Checkpoint and revise your research report until you are satisfied with its focus, content, and organization. Document your sources using the information provided in the Mechanics & Design section of this unit.

MEDIA LINK

 Note carefully the time allotted to business, scientific, and economic reports during a national newscast. What percentage of the overall newscast do these stories represent? Consider also how the information is shaped to present it to the average viewer. What kind of images or visuals are used, and what emotional impact do they convey? If you wanted to get more in-depth coverage of these kinds of stories, where would you go?

Discuss your findings with a partner, and consider what factors make it difficult to present serious economic, business, and scientific stories in mainstream news media. Present your findings in a short report.

ORAL LANGUAGE EXTENSION

One method of obtaining information for a research report is to conduct an interview with a person or a group of people. Working in groups of four, develop a list of guidelines for conducting a research interview. These guidelines should include what should be done before, during, and after the interview. Also provide some information on writing effective questions for interviews. Once completed, share your guidelines with your classmates and, as a class, create a set of class Guidelines for Interviews.

Working in pairs and using the Guidelines for Interviews, arrange to conduct an interview with a member of your family, school, or community. Your purpose is to obtain information on one of your research topics (if applicable) or on some other topic of interest to you (e.g., what knowledge and skills a person needs to do a particular job, how something is made or done, or how something has changed over the years).

Decide what role each of you will play before, during, and after the interview. Use a tape recorder, if available, to record your interview. Following the interview, listen to the tape or look at the notes you recorded during the interview. In point form, list the main points you learned about the topic during the interview as well as the strengths and weaknesses of your interviewing skills.

Grammar

A **misplaced modifier** results when a modifying word, phrase, or clause is placed too far away from the word it modifies.

Learning Goal

- **avoid the use of misplaced and dangling modifiers**

When modifiers are placed too far away from the words they modify, they sometimes appear to modify a word other than the one intended.

Misplaced modifier:	Alexander Fleming wanted to discover how to make penicillin *badly*. (Did he want to make it badly?)
Corrected:	Alexander Fleming *badly* wanted to discover how to make penicillin.
Misplaced modifier:	The child was given antibiotics by the doctor *suffering from a bacterial infection*. (Was the doctor suffering?)
Corrected:	The child *suffering from a bacterial infection* was given antibiotics by the doctor.
Misplaced modifier:	The number of cases *in hospitals* that are resistant to antibiotics is growing. (Are the hospitals resistant?)
Corrected:	*In hospitals,* the number of cases that are resistant to antibiotics is growing.

Confusion can also result when a modifier does not refer to anything in a sentence because the word being modified is left out.

A **dangling modifier** occurs when the word being modified does not appear in the sentence.

Dangling modifier:	When only eight, our doctor gave me my first dose of antibiotics. (Was the doctor only eight?)
Corrected:	When I was only eight, our doctor gave me my first dose of antibiotics.
Dangling modifier:	When ill, the doctor was always willing to help. (Was the doctor ill?)
Corrected:	When patients were ill, the doctor was always willing to help.

1. Rewrite the following sentences, making changes that will correct any misplaced or dangling modifiers.

   a) Some bacteria have become almost resistant to every antibiotic.
   b) I saw bacteria under a microscope on a slide.
   c) Many diseases can be cured by antibiotics that would once have been fatal.
   d) Too many patients are going to doctors with colds and requesting antibiotics.
   e) After years of misuse and abuse by doctors and patients, diseases like tuberculosis are making a comeback.
   f) Aided by research, antibiotics were discovered.

2. Read your research report to ensure that it contains no misplaced or dangling modifiers.

Mechanics & Design

Giving credit to authors' ideas or words you have used in your report is very important. This is usually done within the body of your report in an **in-text citation** and in a **bibliography** section (sometimes titled References or Works Cited) on a separate page at the end of your report.

Your teacher will have specific expectations regarding how you credit your sources in order to avoid plagiarism. The two most common styles of documentation are those of the MLA (Modern Language Association) and the APA (American Psychological Association). In this unit, the MLA style has been used.

Learning Goal

- **use in-text citations and a bibliography to identify borrowed material**

Write **in-text citations** by putting in parentheses the author's last name and the page number(s) on which you found the information. This reference is placed at the end of the last sentence or idea taken from the author. Readers can then refer to the bibliography for the full source information.

Many people still believe in the antibiotic myth, and doctors often give in to demands for antibiotics, even when prescribing them will make no difference to the outcomes. As the saying goes, "An untreated cold goes on for seven days; a treated cold lasts a week" (Levy 106).

If the citation begins with a signal phrase (underlined below) that mentions the author's name, include the page number in the reference.

> As Stuart Levy reports, "Today, everywhere, we see the results of the widespread massive use of antibiotics. Under antibiotic selective pressure, resistant strains have emerged 'victorious' in the world of microbial competition" (75).

If you are simply paraphrasing or summarizing an author's ideas, you do not need to include a page number in the text.

You may be instructed by your teacher to give credit for sources in **footnotes** or **endnotes** rather than in parentheses within the text. While footnotes are written at the bottom of the page on which a source has been used, endnotes (a collection of footnotes) are written at the end of a text on a separate page. Both footnotes and endnotes are signalled in the text by a small raised number (superscript number) at the end of the last sentence or idea to which the note refers.

Sample text reference to a footnote or endnote:
Selman Waksman coined the term *antibiotics* to describe these natural substances that stop the growth of other micro-organisms. [1]

Sample footnote or endnote:

[1] Stuart Levy, *The Antibiotic Paradox: How Miracle Drugs Are Destroying the Miracle* (New York: Plenum Press, 1992) 31.

Should you require footnotes or endnotes in your research report, your teacher will give you more detailed information on their format and use.

> The **bibliography** that appears at the end of a research report contains a detailed list of all the books, articles, videos, people, and other sources you consulted for your report.

The bibliography not only shows readers where the information came from, but it also enables others to find these resources if they want. Examples of bibliography entries in the MLA and APA styles are shown on pages 252 to 255. However, check with your teacher to find out if she or he prefers another style.

1. Write three reasons why sources of information in a research report should be identified.

2. Choose a small section from the model report, paraphrase it, and then write an in-text citation for it in the style your teacher designates.

Usage & Style

The **voice** of a verb tells about the role of the subject in a sentence.

The **active voice** emphasizes the doer of the action.

> Alexander Fleming discovered penicillin.

The active voice should be used most of the time in writing because it is more direct and more efficient.

Learning Goal

- use active and passive voice appropriately

In the **passive voice,** the emphasis is placed on the receiver of the action. Any verb that takes a direct object (transitive verb) can be made passive.

> Penicillin was discovered by Alexander Fleming.

WRITING TIP

Writers often use the passive voice when the focus is on what happened rather than who did something. For this reason, scientific and medical reports often use the passive voice, since what happened or was observed is usually more important than who actually performed it.

> The patient *was treated* using a combination of several antibiotics.

> Several new antibiotics *have been produced* synthetically in the lab.

1. Working in groups of four, identify two sentences in the model that are written in the passive voice and rewrite them in the active voice. Suggest a reason why the author chose to use the passive voice in each case.

2. Identify whether the following sentences are written in the active or passive voice; then recast active sentences as passive and passive sentences as active.

   a) Antibiotics kill most of the bacteria.
   b) The diseases were treated by the doctors.
   c) Scientists throughout the world share information.
   d) Farmers use antibiotics to cure diseases in animals.
   e) Most sinus infections are caused by bacteria.

3. Look through your research report for examples of sentences written in the passive voice. Decide whether its use is justified, and change any sentences that you think should be active.

Word Study & Spelling

Research reports are written on many topics in subject areas across the curriculum. Courses in mathematics, science, technology, history, business, health and physical education, guidance and career education, languages, music, and visual arts all require specialized vocabularies. Since spell checkers may not recognize some of these specialized words, you cannot always depend on your computer to find your spelling errors.

1. The model research report contains some specialized medical vocabulary. Complete the spelling of each of the following words taken from the model by filling in the blank letters. Once you have completed the exercise, check the correct spellings of the words in the model. For those words you spelled incorrectly, apply one of the spelling strategies learned in this text to learn to spell them correctly.

Learning Goal

- **spell scientific terms correctly**

   a) ant_bi_t_cs
   b) _n_umonia
   c) ba_ter_a
   d) pen_ _il_in
   e) org_n_sms
   f) im_ _ne
   g) sa_v_s
   h) inf_ct_o_s

2. The following list contains scientific terms that you have probably used, or at least heard, in your science studies over the past few years.

- analysis
- apparatus
- applications
- chemical
- equipment
- evidence
- experiment
- formulas
- inquiry
- instruments

- investigations
- periodic
- procedures
- processes
- properties
- reactions
- solution
- substance
- systems
- variables

a) With a partner, take turns using each word in a sentence. Have your partner judge whether you have used the word correctly or not.

b) With the same partner, take turns dictating and writing down these words. Compare your work with the list above to find any misspelled words. Then identify a spelling strategy (see page 139) to help you remember the correct spelling.

3. Make a list of 10 words that may cause spelling difficulties from science units you have studied this year. Print the words, leaving out some of the more difficult letters and challenge a classmate to fill in the blanks, while you try to do the same with his or her list. Check your classmate's spelling of the words. (If you are not taking science this year, choose another course that you and a classmate are currently studying.)

WORD ORIGINS

"Microbiologist Selman Waksman coined the term *antibiotics* to describe these natural substances that stop the growth of other micro-organisms (Levy 31)."

New inventions and the use of technology in medicine have resulted in the creation of many words in the last 100 years. Many of these new words have names that describe their function. Use your dictionary to find the meaning of each of the following medical terms.

defibrillator   dialysis machine   fluoroscope   pacemaker

Looking Back

Before handing in your final edited draft, have a classmate check your research report, paying particular attention to the following:

✓ Is the writing free of misplaced and dangling modifiers?

✓ Are sources cited correctly and completely?

✓ Has the passive voice been used only where appropriate?

✓ Have all words, including specialized words, been spelled correctly?

Unit 9 Leaflet

What is a leaflet?

A leaflet is a printed folder or sheet of paper that conveys information about products, services, events, issues, or places. Leaflets are inexpensive because they are usually printed on one piece of paper. They can often be found in places such as government buildings, medical offices, libraries, and travel agencies. The two leaflets shown in this unit use different formats to convey information about health-related issues. The first example is a double-sided flyer (shown on pages 181 to 182) that promotes exercise. The second, which was created by high-school students, is a folded leaflet (shown on pages 183 to 184) that explains the dangers of smoking.

Front

Choose a variety of activities from these three groups:

Endurance

4-7 days a week
Continuous activities for your heart, lungs and circulatory system.

Flexibility

4-7 days a week
Gentle reaching, bending and stretching activities to keep your muscles relaxed and joints mobile.

Strength

2-4 days a week
Activities against resistance to strengthen muscles and bones and improve posture.

Starting slowly is very safe for most people. Not sure? Consult your health professional.

For a copy of the *Guide Handbook* and more information:
1-888-334-9769, or
www.paguide.com

Eating well is also important. Follow *Canada's Food Guide to Healthy Eating* to make wise food choices.

Get Active Your Way, Every Day – For Life!

Scientists say accumulate 60 minutes of physical activity every day to stay healthy or improve your health. As you progress to moderate activities, you can cut down to 30 minutes, 4 days a week. Add up your activities in periods of at least 10 minutes each. Start slowly… and build up.

Time needed depends on effort

Very Light Effort	Light Effort *60 minutes*	Moderate Effort *30-60 minutes*	Vigorous Effort *20-30 minutes*	Maximum Effort
• Strolling • Dusting	• Light walking • Volleyball • Easy gardening • Stretching	• Brisk walking • Biking • Raking leaves • Swimming • Dancing • Water aerobics	• Aerobics • Jogging • Hockey • Basketball • Fast swimming • Fast dancing	• Sprinting • Racing

Range needed to stay healthy

You Can Do It – Getting started is easier than you think

Physical activity doesn't have to be very hard. Build physical activities into your daily routine.

- Walk whenever you can – get off the bus early; use the stairs instead of the elevator.
- Reduce inactivity for long periods, like watching TV.
- Get up from the couch and stretch and bend for a few minutes every hour.
- Play actively with your kids.
- Choose to walk, wheel, or cycle for short trips.

- Start with a 10-minute walk – gradually increase the time.
- Find out about walking and cycling paths nearby and use them.
- Observe a physical activity class to see if you want to try it.
- Try one class to start; you don't have to make a long-term commitment.
- Do the activities you are doing now, more often.

Benefits of regular activity:

- better health
- improved fitness
- better posture and balance
- better self-esteem
- weight control
- stronger muscles and bones
- feeling more energetic
- relaxation and reduced stress
- continued independent living in later life

Health risks of inactivity:

- premature death
- heart disease
- obesity
- high blood pressure
- adult-onset diabetes
- osteoporosis
- stroke
- depression
- colon cancer

Back

I Choose NOT TO Smoke

Please DON'T make me!

1

Council For a Tobacco - Free* Waterloo Region

PROJECT AIR CONTROL

Project Air Control is a youth–driven project co–ordinated by the Council for a Tobacco-Free Waterloo Region, with funding from Health Canada. The Council is a coalition of health groups, youths, and adults interested in promoting nonsmoking.

FOR MORE INFORMATION CALL:

(519) 725-8874

Make it a **RULE···**
Exercise your right to smoke-free air.

Pamphlet by Luciano Panko, Bluevale Collegiate Institute, Waterloo
Logo by Sarah Roxas, St. David's High School, Waterloo
Illustrations by Andy Belanger, Waterloo Collegiate Institute, Waterloo
Photography by James Hertel

6

How does the smoke know where to stop?

Second-hand smoke is the smoke we breathe when we share the air with people who are smoking.

This smoke is harmful to nonsmokers AND smokers.

EXERCISE YOUR RIGHT TO SMOKE-FREE AIR!

5

Read the panels in numerical order.

THE FACTS

Babies exposed to second-hand smoke are more likely to die from Sudden Infant Death Syndrome (crib death)

You're hurting me!

Exposing infants and children to second-hand smoke increases...

... the risk of bronchitis by 46%
... ear infections by 19%
...tonsillectomies by 60-100%
... the risk of asthma by 43%

CHILDREN OF SMOKERS ARE MORE LIKELY TO BECOME SMOKERS THEMSELVES

Two cigarettes a day... and I don't even smoke!

YOU MAY NOT REALIZE HOW YOUR SMOKING AFFECTS YOU AND THE ONES YOU LOVE...

Being exposed to second-hand smoke all day is the same as smoking 2 to 3 cigarettes.

Cigarettes produce 12 minutes of smoke. A smoker inhales only 30 seconds of that.

Second-hand smoke is air pollution that contains more than 4'000 different chemicals. At least 43 of these can cause cancer.

HELP YOUR FAMILY CLEAR THE AIR

It's best to...

... quit, if you smoke, or
... smoke outside to keep the home smoke-free, and
... talk to your children about the dangers of smoking and second-hand smoke

It's good to...

... designate one room in your home for smoking (choose one with a window for ventilation to the outside)

It's NOT so good to...

... rely on ventilation, air cleaners, or smoke-less ashtrays (they can't remove the smoke effectively)
... ignore the issue

4   3   2

Investigating the Models

1. Leaflets are vehicles for providing information to the public. Organizations use leaflets because they are easy to make, are inexpensive to produce and distribute, and can be taken home for future reference. While leaflets often contain a persuasive message, their major function is to disseminate information. Identify the purpose of each of the model leaflets.

2. Leaflets are often targeted at a particular audience. Identify the target audience for each of the models, and suggest where they might be distributed to reach their intended audience.

3. The cover panel of a folded leaflet should catch the reader's eye and identify the topic. Evaluate the cover of the smoking leaflet. How well does it achieve these goals?

4. Leaflets usually rely on a combination of words and visual features to get their message across. In small groups, discuss the use of visuals and words in each of the models. Which leaflet relies more on visual features? How do the visuals in each model enhance the information in the text?

5. The tone of a leaflet should be suited to both the topic and the intended audience. What tone is created in each of the models? Provide examples to support your answer. Why do you think the writers chose to adopt this tone?

6. Leaflets often use design techniques such as headings, lists, and boxes to make information easy to find and understand. Identify which of these and other design techniques and elements are used to make the information accessible in the two models.

7. Leaflets can be a single sheet of paper, or they may be folded in two, three, or even four sections per side. Compare the formats of the model leaflets, and identify the pros and cons of each.

8. The information chosen for inclusion in a leaflet must provide a quick overview of the topic, be easy to understand, and be of interest to the

reader. Assess how well the two model leaflets have achieved these goals. Are there any questions you would have liked to see answered in either of the leaflets?

9. Leaflets usually point the reader to other sources of information on the topic. Identify some of the sources of information in the models. To find where this information is usually placed, compare the models with other leaflets you have collected.

Checkpoint: Leaflet

 As a class, create a checklist of common features of leaflets, based on the models and your own experience. Use the checklist to help you create your own leaflet.

Writer's Workshop

Learning Goal

• **produce a leaflet**

1. Working in groups of four, brainstorm a list of possible topics for a leaflet. Your purpose is to convey information on a topic of interest.

IDEA FILE

Try completing one of the following sentence prompts to get you started:

• The benefits of ...

• So you are thinking about ...

• Making sensible choices about ...

• The facts on ...

• How to protect yourself against ...

2. Decide who would benefit most from the information you are presenting, and prepare a profile of your target audience. Include age, gender, education, and any other relevant characteristics. Use this information to identify the style and content of your leaflet.

3. Make a list of some possible subtopics for information you wish to convey. For example, a leaflet on how to protect yourself from the sun might include the following headings:

- Why Worry About the Sun?
- Types of Ultraviolet Radiation
- Common Myths About Sun Protection
- Your Best Defence
- For Further Information

4. Gather the information you need to support your subtopics. As you gather information, look for illustrations (drawings, photographs, charts, graphs, tables, maps) that you could use to support the information you have gathered.

5. Prepare a draft of each of your subtopics using simple, direct sentences or point-form statements.

6. Create a working layout of your leaflet so that you may test your design ideas. For this preliminary layout, use the same size of paper as you will use for the final product. This will enable you to decide on the size of fonts and illustrations, and their placement in relation to each other.

WRITING TIP

Don't try to put too much information on each panel. If your text and illustrations are cluttered, readers may have difficulty picking out the key points you are trying to make.

7. Format your leaflet, using different fonts, type sizes, graphics, and other techniques to emphasize your titles, key words, and concepts.

8. Exchange your leaflet with two other members of your class and get their feedback. Is the information on the leaflet adequate and clear? What changes would improve the content or style?

 9. Use the list you developed at Checkpoint to revise your leaflet.

ORAL LANGUAGE EXTENSION

Prepare a brief oral presentation comparing the features of the leaflet you prepared in the Writer's Workshop with a leaflet sent to your home, or one you have obtained within your community. Use the following criteria to guide your comparison:

- language used
- balance between text and illustrations
- tone
- use of illustrations
- the effectiveness of the introduction or cover panel

Work in groups of four. Give each group member a chance to present a comparison to the group. After each presentation, other group members may comment on what was said or add their own comments about the leaflets.

Grammar

Learning Goal

- construct simple, compound, complex, and compound-complex sentences

Leaflets must convey a strong message in a limited space. There is not a lot of room for linking ideas or adding supporting details. For this reason, most sentences in a leaflet are either simple or compound in structure. Simple sentences are particularly useful, as they convey a single main thought or idea.

A **simple sentence** is a sentence that contains only one main clause (one subject and one predicate).

Although they contain only one main idea, simple sentences can differ a lot in length. For example, each of the following sentences from the models is a simple sentence.

Increase endurance activities.

Being exposed to second-hand smoke all day is the same as smoking 2 to 3 cigarettes.

1. Find five other simple sentences in the model leaflets.

> A **compound sentence** contains two or more main clauses.

The clauses in a compound sentence can be joined by either a coordinating conjunction (*and, or, not, for, but, so,* or *yet*) or a semicolon.

> Every little bit counts, but more is even better.
>
> Try one class to start; you don't have to make a long-term commitment.

2. Find at least two other examples of compound sentences in the models.

> A **complex sentence** contains one main clause and one or more subordinate clauses.

Always remember to put the most important idea in the main clause of a complex sentence. In the following examples, the main clause is boldface and the subordinate clause is italic.

> *Although you may not realize it,* **your smoking affects you and the ones you love.**
>
> *As you progress to moderate activities,* **you can cut down to 30 minutes, 4 days a week.**

3. Rewrite the following pairs of sentences as a single complex sentence.
   a) Not sure? Consult your health professional.
   b) Increase your endurance, flexibility, and strength. At the same time, reduce the time you spend sitting.
   c) Cigarettes produce 12 minutes of smoke. A smoker inhales only 30 seconds of that.
   d) Don't rely on ventilation, air cleaners, or smokeless ashtrays (they can't remove the smoke effectively).
   e) A lit cigarette gives off second-hand smoke. This smoke is harmful to nonsmokers and smokers.

A **compound-complex sentence** contains at least two main clauses and at least one subordinate clause.

Compound-complex sentences contain a lot of information. They are useful when you want to draw together several ideas and show how they relate to one another, as in an essay or a research report. There are no compound-complex sentences in either of the model leaflets, but here are some examples that draw together information from the models. (The main clauses are boldface and the subordinate clauses are italic.)

Although physical activity is crucial to a healthy lifestyle, **eating well is also important**, so **you should try to improve both your level of activity and your eating habits.**

Children are more likely to become smokers *if their mother or father smokes*, so **parents should try very hard to quit.**

4. Why do you think there are no compound-complex sentences in either of the models? Do you think the sentences above would work well in the leaflets? Why or why not?

5. Construct one example for each of the types of sentences examined in this section. All of your sentences should be about the same topic as your leaflet.

6. Check your leaflet to ensure that you have not used too many complex or compound-complex sentences. Look for ways to simplify your message by using simple or compound sentences.

Mechanics & Design

Learning Goal

- **experiment with design elements**

Designers of leaflets use different design techniques to highlight information and create interest. Here are a few ideas you might want to incorporate into your own leaflet:

- If you are working on a computer, choose fonts (typefaces) that look good together. Try to limit the number of different fonts you use to two or three. Make sure they are easy to read.

- Use larger type to emphasize titles, key words, and important ideas.

- Experiment with bold type and shading to help draw attention to important words, statements, or titles.

- Leave a sufficient amount of white space on the borders and between columns, lists, titles, illustrations, and panels. White space makes it easier to read the words, and makes your leaflet look more appealing.

- Use bullets (dots) to highlight points in a list.

- Try incorporating colour into photographs or drawings, borders, titles or subtitles, charts, graphs, and bullets.

- Choose visual aids such as photographs, drawings, maps, charts, graphs, and lists to break up the text, create interest, and clarify information.

- Add boxes, circles, and lines to separate information and create borders.

TECHNO-TIP

With a computer scanner, you can quickly and professionally copy a photograph into your leaflet. Photographs that have clearly defined lines and colours will produce the best results. (Remember, if you are going to distribute your leaflet, you must get permission to use any photos or artwork that are not your own.)

1. Working with a partner, examine the models and assess their design using the design tips given above. Discuss how each of the features identified in the models contributes to the overall effect and helps to convey the information.

2. Find other leaflets containing effective examples of the design features identified in this section. Try to find an example of each feature. Bring your examples to class and share them with a small group of your classmates. Explain why you think your examples are effective.

3. Assess the design of your own leaflet and make any changes you think will improve it.

MEDIA LINK

Your task is to work in groups of eight or ten to create a 30-second public service commercial based on the topic of one of your leaflets. Start by choosing whose leaflet you will adapt and brainstorming themes or concepts for your video.

Next, create a production proposal. List the jobs involved and assign them. Jobs may include scriptwriter, director, camera person, props master, and actors/hosts/narrators. Also assign a production coordinator who will make sure everyone keeps on schedule.

Set a schedule that takes into account the main stages of production:

- Scripting—writing a treatment, creating the script, revising, polishing
- Pre-production—storyboarding, selecting locations, props, wardrobe preparation
- Shooting—rehearsals, video and audio recording
- Post-production—editing, adding titles, credits, and music

Present your video to your classmates and invite them to critique your work. Be prepared to defend the design and content decisions you made.

Usage & Style

Learning Goal

- select an appropriate level of language to suit the form

Writing a leaflet often involves translating technical information into language everyone can understand. Here are three keys to creating a readable style for your leaflet.

- **Use numbers sparingly.** It is important to present accurate information, and statistics are a good way to make a point. However, people may find it hard to relate to lots of numbers. Before you use statistics in your leaflet, ask yourself if a simple statement using words like "increases," "decreases," or "is higher than" will give your reader enough information. If you do want to include precise numbers, consider using a simple chart or graph to make them easier to understand.

1. Find examples of numbers or statistics in the two model leaflets, and with a partner, discuss how effectively they are used. Can you think of any other ways the information might have been presented?

- **Use the imperative to give readers clear directions for action.** Sentences that use the imperative (commands) almost always begin with a verb.

  Increase strength activities.

  Help your family clear the air.

2. Rewrite the following declarative sentences to make them imperative.
   a) It is important to get some physical activity every day.
   b) Smoking around infants and children should not be allowed.
   c) Your fitness can be improved by getting regular exercise.
   d) Experts agree that it's best to teach children early about the hazards of smoking.

- **Select terms that your readers will understand.** In the smoking leaflet, notice that the author chose to explain the term "Sudden Infant Death Syndrome" as "crib death," a less technical expression meaning the same thing. Similarly, the fitness leaflet talks about endurance activities that help "your heart, lungs, and circulatory system," instead of using the more technical term "cardiopulmonary system."

3. Identify the words or expressions in the leaflets that were used instead of these more technical terms. (Use a dictionary to help you.)
   a) hypertension
   b) carcinogenic
   c) otitis media

4. Using the three points outlined above, reread your leaflet and assess your language style. Make any changes you think are necessary.

Word Study & Spelling

Did you know that the English language contains approximately one million words, and that many new English words are invented each year? The average person has a core vocabulary of about 15 000 words, not including the language specific to jobs, hobbies, sports, activities, and interests of all kinds. These facts imply

Learning Goal

- apply techniques to expand vocabulary and improve spelling of technical terms that you will never stop acquiring new words at school, at work, and in your daily life. Here are some suggestions to help you build your speaking and writing vocabularies.

- **Listen to new words.** Your vocabulary grows when you pick up words by "imitating the talk" of other people. When you hear a new word, find out what it means and try to use it in your speaking and writing several times throughout the day. This way, you will begin to make the word part of your everyday vocabulary.

- **Read, read, read.** Your speaking, reading, and writing vocabularies grow as you see new words used in context. Seeing new words in sentences helps you understand what they mean and how they are used.

- **Keep a list of new words** that you encounter in your listening and reading in a special section of your notebook. Practise using the words in sentences.

- **Play word games,** such as crossword puzzles or word searches.

1. The following list of medical and health-related terms is taken from the models. Although most of these words are specific technical terms, you have probably used many of them, or at least heard them spoken.

   - aerobics
   - asthma
   - bronchitis
   - circulatory
   - diabetes
   - infections
   - obesity
   - osteoporosis
   - tonsillectomies

   a) Before you check in a dictionary, write down your understanding of what each term means; then look it up and compare your definition with that in the dictionary. How accurate were you?
   b) With a partner, take turns dictating the list of words to each other. Switch places, and then compare your lists. Identify a strategy to help you remember any words you misspelled.

2. Make a list of 10 other words from the model leaflets that may cause spelling difficulties for your classmates. Scramble the letters in each word and give them to a classmate to solve.

   Example: scumles—muscles

WORD ORIGINS

"Exposing infants and children to second-hand smoke increases the risk of bronchitis by 46%."

The word **bronchitis** comes from the Greek word *bronchia* meaning "bronchial tubes." Many terms related to science, medicine, physics, and astronomy are Greek in origin. In fact, about 15 percent of English words come from Greek.

Use a dictionary to find the meaning of each of the Greek prefixes, suffixes, and roots below. Then find at least one English word that contains each prefix, suffix, or root.

anthropo- anti-   astro-   auto-   bio-   geo-

hydro-   hyper-   -itis   -logy   mega- photo-

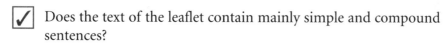

Looking Back

Before handing in your final edited draft, have a classmate check your leaflet, paying particular attention to the following:

☑ Does the text of the leaflet contain mainly simple and compound sentences?

☑ Is the design of the leaflet effective?

☑ Has the writer used simple statements of fact?

☑ Has the writer used the imperative to indicate actions?

☑ Are technical terms used appropriately?

☑ Are all words spelled correctly?

Reflect and Build on Your Learning

Reflecting on Expository Writing Forms

1. Review the Learning Goals on page 145. Which goals do you think you have achieved most successfully? Which goals do you think will require you to do more work? For each goal that will require more work, list one specific action you will take to accomplish the goal.

2. Write a note to your teacher explaining the three most important things you learned about expository writing during the study of this section.

3. Complete each of the following statements about the work you have done in the past three units on exposition.

   - Two things I have done particularly well in this section are ...
   - I have improved as a writer during the study of this section because ...
   - In the future, when I am writing exposition, I will need to be careful to ...
   - I would rate my work in this section as (choose one): weak, fair, okay, good, great.

Looking Over Expository Writing Forms

1. Working with a small group, create a chart summarizing what you know about the features of feature articles, research reports, and leaflets. Include the following headings in your chart: Purpose, Audience, Introduction, Body (content/organization), Conclusion, and Design. The class checklists you developed for each form will help you with this task. Compare your chart with those of other groups. How would you modify your chart based on what they have included in theirs?

Using Expository Writing Forms

1. Outline three methods you would use in writing a feature article, a research report, or a leaflet to make the information in them easy to find and easy to understand.

2. A writer must choose the most appropriate form of writing to communicate her or his message. When would you choose to use each of the following expository forms of writing? Provide one specific example to demonstrate when you might use each form either inside or outside of school.

- comparison
- definition
- explanation
- factual account
- feature article

- hard news story
- instructions
- leaflet
- précis
- research report

3. Imagine that you have to explain the topic of the feature article or research report you wrote in Units 7 and 8 to a group of students in Grade 5. Write a short explanation of how you would communicate and illustrate the information to this younger age group. What would you change? What would you omit? What would you add? How would you change the language? What other methods or aids (e.g., skit, chart, or graphics) might you use to help get your information across? Present your ideas to a group of students in your class for feedback.

4. Working in groups of four, develop a leaflet explaining the steps a student should go through in developing a research report. Use visuals to make your leaflet interesting and easy to read. Share your leaflet with other members of the class, and compare the content and the visual features of the leaflets. Select one leaflet from your class to give to the teacher-librarian in your school for possible reproduction and use by other students.

5. a) Find a hard news story in a local newspaper about an event, issue, or trend that is of interest to you.
   b) Consider how you might use the article as the basis for a feature article. Identify who the audience for such an article would be, what questions you would need to answer, and what experts or other sources you might consult in researching the article. Create a preliminary outline of what your article might look like.
   c) Compare notes with a classmate, and give each other feedback and suggestions that might improve the final article. If you wish, you may go ahead and write the article for submission to the school or local paper.

BUILD ON YOUR LEARNING

Persuasion

Persuasive writing is writing that moves readers to believe or act through logic, argument, or emotional appeal. Ideas used in persuasive writing must be reasonable and reliable, and must be supported with solid evidence. Whether you're giving a speech to urge people to elect you to a position, or trying to persuade an employer that you are the best person for a job, persuasive writing is a way to let people know what you know, what you think, and what you want from them.

The speeches, comparative essay, résumés, and covering letters included in this section all achieve their purposes by using logical and emotional arguments that are suited to the specific audience.

Features of Persuasion

- Persuasive writing aims to move the reader to support a point of view or to act in support of an idea or cause.
- A persuasive piece often begins with a statement of the author's position, then presents arguments and evidence in favour of that position, and concludes with a call to action or a recommendation.
- Persuasive writers arrange their points for maximum impact on their audience.
- Persuasion usually uses a combination of logical and emotional appeals designed to win over a specific audience.

Learning Goals

- use a range of sources to gather information and explore ideas for your written work
- identify and use persuasive forms appropriately in writing a speech, comparative essay, résumé, and covering letter
- use organizational techniques to present ideas and supporting details
- revise your work independently and collaboratively to improve accuracy, clarity, coherence, and style
- edit and proofread to produce final drafts using correct grammar, mechanics, usage, and spelling
- use knowledge of vocabulary and language conventions to write competently and effectively
- develop listening, speaking, and media literacy skills
- read a variety of nonfiction such as speeches, comparative essays, résumés, and covering letters
- identify and understand the elements and style of a variety of nonfiction

Unit 10 Persuasive Speech

What is a persuasive speech?

A persuasive speech is a formal or informal talk given by a speaker to convince members of an audience that they should follow a certain course of action or accept a particular belief or position. A persuasive speech usually combines clear logic (or factual evidence) with emotional appeals to make a convincing argument. Although the two speeches given here are both formal in tone, one was given to mark a serious occasion, while the other takes a more humorous approach.

Learning Goals

- write a persuasive speech
- use parallel constructions for emphasis
- identify ways to include visual aids in a speech
- use effective words and sentence structures
- select words and phrases with appropriate connotations

Ceremony for Decorations for Bravery
June 23, 1995

BY GOVERNOR GENERAL ROMÉO LEBLANC

DISTINGUISHED GUESTS, LADIES, AND GENTLEMEN:

We are gathered in Canada's name to honour you for the courage you have shown. In a moment we will hear citations describing the dangers you faced, whether from fire or smoke, water or ice, minefields or explosions.

But those few words will never describe the full reality, when each of you stood alone at the border of fear, confusion, and danger. You entered situations the rest of us might encounter in our nightmares.

Most of you were leading ordinary quiet lives, but you found the courage to do the extraordinary. You had no special training to instil bravery; it came from within you.

Books have been written about the courage shown in war; and soldiers, sailors, and fliers deserve all the honour they receive. Often they spent years in peril, fighting to preserve freedom.

But most of your acts of bravery took place without the clash of war, and without the stimulus that self-defence can give to courage. You had little if any help, little to gain, and possibly a life to lose. More than the bravery of battle, you showed the courage of giving and self-sacrifice; and that can be an equal or a greater courage.

Some of you may say that others would have acted as bravely. But the rest of us can never be certain. The hope of courage lies in every heart, together with the fear that we will fail.

When the test came, you did not fail. Most of you risked your own lives to save the lives of others. And three of those whom we honour today died in the attempt to help.

As we present these awards to you, you bring to us a greater gift. Amid the pains, distractions, and confusions of daily life, you remind us of the best that lies within the human personality, and you recall to us the ideals of courage for which we all should strive. I wish every Canadian could be in this room.

The nation thanks you for the lives that you have saved. We thank you for the courage you have shown. We thank you for the example you have given. And we thank you for renewing our faith in the higher impulses of the human heart. ∎

My Life as a Procrastinator

BY JENNIFER WILLIAMS

LADIES AND GENTLEMEN, I AM HERE TONIGHT TO MAKE A bid for the esteemed position of President of our Society. I have been in close contact with the members of the Society of Procrastinators for many years now. I realize that I am not yet a member, but this fact is not due to lack of good intent. I have planned to become a member for a long time and just have not found the time to pledge. However, if you elect me President, my first act will be to become a full-fledged member. I feel my tardiness, which could be viewed as a fault by some, simply proves my worth as a procrastinator and makes me all the more deserving of the title of President. Possibly you do not agree. Therefore, I will describe the role procrastination has played in my life.

First, the vicious rumours spread by my opponent are true: I was born two weeks early. I do not try to hide this shocking fact from you; but while I may have entered this world as a nonprocrastinator, I assure you I have never been early since! Throughout my childhood I put things off; I did not learn to ride a bicycle until I was ten and was still sucking my thumb at age eleven; I was always the last child into the school bus, going to school or coming home.

However, my procrastination skills were still not fully developed. Certainly I was late for most events and often used the excuse "Sure Mom, I'll do that later," but no one realized that this behaviour was procrastination.

It was shortly after I began high school that I realized I was a natural procrastinator. Soon after I made this discovery, others began to notice my penchant for putting things off. My skills really surfaced in grade nine when I was given a French project. My teacher assigned the project in February. It was due in May. I did not work on it in February and March because ...

well, it was too cold. In April it was rainy and in May, a week before the project was due, it was warm. Finally, the night before I had to present my project, I got to work. I researched, wrote up, translated, and created an attractive poster, all after dinner (because a *Family Ties* rerun was on after school). I worked two hours past my bedtime. My life as a true procrastinator had begun.

My experience with the French project neatly sums up my high-school career. Tests, essays, projects, exams—all were completed the night before, or in the early morning of the day they were due. However, this pattern did not upset me or my parents. I regularly got high marks and high praise for my superb effort.

This, I believe, is the essence of a good procrastinator: We are not lazy people. We are not people who are always doing things haphazardly and with little care. We are people who do good work. We just have a harder time than most people getting around to things. We are people who work well under pressure.

Notice I say pressure, not panic, as I have heard some nonprocrastinators call our last-minute rushes. My university room-mate used the word *panic* when I almost did not manage to get the rent in on time. She viewed my last-minute flurry of activity with panic, and so believed that I was also panicking. Here, I believe, is what causes the division between procrastinators and nonprocrastinators: we are simply misunderstood. If I am elected President, I will work on programs that will show nonprocrastinators our true natures and so deal a swift blow to the discrimination we so often experience. I believe that we procrastinators are level-headed people who simply work better at the last minute than three weeks early. I intend to prove this truth to the world.

I know procrastination is often a difficult path to choose. I have stepped to the edge of the pit that so many of us have tripped into headlong. I, too, have listened to the endless lectures and clichés: "Time is money," my employer repeats. "I haven't got all day," chastises my sister. "Are you going to take all night getting ready?" questions my boyfriend. And yes, I have been influenced by these people. I do not hide the terrible period in my life when I attempted to be early and to follow the wishes of all those nonprocrastinators. For three whole weeks I worked ahead of deadlines. I was prepared two days ahead of time for work projects, and I always managed to be on time for appointments and outings.

I know what you must be wondering: Was I happy during this time? Let me tell you, I was not. I was constantly tired and miserable. Still, this experience was not completely worthless. People finally realized that procrastination is an integral part of me. They began to accept me as a procrastinator. After those three awful weeks I returned to procrastinating and have felt happy and fulfilled ever since.

I am sure you now agree that I am, indeed, a procrastinator. I have suffered the same trials and social misunderstandings that so many members of this Society have experienced. And still I am proud of my procrastination. I pledge to you today that I will never change my procrastinating manner. I stand before you as a true procrastinator, and as such I hope you will consider me a worthy President for your Society. ∎

Investigating the Models

1. The purpose of a speech may be to persuade, to inform, to amuse, to pay tribute, and/or to provoke action. Identify the purpose(s) of each of the models, and comment on how effectively each model achieves its purpose(s).

2. The intended audience of a speech determines what tone it will take, what arguments will be presented, and in what order they will be arranged. Persuasive speechwriters also try to anticipate any counterarguments the audience may present. Identify the audiences of the two model speeches, and compare how the models' differences in tone and organization reflect their different audiences.

WRITING TIP

If you are writing a humorous speech, two useful techniques that can create humour are

- understatement (i.e., downplaying the humour in a situation)

- hyperbole (i.e., blowing an issue out of proportion by giving it more importance than it actually has, or by overstating its impact)

3. A good speech usually contains a declarative sentence, often called a **thesis statement,** found near the beginning of the speech. This statement provides a clear, concise explanation of the topic and the speaker's purpose. It captures the attention of listeners and sets the tone for what is to come. Identify the thesis statement in each of the models.

4. The supporting evidence for a persuasive speech may take the form of facts and figures, examples, analogies, reasons, comparisons, anecdotes, or quotations. These details are used to prove a point, clarify or illustrate, create interest, or add humour. Analyze the ways in which the speakers have supported the thesis of each model speech. Identify at least two of these elements in each speech and explain why they were used.

5. A speech may contain emotional appeals and language meant to instil pride, or to excite or persuade the audience. Appealing to people's emotions encourages them to care about what you are saying and to take action, if appropriate. Provide one example of an emotional appeal from each of the models.

6. Unlike a reader of an essay or report, the audience of a speech cannot flip back to read what you said earlier. Therefore, you need to find ways to help your listeners remember what you have said and to anticipate what you will say. You can do this by

   - using short paragraphs with lots of pauses
   - stating clearly what you intend to talk about before you begin
   - linking ideas clearly with transition words
   - summarizing what you have said during and after the speech

   Explain how the authors of the model speeches have tried to help their listeners keep track of what they are saying.

7. An effective speech contains a clear, strong conclusion that summarizes, restates the thesis, or motivates the audience to act. Evaluate the conclusions of both models. Explain what functions they serve and assess their effectiveness. Can you suggest another conclusion for each speech?

Checkpoint: Persuasive Speech

 As a class, create a checklist of common features of a persuasive speech, based on the models and your own experience. You can use the checklist to help you write your own speech.

Writer's Workshop

RKSHOP

Learning Goal

- **write a persuasive speech**

1. Look for possible topics for a persuasive speech in feature articles, editorials, and brochures. Everyday occurrences may also give you ideas. Remember to consider the needs and interests of your audience (the students in your class) and to narrow your subject to meet the time constraints imposed by your teacher.

IDEA FILE

- Persuade an audience that something is true or certain (e.g., teenage volunteers contribute a great deal to our community).

- Persuade an audience that something is good, bad, ugly, beautiful, right, or wrong (e.g., Internet use in schools should always be monitored).

- Persuade an audience that something should happen (e.g., the criteria used for the selection of players for our school teams should change).

2. Write a thesis statement for your speech.

3. Gather information to prove your thesis. Begin with ideas or information you already have, without worrying about the correct order. Then use primary and secondary resources to check your facts and gather more information, if necessary.

IDEA FILE

There are books that contain anecdotes and quotations for use in speeches. Check in your school and community libraries for these references. If you choose an anecdote or quotation, make sure that it fits into your speech naturally and that it is directly related to your thesis.

4. Decide on an appropriate order for your ideas. If you think your audience will be sympathetic to your cause, start with your weaker arguments and build up to a strong conclusion that will leave them feeling even more convinced. If your listeners need to be persuaded that your thesis is true, consider beginning with a strong point that will catch their interest. Put any arguments that you think will be less convincing in the middle, and end with another strong point. Remember also to anticipate any counterarguments your listeners may suggest, and address those in your speech.

5. Write a draft of your speech. Begin each paragraph with a topic sentence, and support both the topic sentence and your thesis with examples, arguments, or facts.

6. Write a strong conclusion for your speech.

WRITING TIP

If you are memorizing your speech, use note cards to record the outline. On each card, write the topic sentence of each new paragraph first, followed by some details in point form to support your main ideas. Write out in full any quotations, statistics, or other important details you might need to refer to.

7. Consider using visual aids to support your speech. Refer to the Mechanics & Design section of this unit for ideas.

 8. Refer to the list you created at Checkpoint, and revise and edit your speech until you are satisfied with its focus, content, and organization.

ORAL LANGUAGE EXTENSION

Work in groups of three. Take turns being the speaker, the person introducing the speaker, and the person thanking the speaker. Your introductions and thank-yous should be no longer than one minute apiece. You may use notes, but you will not be allowed to read your speech word for word.

Include the following information in your introductory and thank-you speeches:

Introduction	Thank-you
Give the name of the speaker.	Thank the speaker.
Provide some background on the speaker.	Highlight a few points from the speech.
Give a brief introduction to the topic.	

- Gather information for the introductory speech by interviewing your subject. Try to find some interesting fact that will liven up your introduction.

- For the thank-you speech, you will have to listen carefully and take notes while the person is speaking. Try to identify the main points the speaker is making so you can summarize them in your thank-you speech.

Your teacher will give you further directions on presenting your speeches.

Grammar

Learning Goal

- use parallel constructions for emphasis

Words, phrases, clauses, or sentences with similar grammatical structures or functions are said to be **parallel.** Linking words or ideas through parallel structure and repetition is a powerful way to help your listeners recognize connections among your ideas. It also makes the content easier to read and remember.

Whenever possible, express parallel ideas in a speech in a parallel grammatical form.

Not Parallel: In a moment we will hear citations describing the dangers you faced from fires, smoke inhalation, drowning, ice, walking through minefields, or bomb explosions.

Parallel: In a moment we will hear citations describing the dangers you faced, whether from **fire or smoke, water or ice, minefields or explosions.**

Not Parallel: This, I believe, is the essence of a good procrastinator: We are not lazy people. Procrastinators don't do things haphazardly and with little care. Rather, most of us do good work, but have a harder time than most people getting around to things. Working well under pressure is the procrastinator's strength.

Parallel: This, I believe, is the essence of a good procrastinator: **We are not** lazy people. **We are not** people who are always doing things haphazardly and with little care. **We are people who** do good work. …**We are people who** work well under pressure.

1. Find one other example of parallelism in each of the models and three examples from the short stories and novels you have read this year. Be prepared to explain exactly which elements are parallel.

2. Rewrite each of the following passages to strengthen the parallel structure.

   a) Your bravery can be compared to that of soldiers and sailors, and also can be compared to fliers' courage.

   b) These people showed courage; they showed bravery; and self-sacrifice was also shown by each of them.

   c) It was too cold in February, too rainy in April, and the weather in May was awfully warm.

   d) Preparation for difficult tests or lengthy essays, experiments in the science lab, and important exams always began the night before.

   e) People should recognize the positive traits of procrastinators: We don't panic when the rent is due; we don't fret when the pressure is on; and a vicious rumour being passed around doesn't worry us.

3. Working in pairs, write one short paragraph containing an example of parallelism, which could be added to each of the models.

4. Look for places in your own speech where you might use parallel structures and repetition to emphasize the connections among related ideas.

Mechanics & Design

MECHANICS & DESIGN

Learning Goal

- identify ways to include visual aids in a speech

We know that some people learn better if they see the information (visual learners), while others absorb information better if they hear it (auditory learners). By including visual aids in your speeches and presentations, you make it easier for more people to grasp your message. Visual aids also help you

- focus your audience's attention
- clarify your ideas, including difficult concepts
- make speeches and presentations more persuasive

1. Working in groups of four, discuss other reasons for using visual aids to accompany a speech.

IDEA FILE

You can use many types of aids to enhance your presentation, including your own body. Tone of voice, facial expressions, body movements, and appearance all communicate nonverbally.

Listed below are some other types of visual aids:

- models
- lists
- tables
- photographs
- charts/graphs
- objects
- drawings/diagrams
- maps

2. Which of the visual aids listed above could have been used effectively with the first model, the speech on bravery? Which might have worked with the speech on procrastination? Explain your choices.

Once you have chosen a visual aid, you need to decide how you will present it. Some possibilities include

- overhead transparencies
- videotapes
- slides
- computerized graphics
- poster boards, chalkboards, or flipcharts
- handouts
- objects (to be passed around the room)

TECHNO-TIP

Some computer applications allow you to present slides, photographs, artwork, and other graphics by hooking your computer up to a projector. If your school has access to this kind of program, consider using it to enhance your speech.

3. Identify some of the things you would need to consider when deciding which of the methods listed on page 210 to use.

4. Find two examples of visual aids in a magazine, in a textbook, or on a web site. Analyze their effectiveness in terms of visibility, colour, simplicity, and clarity.

5. Use the information you learned in this section to create a visual aid to support your speech.

MEDIA LINK

Like the persuasive speech, commercials often use emotional appeals to convince the viewer. One method of creating a strong emotional appeal is to use a marketing approach that determines the values, attitudes, and lifestyle (VALs) of the consumer. This study of the things people believe in, the way they live their lives, and their buying patterns is called "psychographics." People are categorized based on the type of products they buy and on their attitudes to work, family, money, the environment, and other social issues.

Watch a currently popular teen television show and list the products you are being persuaded to buy during the show. Choose one commercial that really caught your attention. How much factual information is provided about the product? How does the commercial "hook" you? What needs or emotions does it appeal to? What lifestyle is sold to you along with the product?

Usage & Style

Learning Goal

- use effective words and sentence structures

Choose words and sentence structures that suit your message, your audience, your topic, and the occasion at which you are speaking. Here are some suggestions for choosing effective words and sentence structures to include in your speech:

- **Use short, simple sentences.**

  When the test came, you did not fail. Most of you risked your own lives to save the lives of others. And three of those whom we honour today died in the attempt to help.

  I know you must be wondering: Was I happy during this time? Let me tell you, I was not. I was constantly tired and miserable.

- **Use words that create mental images.** Mental images can be created through the use of figurative language, comparisons, examples, and stories or anecdotes.

  But those few words will never describe the full reality, when each of you stood alone at the border of fear, confusion, and danger. You entered situations the rest of us might encounter in our nightmares.

  I have stepped to the edge of the pit that so many of us have tripped into headlong.

- **Use words that influence feelings and attitudes.**

  I wish every Canadian could be in this room.

  I have suffered the same trials and social misunderstandings that so many members of this Society have experienced.

- **Use words that promote action.** This is especially important if you are trying to persuade your audience to do something.

  However, if you elect me President, my first act will be to become a full-fledged member.

  I feel my tardiness, which could be viewed as a fault by some, simply proves my worth as a procrastinator and makes me all the more deserving of the title of President.

- **Repeat key words and ideas.** Notice how the word *courage* is repeated in the first speech and *procrastinator* or *procrastination* in the second.

1. Find one more illustration of each of these points in the models.

2. Rewrite each of the following sentences, following the guidelines in parentheses to help improve their effectiveness.

   a) You should vote for me because I was a procrastinator during my early years, when I attended high school, when I attended university, and even today, I continue to be a true procrastinator. (Use short, simple words, phrases, and sentences.)

   b) You showed great courage. (Use words that create mental images.)

   c) I will work hard for the Society and make you glad you elected me President. (Use words that influence feelings and attitudes.)

   d) I know that you will do the right thing and make me your President. (Use words that promote action.)

3. Check your own speech to make sure that you have used effective words.

WRITING TIP

A good technique for engaging your audience in a speech is to use rhetorical questions—that is, questions that do not really require an answer. For example, Jennifer Williams might have used the following rhetorical question in her bid to become President:

> Why should I be ashamed of my early birth? Doesn't it simply show how far I have come?

> Can you imagine how I felt after denying my true nature for three whole weeks?

Word Study & Spelling

When you are choosing words, it is important to consider both their denotative and their connotative meanings.

The **denotative** meaning of a word is the objective meaning—the meaning you would find in the dictionary.

Learning Goal

- select words and phrases with appropriate connotations

> The **connotative** meaning is the emotional meaning of the word, the feelings you experience and the associations you make when you see the word in print or hear it spoken.

Here are two examples from the models to illustrate the importance of word connotations.

> Most of you were leading *ordinary quiet* lives ...

Roméo LeBlanc might have chosen to describe his listeners' lives as "dull and boring" or "unexceptional." Instead, he preferred to use words with a more neutral or positive connotation so as not to insult or belittle his audience.

> Notice I say pressure, not *panic*, as I have heard some nonprocrastinators call our *last-minute rushes*.

A *last-minute rush* has a more positive connotation than a *panic*; it implies that the person rushing is in control of the situation, whereas someone in a panic certainly is not.

1. The sentences below might have appeared in a draft of one of the model speeches. Rewrite the sentences, replacing the italicized words and phrases with others that have more appropriate connotations.

   a) You were very *foolhardy* in your attempts to save others.
   b) Your *stubbornness* was amazing; you did not give up when obstacles got in your way.
   c) We, the nation, can never hope to *even the score.*
   d) I *beg* you to vote for me.
   e) I have access to *money* and will listen to all your *demands.*
   f) My opponent is *stupid* if he thinks he can beat me.

2. When you choose words, choose those that connote just the right intensity for your purpose, the audience, and the occasion. In groups, discuss the words in italics in the following sentences. Do you think these words are appropriate to the context, purpose, and audience? Which of the words listed in parentheses might also have worked? Which would not have been appropriate? Why?

   a) I am here tonight to make a bid for the *esteemed* position of President of our Society. (important, respected, distinguished)
   b) I regularly got high marks and praise for my *superb* effort. (great, wonderful, excellent, outstanding)

3. Check your persuasive speech to make sure that the words you have used evoke emotion and contain the right degree of intensity.

WORD ORIGINS

The word **procrastination** comes from the Latin word *procrastinare* (*pro* meaning "forward" + *crastinus* meaning "of tomorrow").

Each of the words below contains the prefix *pro*. Using your own knowledge and a dictionary, explain what each of these words has to do with "moving something forward."

proceed	procedure	process
produce	profit	prognosis

Looking Back

Before giving your speech in front of an audience (or handing it in), have a classmate listen to it and then read it, paying particular attention to the following:

☑ Does the speech include parallel structures to emphasize connections among ideas?

☑ Does the speaker use body language and/or visual aids effectively?

☑ Does the speaker use techniques to help the listener follow the argument and anticipate what will come (e.g., short sentences, figurative language, words that evoke feelings)?

☑ Does the speech include words that create mental images and that influence feelings and attitudes?

☑ Does the speaker use words with appropriate connotations?

☑ Are all words spelled correctly?

Unit ⑪ Comparative Essay

What is a comparative essay?

An essay is a formal or informal piece of writing of several paragraphs that expresses points of view, insights, or opinions on a topic. A comparative essay shows the relationship (similarities and/or differences) between or among two or more people, places, actions, ideas, or things.

Learning Goals

- write a comparative essay
- use subject–verb agreement correctly and make pronouns agree with their antecedents
- write quotations correctly
- identify examples and explain the use of formal English, informal English, dialect, colloquialisms, slang, idioms, and clichés
- understand and use academic and sophisticated words

Reach for the Sky

BY BILL ANDERSON

THE DESIRE TO CHALLENGE THE LIMITS imposed by nature, and to contemplate possibilities considered beyond our capabilities is a timeless theme. This theme inspired the Greek myth of Daedalus and Icarus, as well as at least one of the West African folk tales about Ananse the Spider. Both Horace Gregory's translation of Ovid's version of the Daedalus story (<u>The Metamorphoses</u>, Book 8, pp. 219–222) and Peggy Appiah's account of Ananse's striving to fly in the story "Why Kwaku Ananse Stays on the Ceiling" from the collection <u>Ananse the Spider: Tales From an Ashanti Village</u> deal with this theme, but from the perspectives of very different characters: Icarus and Ananse—man and spider. Both characters test the limits of what is natural, and although their destinies are very different, the lesson to the reader is the same: overreaching can lead to failure and loss.

"UP THEY ROSE, THE BOY AFTER HIS FATHER"

In both tales, the ruler of the land presents a challenge to which the main character responds. Daedalus, a father, "well known for artful craft and wit" (219) agrees to construct a labyrinth at the request of King Minos. When the labyrinth fails to serve its purpose, King Minos imprisons Daedalus and his son, Icarus, on the island of Crete.

Ananse, too, takes up his ruler's challenge as he responds to the lion's need to determine, once and for all, which of his subjects is the cleverest. Ananse's claim to be the wisest and cleverest of the king's subjects is met with doubt and reservation, especially by the birds. Annoyed at their taunts, Ananse boasts, "'Oh yes I can … these foolish creatures think I cannot fly, but they are wrong'" (142).

Both Daedalus and Ananse consider flight as a solution to their predicaments, but for different reasons. Daedalus, aware that "Minos owns this island [and] rules the waves" (220), contemplates making his escape by means of the open skies. He, therefore, considers flight as a way of escaping his imprisonment. Ananse, on the other hand, sees flight as a way to fulfil his boasts and substantiate his claim to be preeminent among the animals.

Both characters are clever enough to look to the creatures of the air for ideas about how to overcome their earth-bound status:

> So Daedalus turned his mind to subtle craft,
> An unknown art that seemed to outwit nature:
> He placed a row of feathers in neat order,
> Each longer than the one that came before it
> Until the feathers traced an inclined plane (220).

Ananse sets traps, and catches and kills many birds. He then plucks their feathers and uses latex to stick them all over his body.

Although Daedalus and Ananse both have sons who play prominent parts in the stories, the role assigned to each is considerably different. Daedalus's son, Icarus, is presented as an enthusiastic protégé of his father. "He taught his son the trick" (221) and instructed him to fly midway between the waves and the sun. "He gave [his son] instructions how to fly / and made a pair of wings to fit the boy" (221). Ananse's son, Ntikuma, has no such opportunity. He acts as assistant and messenger, and helps his mother stick the feathers all over his father. Moreover, when he goes to tell the King that Ananse is ready to demonstrate his ability to fly, he is held hostage in case his father should be tempted to run away.

The stories are similar in that they both mention the reaction of those who witness the spectacle of normally flightless beings in flight. Ovid's version has a stray fisherman, a bland shepherd, and a dazed farmer all equally amazed to see the pair of mortals floating through the sky. They assumed them to be gods. Appiah's tale talks of animals and birds startled to see "the most extraordinary looking creature, flying round and round in the sky" (144).

There is evidence of excessive pride occurring in both stories, as well. Icarus begins "to feel the joy / Of beating wings in air and steered his course / Beyond his father's lead" (221–222). Ovid mentions that Icarus was tempted by the wide sky as he steered toward heaven. Similarly, the eagle, the king of birds, calls on Ananse "to follow him and show that he really could fly" (144). As "Higher and higher climbed the eagle, Ananse [was] always following close behind" (144). Both Icarus and Ananse are lured toward the heat of the sun and, as a result of their character weakness, fall victim to the effects of the burning orb.

Ananse tumbles down to earth but miraculously survives the plunge by landing on the soft palm branches of the roof of a house. Icarus is not so fortunate. Daedalus spots "the boy's torn wings washed on the climbing waves" (222), recovers Icarus's body from the sea, and places it in a tomb. Thus, Daedalus loses his only son and is left to damn "his wretched cleverness" (222) as he accepts responsibility for this tragedy. Ananse, for his part, loses only his dignity. He refuses to come down from the roof and ceiling, so ashamed is he of his act of vanity.

Perhaps it is an inevitable human characteristic, to attempt to rise above our natural limitations. The myth of Icarus illustrates this theme with its tragic consequences: Icarus fails to escape imprisonment and loses his life. The tale of Ananse includes comic overtones relating to his identity as a spider and his boastfulness, but ends with his failure to fly and prove his superiority, and his loss of personal dignity.

BIBLIOGRAPHY

Appiah, Peggy. <u>Ananse the Spider: Tales From an Ashanti Village</u>. New York: Pantheon, 1966.

Ovid. <u>Metamorphoses</u>. Trans. by Horace Gregory. New York: Penguin, 1960. ∎

Investigating the Model

1. The purpose of a comparative essay is to examine similarities and/or differences that characterize two or more people, places, actions, or things. However, even when the focus is on differences, the subjects of the comparison must have something in common. What do the books mentioned in the essay have in common? Does the essay focus on their similarities, their differences, or both? Give examples.

2. A comparative essay usually contains a thesis statement near the beginning in which the author identifies a point of view (angle) and establishes what will be compared. Sometimes the thesis statement is implied, but not stated. Find the thesis statement in the model.

3. Points for comparison may be based on direct observation, analysis, or research. On what basis does the author of the model make his comparison?

4. Comparisons are usually organized in one of two ways:

   • The **block method,** in which all of the characteristics of one subject are explained before moving on to an explanation of the characteristics of the second subject.
   • The **point-by-point method,** in which one characteristic of the first subject is explained and then compared with the same characteristic of the second subject.

   Which of these two methods does Bill Anderson use? Why do you think he chose this method over the other?

5. The conclusion of a comparative essay reiterates the thesis provided at the beginning of the essay. Comment on the model's effectiveness in reiterating the thesis in the conclusion.

Checkpoint: Comparative Essay

 As a class, create a checklist of common features of a comparative essay, based on the model and your own experience. Use the checklist to help you write your own comparative essay.

Writer's Workshop

1. For this assignment, you will compare two or more different characters, settings, or themes in a novel or novels that you have either studied in class or read independently this year. Your audience will be your teacher.

2. In order to determine whether you should compare the similarities or differences (or both) of your subjects, set up two pages in your notebook using the sample charts on the following page. One example, comparing two hypothetical characters, has been included in each chart.

Chart A	
Similarities	**Subjects A and B**
Objective of characters	To escape from their captives

Chart B		
Differences	**Subject A**	**Subject B**
What happens to them	Escapes successfully	Is killed during escape

3. After you have completed your charts, look over the lists of items you have developed. The quantity and quality of the items should help you decide whether you will write about similarities, differences, or both. Once you have decided, select those items from the charts that you will use in your comparison, and number the items in the order in which you will write about them.

4. Write a thesis statement identifying your point of view and establishing what will be compared (similarities, differences, or both). For example, "Although both x and y share the characteristic _____, they differ with respect to _____, _____, and _____."

> *Learning Goal*
>
> • **write a comparative essay**

5. Decide whether you will use the block or point-by-point method of organization.

6. Write a draft of your essay. As you write, make sure that you provide enough details from the stories to support each point you make. Use at least two direct quotations from the short story or novel as backup.

7. Write an introduction (one or two paragraphs including your thesis) and a conclusion (usually one paragraph) that restates or summarizes your topic.

✓ 8. Refer back to the list you created at Checkpoint, and revise and edit your comparative essay until you are satisfied with its focus, content, and organization.

ORAL LANGUAGE EXTENSION

A **debate** is a controlled argument in which two groups take sides (pro and con) on a proposition. A **proposition** is a positive statement that is debatable, much like a thesis.

For this activity, your class will be divided into groups of four. Each group will meet and choose a proposition for debate. Then you will choose two members of your group to support the proposition (the "yes" team) and two members to argue against it (the "no" team). Each team then works on its own.

- Working with your partner, draw a line down the centre of a piece of paper. On the left-hand side of the page, list arguments you could use to support your position. Under each argument, record any supporting facts, examples, or illustrations. Choose your four best arguments and prepare to present them. On the right-hand side of the paper, record any possible arguments your opposition might use against you. Under each argument, list ideas for refuting (arguing against) it. Be prepared to present your arguments.

- Decide with your partner who will speak first and who will speak second. Check with your teacher to find out how much time you have for each part of the debate. Practise your arguments, bearing in mind the following roles:

  — The first speaker for the "yes" team will state the proposition and then outline the team's two strongest arguments in support of the proposition, including evidence to support them.

  — The first speaker for the "no" team will present the team's two strongest arguments against the proposition and refute the arguments of the first "yes" speaker.

  — The second speaker for the "yes" team will then give two more arguments to support the proposition and refute the arguments of the first "no" speaker.

  — The second speaker for the "no" team will provide two further arguments against the proposition, will refute the arguments of the second "yes" speaker, and will summarize the position of the "no" side.   *(continues)*

(continued)

— The first speaker for the "yes" team then has the opportunity to summarize the position of the "yes" team.

Your teacher will provide you with information about the audience and the judges for your debate, and will also assign a chairperson to announce the topic, introduce the speakers, explain the time limits, and announce the judges' decision.

Grammar

Agreement refers to the relationship between two elements in a sentence. A verb must agree with its subject, and a pronoun must agree with its antecedent (the word it replaces).

If the subject is singular, the verb must be singular; if the subject is plural, the verb must be, too. Similarly, a pronoun must agree with the number, case, and sometimes gender of the word it replaces.

Problems with agreement sometimes arise when the subject or object of a sentence is compound (two nouns or pronouns joined by a conjunction such as *and*). Here are some rules to help you choose the right verb or pronoun in sentences with compounds.

Learning Goal

- **use subject–verb agreement correctly and make pronouns agree with their antecedents**

- When two nouns joined by *and* form a compound subject, the verb is usually plural.

Both <u>Daedalus</u> and <u>Ananse</u> **consider** flight as a solution.

However, note that when a compound subject is joined by *or*, or by an expression such as *either ... or, neither ... nor,* or *not only ... but also,* the verb agrees with the noun nearest to it.

Not only Ovid, but also many modern <u>writers</u> **have given** their interpretations of the myth.

- Use the subjective case (*I, you, he, she, it, we, they*) for pronouns that are part of a subject or subject complement. Use the objective case (*me, you, him, her, it, us, them*) for pronouns that function as part of a direct or indirect object. Be particularly careful in sentences with a subject complement. Remember to use the subjective case after the verb *to be*.

Subject: *Icarus* and <u>he</u> long to escape from the island.

Subject complement: It is <u>he</u> who brings about his own downfall.

Object: King Minos is holding <u>him</u> and *Icarus* captive.

1. Rewrite the following sentences, correcting any agreement errors.
   a) Daedalus and him plans to escape by flying.
   b) It is us, the readers, who must draw the moral from the myth.
   c) Neither Icarus nor Daedalus escape without harm.
   d) Some versions of the myth considers Daedalus to be at fault; however, Ovid paints both Icarus and he as tragic heroes.

In addition to compounds, a few other factors may cause agreement problems. Watch out for sentences that contain

- indefinite pronouns
- collective nouns
- phrases that separate the subject and verb or pronoun and antecedent

The following sections will look at each of these in turn.

- Indefinite pronouns are usually considered singular when they act as subjects or antecedents and, therefore, require a singular verb or pronoun. The exceptions are the pronouns *both, few, many, others,* and *several,* which are plural, and *all, any, more, most, none,* and *some,* which can be singular or plural depending on the sentence.

singular subject = **singular verb**

Each **treats** the myth in <u>his or her</u> own way.

Singular antecedent   =   <u>singular pronoun</u>

plural subject = **plural verb**

Of the writers discussed, *most* **have given** the myth <u>their</u> own interpretations.

plural antecedent   =   <u>plural pronoun</u>

In informal writing or speech, we often use *they* or *their* to avoid the awkwardness of *she or he* and *her or his*. However, in formal writing, this usage is not acceptable with a singular antecedent.

Informal: *Each* of these authors has <u>their</u> own interpretation of the Icarus myth.

Formal: *Each* of these authors has <u>her or his</u> own interpretation of the Icarus myth.

Or: *All* of these authors have <u>their</u> own interpretations of the Icarus myth.

- Collective nouns such as *crowd, group, class, team,* or *herd* are usually considered singular and, therefore, require a singular verb or pronoun.

  The *class* **is** presenting <u>its</u> interpretation of the play to the whole school.

  However, when the sentence emphasizes the actions of individuals, the collective noun is considered plural.

  The *class* **are** presenting <u>their</u> speeches to the teacher.

- Phrases that come between a subject and a verb, or a pronoun and its antecedent, are not the true subject or antecedent.

  <u>phrase</u>

  These *shelves* <u>in the library</u> **contain** books on science.

  <u>phrase</u>

  None <u>of the female characters in this novel</u> **has** control over <u>her</u> own life.

2. Rewrite the following sentences, correcting any agreement errors.

   a) The moral of both these stories are "avoid excess."
   b) Icarus's death in the icy waters are captured poignantly by the illustrator.
   c) Both of the characters reveal something about his past.
   d) Every character in this book has their own problems to deal with.
   e) Neither of the male heroes in these books use violence to attain their end.

f) One of the heroes sacrifices their own life for a friend.

g) Some of the stories in this collection is better than others.

h) Each of these writers treat the myth in their own way.

i) This series of books have given me hours of pleasure.

3. Check your comparative essay for any mistakes in pronoun–antecedent and subject–verb agreement.

Mechanics & Design

Learning Goal

• **write quotations correctly**

Direct quotations are an important part of essays and research reports. They are used to create interest, to illustrate or reinforce a point or argument, or to add credibility to the ideas presented. Here are some guidelines to help you incorporate quotations into your essay.

• Make sure the text you are quoting is relevant to the point you are trying to make, and use only as much of the quotation as you need to make your point.

• Quotations of fewer than four typed lines should be incorporated into the text of the essay and enclosed in double quotation marks.

  Daedalus, a father, "well known for artful craft and wit" (219) agrees to construct a labyrinth at the request of King Minos.

• Longer quotations should be indented, separated from the text, and single-spaced. You do not need to use quotation marks when the quotation is set apart in this way.

  Both characters are clever enough to look to the creatures of the air for ideas about how to overcome their earth-bound status:

    So Daedalus turned his mind to subtle craft,
    An unknown art that seemed to outwit nature:
    He placed a row of feathers in neat order,
    Each longer than the one that came before it
    Until the feathers traced an inclined plane (220).

- If you omit any part of a quotation, use an ellipsis (...) to indicate that something has been left out. If the part left out comes at the end of your quotation, some style guides suggest adding a period to the ellipsis (....).

  Annoyed at their taunts, Ananse boasts, "'Oh yes I can ... these foolish creatures think I cannot fly, but they are wrong'" (142).

- If you have to insert your own words into a quotation, enclose them in square brackets [ ].

  Daedalus's son, Icarus, is presented as an enthusiastic protégé of his father. "He taught his son the trick" (221) and instructed him to fly midway between the waves and the sun. "He gave [his son] instructions how to fly / and made a pair of wings to fit the boy" (221).

- The sources of all quotations should be documented. The in-text citations and bibliography in the model are based on the Modern Language Association (MLA) style. You will find more information on both MLA and APA (American Psychological Association) styles on pages 252 to 255 of this textbook. While these methods of documentation are widely used, check with your teacher to find out if she or he has another preference.

1. Use the short story in Unit 2 for the following activity:
   a) Working with a partner, select a passage of up to three typed lines. Write a sentence (using these lines as a quotation) that shows how a direct quotation should be incorporated within an essay. Remember to introduce the quotation with a relevant comment.
   b) Select a passage of four or more typed lines to demonstrate how a direct quotation is set apart from the text in an essay.
   c) Select a passage of two or three typed lines and create a third example to demonstrate how to use an ellipsis. Make sure the quotation makes sense with the words removed, and that it is directly related to your introductory comment.
   d) Select one more passage and use it to demonstrate the use of square brackets.

2. Check to make sure that any direct quotations you have used in your essay follow the rules outlined in this section.

Usage & Style

Academic essays, such as the one you have written in this unit, are usually written in formal English. **Formal English** is the language used for most legal documents, textbooks, essays, business letters, and research reports. Although there are degrees of formality, some of the features that characterize more formal writing are as follows:

- Formal writing may contain lengthy sentences, complex sentence structures, and specialized or sophisticated vocabulary.
- No contractions are used in formal writing.
- Abbreviations are used sparingly (*Mr.* or *Mrs.* is acceptable, but *e.g., i.e.,* and most others are not).
- Formal writing makes no concessions in its use of proper grammar, spelling, and punctuation.
- Formal writing prefers an impersonal tone to a more relaxed, conversational tone.

Learning Goal

- identify examples and explain the use of formal English, informal English, dialect, colloquialisms, slang, idioms, and clichés

Informal English, by contrast, is the type of language you might use in diaries, journals, friendly letters, or dialogue. Informal writing may contain examples of the following nonstandard forms of language:

- **Dialect** is a form of speech in which vocabulary and pronunciation are peculiar to a region or a class of people. While many people speak English across the world, the pronunciation and vocabulary, as well as the grammar used, may vary from country to country, or even from region to region. Dialect is often used by fiction writers and playwrights to give a sense of the speaker's character.

Dialect: Ain't them pants tight fer yuh?

Standard English: Are those pants tight on you?

- **Colloquialisms** are informal words and phases used in informal language. The expression *fixings* for the condiments you would put on a hamburger is an example of a colloquialism. Authors often use colloquial language in dialogue to make the language of the speaker sound more natural.

- **Slang** is language used by a particular group of people. It is a highly informal language that sometimes only the people using it can understand. Slang is usually spoken; words and expressions are added and dropped frequently, so writers seldom use it. Words like *groovy* and *far out* are examples of slang words that were used in the 1960s. Advertisers sometimes incorporate slang into their ads to attract a particular market.

- **Idioms** are phrases or expressions whose meaning cannot be deduced from the words themselves. Expressions like "the ball's in your court" and "don't bite off more than you can chew" are examples of idioms. While idioms are generally acceptable in informal writing, they are best avoided in more formal work.

- **Clichés** are words or phrases that are overused. Many clichés are metaphors or similes (e.g., "as sweet as sugar"; "as hard as a rock") that have been used so often that they no longer conjure up an image or comparison. Clichés are best avoided in both formal and informal writing.

WRITING TIP

Avoid the temptation of putting colloquial, slang, or other informal expressions or words in quotation marks to make them acceptable in formal writing. If you are unsure about the appropriateness of a word or expression, don't use it. If you do use it, omit the quotation marks unless it is a direct quotation.

Unacceptable: The author of this book has a "totally awesome" gift for storytelling.

Informal: The author of this book has a totally awesome gift for storytelling.

Formal: The author of this book has a remarkable gift for storytelling.

1. Write a sentence to illustrate each of the following forms of language:
   a) dialect
   b) colloquialism
   c) slang
   d) idiom
   e) cliché

2. The following paragraph comparing two characters is written in informal language. Rewrite the paragraph in formal language.

   Like, these two characters in this novel are like day and night. They goof around together but they are sorta different. They both dig science, but Thomas, who is the party animal, is more interested in tearin' things apart than puttin' things together. Todd is different. He is only interested in making new contraptions that are superweird. The kinda things you won't find in your average big box store.

3. Check your comparative essay to ensure that you have used formal language. If you have used informal language, replace the words or phrases with more appropriate words.

MEDIA LINK

We learn about characters in movies and in television shows by *what* they say and *how* they say it. Accents or dialect can indicate social class and ethnic background, and the use of slang, colloquialisms, and nonstandard English can indicate the characters' level of education, their social status, and the historical time frame in which they are living.

Choose one scene from two movies of the same genre (e.g., mystery, romance, adventure) set in different eras. List specific examples of language in each film that reflect the time period in which the film was set. Identify the characters by name, and show how *what* they say and *how* they say it (e.g., use of slang, accents, nonstandard English, and colloquialisms) reveal character. How realistic is their style of speech?

Word Study & Spelling

In addition to using formal English, academic essays often contain specialized language that relates to a particular discipline. The study of literature is no exception. The list below contains some academic terms that are often used in English essays:

- myth
- character
- pattern
- motif
- allusion
- metaphor

- theme
- protagonist
- antagonist
- climax
- conflict
- symbolism

- crisis
- fiction
- mood
- plot
- thesis

1. **a)** Write the meaning of any terms in the list you already know. Check your definitions with those of another student.
   b) Then look up in a dictionary the meaning of the words you don't know and add those definitions to your list. Use your list to create a Glossary of Literary Terms.
   c) With a partner, try to find other literary terms to add to the glossary.

2. Take turns testing each other on the spelling of each of the words in your glossary. Develop strategies to help you remember the correct spelling of those you misspell.

Academic language (such as the literary terminology given here) serves a specific purpose; the specialized words have no exact equivalent in everyday language. For the same reason, academic writers often use a more sophisticated vocabulary than you would find in writing aimed at a more general audience.

Learning Goal

- **understand and use academic and sophisticated words**

TECHNO-TIP

If your teacher requires you to write an essay of a certain length, use the word count function of your word-processing program to get an accurate count.

3. a) The author of the model uses some sophisticated words in his essay. Match the words on the left with the meanings on the right. It may help you to read through the model again to see the words in context.

contemplate	unpleasant, trying, or dangerous situations
imposed	person of whom another is protector or patron
labyrinth	support the truth of
predicaments	view mentally
substantiate	empty pride, conceit
preeminent	exerted influence on a person
protégé	distinguished beyond others in some quality
vanity	complicated irregular structure with many confusing passages; a maze

b) Find three words in the list above that could have been replaced by a simpler term. Discuss with a partner why you think the author chose the word he did. Do you agree with the author's decision? Why or why not?

WRITING TIP

While specialized vocabularies and sophisticated words have a place in formal writing, you should not use large words just for the sake of impressing someone. Rather, choose the word that best conveys your intended meaning. Formal writing does not have to be pompous or stuffy.

4. Check your essay to see that you have used academic literary terminology correctly and that the words you have used are the best words to relay your message.

WORD ORIGINS

The cliché "don't cry over spilled milk" comes from the fable of a milkmaid who wanted to make money selling milk. When she tripped and spilled the milk, she decided there was no use crying about it. We now use the expression to point out the futility of feeling bad about misfortunes we cannot change.

Following are the origins of three clichés and colloquial expressions. Try to identify each expression.

- This expression originated in World War II. It was used to describe a soldier willing to take on any new task. It contains the name of a very industrious animal.

- Long ago, attendance at a meeting was taken by cutting a notch or nick on a wooden stick as each person entered. This expression describes someone who got there just before the meeting started.

- This expression goes back to the days of knights. A knight's bodyguard would stand on the right-hand side of his master, so his own right hand would be free to use his sword to defend his master.

Looking Back

Before handing in your final edited draft, have a classmate check your essay, paying particular attention to the following:

- ☑ Is the essay free of agreement errors, especially in sentences with compound subjects or objects?

- ☑ Are direct quotations relevant and properly punctuated?

- ☑ Is the essay written in formal English, free of inappropriate words or expressions?

- ☑ Does the essay use academic language correctly and appropriately?

- ☑ Are all words spelled correctly?

Unit 12 — Résumé and Covering Letter

What are a résumé and covering letter?

A résumé is an organized summary of your skills, knowledge, and qualifications. The main purpose of a résumé is to persuade a potential employer to call you for an interview. A covering letter is a brief introduction to you and your résumé. The main purpose of the covering letter is to encourage the potential employer to read your résumé. The two résumés and covering letters in this unit show how two students set about selling their skills to potential employers.

Learning Goals

- write a résumé and covering letter
- use verbs effectively and correctly
- learn the uses of the semicolon
- use formal language to write a résumé and covering letter
- review useful spelling rules

Robin Ashoona
286 Pine Street
Banff, Alberta
T2J 4D7
Telephone: 555-4444
E-mail: rashoona@golden.ca

Objective
To become a summer playground instructor for the Town of Banff

Education

1998–2000	Central Collegiate High School
	Presently in Grade 10
	Average: 78%
	Relevant Courses: Physical Education and Health;
	First Aid and CPR Training

Work Experience

1999–Present   Caribou Lodge Day-Care Centre
 • supervise children and prepare educational experiences
   for them for ninety minutes, three days a week

1998–1999   Volunteer, Dover Nursing Home
 • visited with elderly tenants
 • read letters and newspapers to those who needed help

1997–1998   Babysitter, Ms. Theresa Schafer, Banff
 • cared for children, ages four, five, and eight, as requested
 • travelled with family for one-week holiday to help
   supervise children and to babysit

Interests and Accomplishments

1999–2000	Intramural basketball team
1999	Grade 9 Citizenship Award
1997	St. John Ambulance babysitting course
1994–1998	Member of a First Nations dance troupe

References
Available upon request

May 14, 2000

Mr. S. Holmes, Supervisor of Playgrounds
Banff Parks and Recreation Department
1864 Banff Avenue
Banff, Alberta
T0L 0C0

Dear Mr. Holmes:

I am writing to apply for the job of instructor at one of the summer playgrounds. I understand from phoning your department that you have two such positions available this summer. The enclosed résumé will show you the experience I have working with children.

My experiences as a babysitter and day-care worker have taught me that people who work with children must be caring, responsible, and dependable; that children need a safe environment where they can play, learn, and grow; and that parents need to know that their children are being well cared for and stimulated. I am the person who can provide these services for you.

I would like to arrange an interview at your convenience to learn more about your expectations for summer playground instructors. You may reach me at 555-4444 after 6:00 p.m. or by leaving a message on my family's answering machine. You may also send me a message using my e-mail address: rashoona@golden.ca. Thank you for considering my application.

Sincerely,

Robin Ashoona

Robin Ashoona

DALE BOOSLOWSKI

**14–2309 Brunswick Towers
Halifax, Nova Scotia B3K 2Z1
Telephone: 999-1111
E-mail: dboslo@istar.ca**

OBJECTIVE

Summer job with automotive repair or body shop

SKILLS

Auto Repair

- trained in proper methods for minor repairs at high school auto shop
- assisted friend of family in doing body work on car
- perform regular routine maintenance on the family car: oil changes, tune-ups, minor mechanical repairs, and tire rotations

General Work Skills

- good team worker
- able to complete tasks with minimal supervision
- punctual
- courteous
- hard-working

EXPERIENCE

Silverheights High School Auto Shop 1998–present
Duties: tune-ups; oil changes; diagnosis and repair of minor mechanical problems on cars, trucks, and vans; and minor body repairs

EDUCATION

Silverheights High School, Halifax, 1998–present
Currently completing Grade 10

INTERESTS

School hockey team (1999–2000)
Intramural basketball (1998–2000)
Reading car magazines

REFERENCES

Available upon request

14–2309 Brunswick Towers
Halifax, Nova Scotia B3K 2Z1

May 22, 2000

Mr. Wally Pietraszko
3 Bay Sales & Service
17 Queens Way Place
Halifax, Nova Scotia
B6R 2K3

Dear Mr. Pietraszko:

I am writing to request the opportunity to work for you at your car repair shop. I understand from speaking to your nephew, Jamie, that you are in need of a student to assist your trained staff with automobile repairs and body work.

As the enclosed résumé indicates, I have received some training in both mechanical work and body repair. Working for a business like yours will give me an opportunity to put my skills to work. I am a hard worker who takes pride in doing the best possible job at whatever task I take on; furthermore, my friendly nature would enable me to get along well with the rest of your staff.

I am serious about becoming an apprentice mechanic at the completion of high school. A position with your company would give me the opportunity to experience first hand the duties associated with this type of work.

I would very much appreciate the opportunity to meet with you at your convenience. I am eager to put my skills to work for your business. If necessary, I could begin working part time immediately. I can be reached at 999-1111 after 5:00 p.m. or through e-mail at dboslo@istar.ca.

Sincerely,

Dale Booslowski

Dale Booslowski

Investigating the Models

Résumé

1. The main purpose of a résumé is to persuade the employer to give you an interview. The details provided and the way they are presented are intended to highlight both the candidate's skills and her or his qualities as a good employee: dependability, responsibility, and organization. Use specific examples to show how the model résumés achieve this purpose.

2. Each résumé is designed for a particular job. The work experience, skills, and educational courses you would include in your résumé when applying for a job as a waiter would be quite different from those you would use when applying for a job repairing computers. Provide two examples of items listed in each model that are specific to the job applied for.

3. The two main methods for organizing résumés are **chronological** and **functional.** In a chronological résumé, the most common type, all work experience is listed in chronological order, with the most recent experience first. The functional résumé is not organized chronologically, but by skill. Identify the organization used in each of the models. Why do you think each student chose that type of organization?

4. The design of a résumé should make it easy to find relevant information. Employers often have many résumés to read, and little time, so the résumé should be as concise and as organized as possible. Identify the models' design features that would help a busy employer find relevant information quickly.

5. Most résumés include the following headings:
   - Education
   - Work Experience
   - References

   A résumé *may* also contain some of the following headings:
   - Objective (usually comes just below your name and address)
   - Skills (usually comes before Work Experience and Education)
   - Achievements (usually comes after Work Experience and Education)
   - Interests and Activities (usually comes after Work Experience and Education)

Look through the models and identify which of the optional headings each student has decided to include; then analyze what impression the additional information would make on a potential employer.

Covering Letter

6. The main purpose of a covering letter—also called a letter of application—is to persuade the employer to read your résumé. It is also a way of introducing yourself, highlighting why you want to work for the employer, and expanding on the information in your résumé. Comment on how effectively the model covering letters accomplish these purposes.

7. A covering letter should be no longer than one page, and each paragraph should have a particular purpose, usually expressed in a topic sentence (although sometimes the topic sentence is implied). Identify the topic sentence of each paragraph in Robin's and Dale's letters. If a paragraph has no stated topic sentence, write one that sums up the purpose of the paragraph.

8. The tone of a covering letter should be polite, businesslike, and direct. An employer will form an opinion of you based on the language you use. Provide an example from each model that demonstrates that the tone used is polite, businesslike, and direct.

9. A covering letter should be written using the correct form for a business letter. In your notebook, list the parts of a business letter, and provide an example of each part from the models.

10. A covering letter must contain the following information:
    • the reason you are writing
    • how you heard about the job or company
    • the specific position you are applying for (if possible)
    • a request for a follow-up interview
    • how and when the employer can contact you

    Based on the two models, identify where this information is usually found.

11. The knowledge, skills, and work experience that are highlighted in the covering letter should be chosen for their relevance to the specific job you are applying for. How relevant is the information that Robin and

Dale chose to highlight in their letters? Name one other fact from each résumé that they might have chosen to expand upon.

Checkpoint: Résumé and Covering Letter

 As a class, create a checklist of common features of a résumé and covering letter, based on the models and your own experience. You can use the checklist to help you write your own résumé and covering letter.

Writer's Workshop

1. Before you begin, take inventory of yourself. Make a chart with these headings: Experience, Skills, Knowledge, and Character Traits. In the first column, list experiences you have had—through jobs, school, clubs, or personal interests. As you list each experience, make point-form notes in the next three columns listing what specific skills, knowledge, or character traits you required for or developed from that experience.

Learning Goal

- **write a résumé and covering letter**

IDEA FILE

Even if you have no previous work experience, you may be able to demonstrate that you are qualified for a job. For example, running in a marathon shows you have the determination and willingness to work toward a goal. Being a member of a Scout troop every year since you were old enough to join shows that you are reliable and probably have well-developed social skills. Taking a babysitting course means you have some concrete knowledge that you can apply in a child-care job. Consider the following types of experiences when you make your inventory:

- part-time or full-time jobs
- babysitting
- clubs
- committees
- hobbies
- sports activities or teams
- school awards
- volunteer work
- extracurricular activities
- travel experiences

2. Decide on a job you would like to apply for. This may be a full-time job that you are seeking this summer or a part-time job you want during the next school year. It could be a job related to an occupation you hope to pursue in the future, or it could be a job you find in the "Help Wanted" section of a newspaper.

3. In your notebook, list the skills, knowledge, and character traits you think the job you are applying for requires. (If you are replying to an ad or job posting, take careful note of any qualifications listed by the employer.) Compare this list with your personal inventory. Can you demonstrate to an employer that you have at least some of the requirements based on your experience? If so, highlight the experiences listed in your inventory that demonstrate these qualifications.

4. Decide whether you will use the chronological or functional organization for your résumé. Use the chronological organization if you have considerable paid work experience. Use the functional arrangement if you have little or no job experience, or if you feel your most important qualifications for the job are related to unpaid experiences, such as clubs, hobbies, and volunteer work.

5. Make a chronological list (starting with the most recent information) of your work experience, including a brief description of your duties. Be sure to include the name and address of each employer you worked for.

6. List your educational achievements. Be sure to include the name and address of the schools you have attended (you don't need to list elementary schools). Also be sure to include what grade you are currently in, and mention any courses you have taken that relate to the job.

WRITING TIP

References are not usually listed on a résumé, but you should have a list of three names ready before you hand in your job application. Your reference list should include each person's name, position, place of work, address (including postal code), and phone number. Do not use relatives unless absolutely necessary. Also, make sure you have checked with the people whose names you are using to make sure they feel comfortable being used as a reference.

7. Decide what optional headings you will use and what information you will include under them. (Remember that your goal is to highlight your most relevant experience.) Then use the information you have gathered to write a draft of your résumé.

8. Write a covering letter for your résumé. Choose one or two of your most relevant qualifications from your inventory and expand on them in the body of the letter. Make sure the tone of the letter is polite, businesslike, and direct.

9. Format your letter and résumé. Use standard-size paper and a business-like font such as Ariel, Times Roman, or Helvetica. (Don't use more than two different fonts in your letter or résumé.) See the Appendix on page 256 for more detailed information on how to format your résumé and letter. Make sure your résumé and letter each fit on a single page, that they are attractive and inviting, and that information is easy to find.

TECHNO-TIP

Some word-processing programs include a choice of designs and layouts for covering letters and résumés called templates. All you have to do is select the appropriate template, key in the text of your résumé or covering letter, and the application will automatically format the document.

 10. Ask a classmate to read and comment on your résumé and letter. Use her or his suggestions and the list you created at Checkpoint to help you revise your draft. Proofread it very carefully for spelling and grammatical errors.

ORAL LANGUAGE EXTENSION

Robin telephoned the employer to see if any jobs were available as a playground instructor. Calls to inquire about jobs need to be planned carefully because the person you speak to may be the person doing the hiring.

Working with a partner, take turns role-playing the person making a call and the person receiving the call (the employer). As the person making the call, use the résumé you prepared in the Writer's Workshop as the basis for the call. As the employer, make up questions to ask the person calling.

MEDIA LINK

In a résumé, you present an image of yourself as a serious, responsible worker. You target your message to appeal to the employer's needs. Most magazines also target themselves at a particular reader. By doing so, they become more appealing to advertisers, who can choose just the right medium for their message.

Bring in at least two copies of a magazine that is popular with students your age. Count the total number of pages and the number of pages of advertisements. What percentage of the magazine is advertising? List the different categories of ads and count the number of ads in each category. Next, consult the contents page, and group the articles into categories according to theme or subject matter. How many articles are found in each group? Record your findings to report to the class.

Basing your conclusions on your analysis of the ads and articles, create a profile of the typical reader of this magazine (age, gender, social status, lifestyle, values, desires, needs, and dominant interests). Create a collage of images from the magazine that clearly illustrates this profile. Present your collage to the class together with your earlier findings.

Grammar

Verbs are important in any piece of writing, but they are especially significant in résumés. For the sake of efficiency and to avoid beginning every point with "I," résumé writers often list duties, responsibilities, and achievements in point form, beginning each point with a verb.

- [I] **assisted** friend of family in doing body work on car

Learning Goal

- **use verbs effectively and correctly**

Notice in the model résumés that some verbs are in the present tense (e.g., *supervise, perform*) and some verbs are in the past tense (e.g., *travelled, assisted*). Use the present tense to describe work that you have done and are still doing; use the past tense for work you did in the past.

1. Change the following verbs to the past tense if they are currently in the present tense and to the present tense if they are currently in the past tense. Use the verb in each answer to write a point-form description that might appear in a résumé.

   Example: load—loaded   • loaded trucks each morning

   a) organize   **b)** inspect   **c)** distributed
   d) maintain   **e)** designed   **f)** coordinated

When you use the past tense, be sure to use the correct form of the verb. Remember that some verbs have irregular past tenses and past participles.

> A verb is **irregular** if it does not form the past tense and/or the past participle in the usual way.

Regular verbs form the past tense and past participle by adding -*d* or -*ed* to the root (e.g., *supervised, travelled*). Most verbs are regular. Irregular verbs, however, follow a variety of patterns.

Present Tense	Past Tense	Past Participle
write	wrote	written
send	sent	sent
be	was	been

2. In your notebook, make a chart with the following headings: Present Tense, Past Tense, and Past Participle. Enter each of the following present-tense verbs in the first column, and complete the remaining columns.

   a) begin   **b)** blow   **c)** break   **d)** choose
   e) drink   **f)** fight   **g)** fly   **h)** give
   i) know   **j)** set   **k)** show   **l)** sing
   m) steal   **n)** throw

3. Correct the past-tense verb form in each of the following résumé descriptions. If the verb is already correct, write C.

   a) teached social skills to a six-year-old child with special needs
   b) driven a delivery van for a pizza restaurant
   c) swum in a 50-m race as a school representative
   d) writ letters for senior citizens with impaired vision
   e) brought students' concerns to the school administrators when necessary

f) done odd jobs for neighbours

g) begun with local Brownie troop at age five; have been a member of Guides and Brownies for the past 11 years

h) lay tile for a residential tiling company

i) set up a computer program for designing the school newsletter

Mechanics & Design

Learning Goal

- **learn the uses of the semicolon**

The semicolon, like a comma and a period, signifies a break in a sentence. It is stronger than a comma, but weaker than a period, question mark, or exclamation mark. As you will see in the first use below, you sometimes have the option of using a comma, a semicolon, or a period to achieve the same purpose.

There are three main uses for the semicolon:

- **Join independent clauses *without* a coordinating conjunction** (e.g., *and, or, nor, for, but, so, yet*). Examine the three sentences below. In the first sentence, the two independent clauses are joined by the coordinating conjunction *but;* in the second sentence, the clauses are joined by a semicolon; and in the third sentence, the clauses are separated into two sentences with a period.

   Robin has submitted a résumé, but Dale has not yet done so.

   Robin has submitted a résumé; Dale has not yet done so.

   Robin has submitted a résumé. Dale has not yet done so.

- **Join two main clauses when the second clause begins with a conjunctive adverb** (e.g., *however, therefore, furthermore*).

   I am a hard worker who takes pride in doing the best possible job at whatever task I take on; furthermore, my friendly nature would enable me to get along well with the rest of your staff.

- **Separate items in a series** if one or more of these items contain commas.

   My experiences as a babysitter and day-care worker have taught me that people who work with children must be caring, responsible, and dependable; that children need a safe environment where they can play, learn, and grow; and that parents need to know that their children are being well cared for and stimulated.

1. Rewrite the following sentences, inserting semicolons where necessary.

   a) I know I can be an asset to your business, I would like the opportunity to prove it to you.
   b) I know I can be an asset to your business, therefore I would like the opportunity to prove it to you.
   c) I am available to work after school from 4:00 to 6:00 p.m. on weekdays from 8:00 a.m. to 6:00 p.m. on Saturdays, Sundays, and holidays and any combination of day, evening, or night shifts during the summer vacation.

2. Write three sentences that might have appeared in your covering letter to demonstrate the three main uses of the semicolon.

WRITING TIP

Using semicolons in place of periods to join related sentences can add variety to your writing. In addition, the semicolon makes the reader look ahead to the next sentence; it is a good way to emphasize logical connections, for example, between your skills and the employer's needs!

> My references will vouch that I am punctual, reliable, and hardworking; please give me the chance to put these qualities to work for you.

Usage & Style

Strong verbs are important in all writing. In a résumé, however, the verbs you choose to describe your duties and experience can make the difference between a successful or unsuccessful job application. By using strong action verbs at the beginning of each point, you emphasize that you were productive in the work you did.

Learning Goal

- use formal language to write a résumé and covering letter

Read the two point-form job descriptions that follow. The first example is something Robin may have written as a first draft résumé; the second example is what was written in the final copy.

- *watch* children and *give* educational experiences to them for ninety minutes, three days a week
- *supervise* children and *prepare* educational experiences for them for ninety minutes, three days a week

The verbs *supervise* and *prepare* are not only more precise than *watch* and *give*, they also sound more impressive.

1. Find five more examples of strong action verbs in the model résumés.

2. Working with a partner, list 10 other strong action verbs that could be used in a résumé to describe work experiences. Share your list with your classmates and compile a class list of Effective Words for Résumés.

3. Check the verbs you have used in your own résumé. Use the class list you created in activity 2 to improve your choices, if appropriate.

Word Study & Spelling

Learning Goal

- review useful spelling rules

1. There are many rules for spelling, but only a small number of them are regular enough to be really useful. Test your knowledge by filling in the blanks below.

a) The letter *q* is always followed by the letter ___.
Example: queen

b) Every syllable has a _____ or *y*.
Examples: ex-per-i-ence, el-der-ly

c) Use___ before ___ except after ___ or when it sounds like the letter *a*.
Examples: receives, neighbour

d) When a ___ at the beginning of a word is followed by *e*, *i*, or *y*, it is _____ (like the "s" sound); otherwise, it is _____ (like the "k" sound).
Examples: centre, convenience

e) When words end in a consonant plus _____, change the _____ to _____ before adding a suffix other than *-ing*.
Examples: family, families

f) Drop the silent _____ from a root word before adding *-ing*.
Examples: becoming, associating

g) For one-syllable words with a _____ vowel, _____ the final _____ before adding an ending.
Examples: getting, letting

2. Check your own résumé and covering letter carefully to find examples of as many spelling rules as possible. Be sure that you have spelled each word correctly.

WORD ORIGINS

The word **résumé** comes from the French word *résumé*, the past participle of *résumer* meaning "to summarize." Many other English words have their origins in the French language, and many are spelled very much like the French words they come from.

Listed below are French words from which some English words are derived. The original meaning of the word is in parentheses. Try to guess the modern English word that evolved from each French word and use each in a sentence.

- **bouteillier** (a person who puts wine into bottles so it can be served)
- **caissier** (treasurer)
- **Gênes** (the city of Genoa, where this cloth was first made)
- **étincelle** (spark)

Looking Back

Before handing in your final edited draft, have a classmate check your résumé and covering letter, paying particular attention to the following:

☑ Do the résumé and covering letter contain strong, active verbs in the correct form?

☑ Are semicolons used correctly?

☑ Has the writer used formal language throughout?

☑ Are all words spelled correctly?

Reflect and Build on Your Learning

Reflecting on Persuasive Writing Forms

1. Review the Learning Goals on page 199. Which goals do you think you have achieved most successfully? Which goals do you think will require you to do more work? For each goal that will require more work, list one specific action you will take to accomplish the goal.

2. Write a note to your parent or guardian explaining the three most important things you learned about persuasive writing during the study of this section.

3. Complete each of the following statements about the work you have done in the past three units on persuasion.

   • The best piece of writing I wrote in this section was ... It was my best piece because ...
   • Two things I found challenging in this section were ...
   • In the future, I will use the knowledge and skills I learned in this section to ...
   • I have improved as a writer during the study of this section because ...

Looking Over Persuasive Writing Forms

1. Working with a small group, create a chart summarizing what you know about the features of persuasive speeches, comparative essays, and résumés and covering letters. Include the following headings in your chart: Purpose, Audience, Introduction, Body (content/organization), and Conclusion. The class checklists you developed for each form will help you with this task. Compare your chart with those of other groups. How would you modify your chart based on what they have included in theirs?

Using Persuasive Writing Forms

1. Persuasive writing requires the writer to convince someone to act or think in a certain way. Outline three methods you might use in a

speech, comparative essay, or résumé and covering letter that would help you convince someone to do something or to act or think in a particular way.

2. A writer must choose the most appropriate form of writing to communicate her or his message. When would you choose to use each of the following persuasive forms of writing? Provide one specific example to demonstrate when you might use each form either inside or outside of school.

- opinion piece or editorial
- advertisement
- review
- comparative essay
- letter
- speech
- résumé/covering letter

3. Working in groups of four, debate the following proposition: In the world outside of school, persuasive writing is much more important than narrative, descriptive, or expository writing. Use the format on pages 222 to 223 to develop and conduct your debate. At the end of your debates, have each member of the class vote for or against the proposition.

4. Working with a small group, discuss the following thesis: People who provide false information on résumés do damage to themselves and to their prospective employers. Following the discussion, write a brief speech on this topic. Once completed, present your speech to a group of classmates.

5. Speeches can be read, partially memorized and read, or memorized. Working with a partner, provide two examples of situations to demonstrate when each of these methods of presentation would be appropriate. Be prepared to defend your answers.

6. You have decided to apply for a part-time job for which you have very little background knowledge or experience. How would this lack of knowledge and experience influence the content and organization of your résumé, and the content of your covering letter?

7. Write a brief comparative essay comparing your life now with your life 10 years from now. Your purpose is to persuade your family that you have plans for the future and know where you are going. Before you begin, make a list of those things you would like to compare. For example, you might compare your living accommodations, places of work/school, friends, attitudes and beliefs, and leisure activities. Share your completed comparison with the members of your family.

MLA Style for Bibliographies

The Modern Language Association (MLA) developed a style of documentation that is used most frequently in the humanities for disciplines such as language arts. For example, this style was used to format the references for the research report in Unit 8 and the comparative essay in Unit 11.

Here are other examples of MLA citations for a bibliography, based on the *MLA Handbook for Writers of Research Papers,* Fifth Edition, 1999.

A book by a single author
Include the author's name, the title of the book, the place of publication, the publisher, and the date of publication. You will find this information on the copyright page.

Urquhart, Jane. The Underpainter. Toronto: McClelland & Stewart Inc., 1997.

A book by two or more authors
Aker, Don, and David Hodgkinson. Language & Writing 10. Toronto: Nelson Thomson Learning, 2000.

A work in an anthology
Hughes, Matt. "Bearing Up." Takes: Stories for Young Adults. Ed. R. P. McIntyre. Saskatoon: Thistledown Press, 1996. 21–32.

A work in several volumes
MLA recommends using arabic numerals, even if the original source uses roman numerals (e.g., *Book 6* instead of *Book VI).*

Brewer, Wilmon. Ovid's Metamorphoses in European Culture. Boston: Marshall Jones, 1941. Books 6, 7, 8, 9, 10.

A reference book
If the article is signed by an author, start the entry with the author's name. Otherwise, begin with the title of the article itself.

Faro, David. "Addicted to Antibiotics." The New Science. Ed. Margaret Teal. Vancouver: Pinegrove Press, 2000.

"A New Epidemic." World Health Matters. London: Tybolt Publishers, 1997.

A leaflet
Canada's Physical Activity Guide. Ottawa: Health Canada and Canadian
 Society for Exercise Physiology, 1999.

A newspaper or magazine article
Always show the date of the newspaper article along with the section and
page number.

Moran, John M. "Eye Spy." Saturday Record 14 Aug. 1999: Perspectives 1.

If the magazine article is continued on subsequent pages, write a plus sign
after the first page number, as shown.

Harris, Jane. "Sonnets and Ballads." Canadian Literary Magazine April–May
 1998: 16+.

A CD-ROM
If a CD-ROM is published in addition to a print version, show the print
version first, ending with the page numbers.

"Résumés and Covering Letters." Media Report. 20 Feb. 1995: 38–40.
 Résumés and Covering Letters. CD-ROM. Compact Publishing, 1998.

Sometimes a CD-ROM is produced on its own, without a print version.

Jackson, Penelope. Wings of Icarus. CD-ROM. Compact Publishing, 1997.

A web site
Include the date you retrieved the information and enclose the web address
in angle brackets: <   >.

Linenger, Jerry. "It's All Downhill From Here." Letters to My Son. (1997).
 12 Oct. 1999 <http://38.201.67.77/history/shuttle-mir/ops/crew/
 letters/linenger/letter60.html>

A speech, lecture, or address
LeBlanc, Roméo. Address. Ceremony for Decorations for Bravery. Rideau
 Hall, Ottawa, 23 June 1995.

A film or video
William Shakespeare's Romeo & Juliet. By Craig Pearce and Baz Luhrmann.
 Dir. Baz Luhrmann. Twentieth Century Fox, 1997.

APA Style for Bibliographies

The American Psychological Association (APA) developed a style of documentation that is used most frequently in the social sciences for disciplines such as psychology and sociology. Here are some examples of APA citations for a bibliography, based on the *APA Publication Manual*, Fourth Edition, 1994.

A book by a single author
Include the author's name, the date of publication, the title of the book, the place of publication, and the publisher. You will find this information on the copyright page.

Urquhart, J. (1997). <u>The underpainter</u>. Toronto: McClelland & Stewart Inc.

A book by two or more authors
Aker, D., & Hodgkinson, D. (2000). <u>Language & writing 10</u>. Toronto: Nelson Thomson Learning.

A work in an anthology
Hughes, M. (1996). Bearing up. In R. P. McIntyre (Ed.), <u>Takes: Stories for young adults</u> (pp. 21–32). Saskatoon, SK: Thistledown Press.

A work in several volumes
Brewer, W. (1941). <u>Ovid's metamorphoses in European culture</u> (Books VI, VII, VIII, IX, X). Boston: Marshall Jones.

A reference book
If the article is signed by an author, start the entry with the author's name. Otherwise, begin with the title of the article itself.

Faro, D. (2000). Addicted to antibiotics. In M. Teal (Ed.), <u>The New Science</u>. Vancouver: Pinegrove Press.

A new epidemic. (1997). In <u>World health matters</u>. London: Tybolt Publishers.

A leaflet
Canada's physical activity guide. (1999). Ottawa: Health Canada and
  Canadian Society for Exercise Physiology.

A newspaper or magazine article
Always show the date of the article, the page number, and the section,
if applicable.

Moran, J. M. (1999, August 14). Eye spy. Saturday Record, Perspectives p. 1.

Harris, J. (1998, April–May). Sonnets and ballads. Canadian Literary
  Magazine, pp. 16, 27–28.

A CD-ROM
If a CD-ROM is published in addition to a print version, show the print
version first, ending with the page numbers.

Résumés and covering letters. (1995, February 20). Media Report, pp. 38–40.
  Résumés and covering letters. (1998). [CD-ROM]. Compact Publishing.

Sometimes a CD-ROM is produced on its own, without a print version.

Jackson, P. Wings of Icarus. (1997). [CD-ROM]. Compact Publishing.

A web site
Always include the date you retrieved the information.

Linenger, J. (1997). It's all downhill from here. Letters to my son. Retrieved
  October 12, 1999 from the World Wide Web: http://38.201.67.77/
  history/shuttle-mir/ops/crew/letters/linenger/letter60.html

A speech, lecture, or address
LeBlanc, R. (1995, June 23). Address. Ceremony for decorations for bravery.
  Rideau Hall, Ottawa.

A film or video
Pearce, C., & Luhrmann, B. (Writers), & Luhrmann, B. (Director). (1997).
  William Shakespeare's Romeo & Juliet. [Film]. Twentieth Century Fox.

Guidelines for Business Letters

- Use one of the following formats for a business letter:

Block	**Modified Block**	**Semiblock**

Block:
```
————————
————————
————————

Dear _____:
————————————
————————————
————————————
————————————
————————————

Yours truly,
————————
```

Modified Block:
```
            ————————
            ————————
            ————————

Dear _____:
————————————
————————————
————————————

            Yours truly,
            ————————
```

Semiblock:
```
            ————————
            ————————
            ————————

Dear _____:
    ————————————
    ————————————
    ——————————
        ————————————
        ————————

Yours truly,
————————
```

- Use good quality, standard-sized paper.
- Provide enough white space to ensure that your information does not look crowded.
- Leave a comfortable margin on the sides, top, and bottom of the page.
- Be consistent in the size of type you use for any main headings and less important headings, and make sure that these headings are capitalized and aligned correctly.
- Make sure that you have included all parts of a business letter (your address and date, the receiver's address, salutation, body, complimentary closing, and your signature) and that the proper punctuation has been used for each.
- If you send your letter by surface mail (rather than e-mail), address the envelope as follows:

```
MR. KIAN MERRIKH
987 DEER CROSSING
VICTORIA BC  Z6T 8L3

                THE VICTORIA BANNER
                214 HAMPTON STREET
                VICTORIA BC  Z6T 4T5

                ATTENTION: LETTERS EDITOR
```

Handbook

Table of Contents

HANDBOOK

Handbook

Noun

A **noun** is a word that names a person, place, thing, quality, or idea.

Person	Place	Thing	Quality	Idea
teacher	classroom	train	honesty	poverty

A **proper noun** is the name of a specific person, place, or thing. All other nouns are **common nouns.**

Specific Person	Specific Place	Specific Thing
Wayne Gretzky	Toronto	Windows 2000

Abstract nouns refer to qualities or ideas while **concrete nouns** refer to entities that can be experienced using the senses.

Abstract Nouns	Concrete Nouns
courage	house
pride	forest
truth	thunder

Count nouns refer to people, places, and things that can be counted. **Noncount nouns** refer to entities that cannot be counted. **Collective nouns** name a group of people or things.

Count Nouns	Noncount Nouns	Collective Nouns
girls	soil	team
countries	wood	audience
cups	cheese	committee
butterflies	salt	flock
stones	knowledge	herd

A **singular noun** refers to one entity while a **plural noun** refers to two or more entities.

Singular Nouns	Plural Nouns
woman	women
city	cities
brick	bricks

A **compound noun** is formed by combining two or more words.

weightlifter	waterspout

The **gender** of a noun may be **masculine, feminine, indefinite,** or **neuter.**

Masculine	Feminine	Indefinite	Neuter
man	actress	child	book
uncle	niece	youth	car

Verb

A **verb** is a word that shows action (**action verb**) or a state of being (**linking verb**).

Carlos **pointed** at a child who <u>appeared</u> lost.

    action verb   <u>linking verb</u>

Sometimes a verb may be made up of more than one word: a **main verb** and one or more **helping** (or **auxiliary**) **verbs.**

The soccer team **had been** <u>competing</u> for the regional title.

           helping verb   <u>main verb</u>

Common Action Verbs	Common Linking Verbs	Common Helping Verbs
walk	be	have
swim	become	be
run	appear	do
jump	seem	can
dance	feel	shall
sing	remain	will

A **transitive verb** requires a noun phrase (called a direct object) to complete its meaning. An **intransitive verb** does not require a direct object.

As I **described** *the problem*, Father <u>grinned</u>.

  transitive verb *direct object*   <u>intransitive verb</u>

A verb may be either **singular** or **plural**, depending on the number of its subject.

Singular verb: The dog **barks** at the approaching mail carrier.
Plural verb: The dogs **bark** at the approaching mail carrier.

The **tense** of a verb expresses the time of its action. There are three **simple verb tenses: present, past,** and **future.**

Simple present: I **exercise** every day.
Simple past: I **exercised** with Leigh yesterday.
Simple future: I **will exercise** with Joaquin tomorrow.

More complex time relations are indicated by the **perfect tenses:**

Present perfect: I **have exercised** for several years.
Past perfect: I **had exercised** sporadically before joining a gym.
Future perfect: By the end of this month, I **will have exercised** more than any of my team members.

Progressive forms are used to indicate continuing actions:

Present progressive:	I **am exercising** now.
Past progressive:	I **was exercising** when Julia arrived.
Future progressive:	I **will be exercising** later this evening.
Present perfect progressive:	I **have been exercising** all morning.
Past perfect progressive:	I **had been exercising**, but I stopped to take a shower.
Future perfect progressive:	When the timer rings, I **will have been exercising** for two hours.

The -*ing* form of the verb is called the **present participle** while the **past participle** is the form of the verb usually ending in -*d, -ed, -n, -en,* or -*t.*

Helene was **studying** for the test that everyone else had <u>written</u> last week.

        present participle   **past participle**

For **regular verbs**, the past tense is formed by adding -*ed* or -*d* to the verb; the past-tense and past-participle forms are the same. This is not true of **irregular verbs**.

Regular Verbs			Irregular Verbs		
Present Tense	Past Tense	Past Participle	Present Tense	Past Tense	Past Participle
walk	walked	walked	ride	rode	ridden
plan	planned	planned	break	broke	broken
toss	tossed	tossed	draw	drew	drawn
wrap	wrapped	wrapped	eat	ate	eaten

The **voice** of a verb tells about the role of the subject in a sentence. The **active voice** emphasizes the *doer* of the action, while the **passive voice** emphasizes the *receiver* of the action.

Active voice:	Vandals **ruined** the graduation decorations.
Passive voice:	The graduation decorations **were ruined** by vandals.

Adjective

An **adjective** is a word that describes a noun or pronoun. Adjectives give information such as *which one? what kind? how much? how many?*

A, an, and *the* are adjectives called **articles**. *The* is a **definite article** because it indicates a particular person, place, or thing.

The goalie caught **the** soccer ball in mid-leap.

A and *an* are **indefinite articles** because they do not refer to particular people, places, or things.

A goalie caught **a** soccer ball in mid-leap.

Proper adjectives are formed from proper nouns and are capitalized.

The **Spanish** class was postponed.

Predicate adjectives follow linking verbs and give information about the subject of the sentence.

This spaghetti sauce tastes **delicious**.

Compound adjectives are formed by joining words used to describe a noun.

Rejeane bought an **eighteen-speed** bicycle.

Most adjectives and adverbs have three forms, or **degrees: positive, comparative,** and **superlative:**

Positive	Comparative	Superlative
slow	slower	slowest
big	bigger	biggest
good	better	best

Adverb

An **adverb** is a word that describes a verb, an adjective, or another adverb. When describing verbs, adverbs tell *how, when,* or *where.*

Describes a verb:	Gillian skated **effortlessly** across the ice.
Describes an adjective:	The judges were **quite** impressed by her performance.
Describes an adverb:	The audience clapped **very** loudly when her performance ended.

The **degree** of an adjective or adverb refers to the number of items being described. An adjective or adverb in the **positive degree** describes items but does not make a comparison.

All six competitors ran **fast**.

In the **comparative degree**, an adjective or adverb compares two items.

Erica ran **faster** than Justine.

In the **superlative degree**, an adjective or adverb compares three or more items.

Of the six competitors, Frances ran **fastest**.

Adjectives that are more than two syllables long and adverbs ending in *-ly* usually use *more* and *most* to form the comparative and superlative forms.

Positive:	The leaves fell **rapidly**.
Comparative:	The maple tree lost its leaves **more rapidly** than the oak tree.
Superlative:	The mountain ash lost its leaves most rapidly.

Pronoun

A **pronoun** is a word that takes the place of a noun. (Refer to the chart on page 50 for lists of examples.) The noun that the pronoun replaces is called the **antecedent** of the pronoun.

Personal pronouns refer to specific people or things.

Sandi asked Mike to take notes for **her**.

antecedent   personal pronoun

Indefinite pronouns refer to nonspecific people or things.

Somebody left Michelle a message.

Reflexive and **intensive pronouns** can only be used when they refer to another word in the sentence. **Reflexive pronouns** name a receiver of an action that is identical to the doer of the action.

After seeing his test score, Joey told **himself** he would study harder next time.

Intensive pronouns emphasize a noun or pronoun.

The mayor **herself** apologized for the garbage on the streets.

Relative pronouns introduce subordinate clauses that function as adjectives, referring back to the noun or pronoun that the clause describes.

The man **whose** wallet was stolen waited to see the detective.

Demonstrative pronouns identify or point to nouns. Besides taking the place of nouns, they may act as adjectives.

Demonstrative pronoun: **That** is my favourite video.
Adjective: **That** video is my favourite.

Interrogative pronouns are used in asking questions.

Which is the correct answer?

Personal pronouns change form, or **case**, depending on their use in a sentence. When a pronoun is used as a *subject*, choose the **subjective case**.

Subjective case: **She** waited until 4:00. (subject of *waited*)

When a pronoun is used as an *object*, choose the **objective case**.

Objective case: Terry gave **her** the textbook. (indirect object of *gave*)

Choose the **possessive case** when indicating *ownership*.

Possessive case: The decision was **hers** to make.

HANDBOOK

	Subjective	Objective	Possessive
First-person singular	I	me	my, mine
Second-person singular	you	you	your, yours
Third-person singular	she, he, it	her, him, it	her, hers, his, its
First-person plural	we	us	our, ours
Second-person plural	you	you	your, yours
Third-person plural	they	them	their, theirs

Preposition

A **preposition** is a word that shows the relationship between two words in a sentence. Usually, the word or phrase following a preposition (known as the **object of the preposition**) is a noun (phrase) or pronoun.

> The volume **of** the music was unacceptable.
>
> preposition   object of the preposition

However, a preposition can also be followed by a verb (to form the infinitive), by an adjective, or by an adverb.

> Tracy wanted **to** see the new James Bond film. (verb)
>
> Karen's travel experiences went **from** bad **to** worse. (adjective)
>
> Jorge recalled an experience **from** earlier in the year. (adverb)

Prepositional phrases almost always function as adjectives or adverbs. When a prepositional phrase functions as an adjective, it immediately follows the noun or pronoun it describes.

> The girl **on the bicycle** looked familiar. (describes the noun *girl*)

When a prepositional phrase functions as an adverb, it may or may not appear next to the verb it describes.

> The girl rode several miles **on the bicycle**. (describes the verb *rode*)

Conjunction

A **conjunction** is a word that joins two or more words, phrases, or main clauses. There are two kinds of conjunctions. **Coordinating conjunctions** join two or more words, phrases, or complete sentences.

> You might want to talk to Silas **or** Ray about the tournament. (joins words)
>
> Relaxing on the beach **and** reading a book are two of my favourite activities. (joins phrases)
>
> The engine sputtered and backfired, **but** the car still would not start. (joins main clauses)

The most common coordinating conjunctions are *and, but, nor,* and *or.*

Correlative conjunctions are pairs of conjunctions that join grammatically equal elements in a sentence.

Neither Fredda **nor** her parents enjoyed the performance.

Both the basketball team **and** the soccer team won district championships.

Subordinating conjunctions only join clauses, one of which functions as a noun, adjective, or adverb and cannot stand alone. Subordinating conjunctions can appear either at the beginning or in the middle of a sentence.

Before <u>the train left,</u> <u>we bought souvenirs at the gift shop.</u>

<u>The storm arrived</u> **before** <u>we were prepared for it.</u>

Some common subordinating conjunctions are *as, although, because, since, unless, until, whenever,* and *while.*

Interjection

An **interjection** is a word that indicates strong feeling or sudden emotion.

Hey! The game has already started!

Rubbish! There is no such thing as a ghost.

Ouch! That hurts!

Verbal

A **verbal** is a verb form that functions as a part of speech other than a verb. The three main types of verbals are **participles, gerunds,** and **infinitives**.

A **participle** is a verb form that can act as a verb only when it is accompanied by a helping verb (e.g., a form of *be* or *have*). A participle on its own can also function as an adjective. (Refer to page 260 of this handbook for more information about participles.)

Participle acting as a verb: The class *was* **attending** the science fair.

                                            helping verb   **participle**

Participle acting as an adjective: **Attending** the science fair, the class learned about new forms of computer software now available.

A **gerund** is an *-ing* verb form that functions as a noun.

Walking is one of the most effective cardiovascular exercises. (subject of the verb *is*)

Elise stopped **walking** and waited for Dennis to catch up. (direct object of the verb *stopped*)

The **infinitive** is the basic form of the verb used with *to.* Infinitives can function as adjectives, adverbs, or nouns.

To ensure our safety, Etienne suggested that we all wear reflective clothing. (adjective describing *Etienne*)

Grady called **to see** if Marianne wanted to join us. (adverb modifying *called*)

Everyone wanted **to hike** until nightfall. (direct object of *wanted*)

GRAMMAR Parts of a Sentence

Subject

The **subject** is the noun phrase that tells who or what the sentence is about. The **simple subject** is the main noun (or pronoun) by itself; the **complete subject** includes all the words that describe or modify that noun or pronoun.

The bright red **sunset** indicated fine weather for the following day.
complete subject **simple subject**

A sentence may have a **compound subject** that contains two or more simple subjects joined with a coordinating conjunction.

Hard work and **patience** are requirements for success.
compound subject

Predicate

The **predicate** is the verb phrase that either tells the action the subject is performing or explains the condition or effect of the subject. The **simple predicate** is the main verb by itself; the **complete predicate** includes any words or phrases that modify the verb.

Four large dogs **raced** across the golf course.
simple predicate complete predicate

A **compound predicate** includes two or more predicates joined with a coordinating conjunction.

The dogs **barked annoyingly at several golfers** and **dug holes in the fairways**.
compound predicate

Direct and Indirect Object

A **direct object** is a noun phrase that completes the meaning of a transitive verb. The direct object answers *whom* or *what* about the verb. A transitive verb may also take an **indirect object,** which answers *to whom, for whom, to what,* or *for what* about the verb.

Kelly gave *Eileen* **a book about calligraphy.**
indirect object **direct object**

Subject Complement

A **subject complement** is a noun or adjective used after a linking verb; it describes or renames the subject.

Subject	Linking Verb	Subject Complement
The horses	appeared	restless.
The leader of the herd	was	a palomino.

Phrase

A **phrase** is a group of words that lacks either a verb, a subject, or both, and functions as a single unit in a sentence. There are many different types of phrases, each identified by the function it performs.

A herd of gazelles grazed peacefully on the African plain. (noun phrase)

The conflict **has ended** without incident. (verb phrase)

Three large, mysterious shapes loomed over them. (adjective phrase modifying *shapes*)

Julian opened the package **very carefully.** (adverb phrase modifying *opened*)

Hundreds **of people** waited impatiently as the delay continued. (prepositional phrase)

Splashing about in the pool, the twins attracted considerable attention. (participial phrase)

Several seniors began **walking regularly in the mall**. (gerund phrase)

Gerry waited **to see his final score.** (infinitive phrase)

An **appositive phrase** is a noun phrase that renames a nearby noun.

Margaret Atwood, **the author of Alias Grace,** is one of Canada's finest writers.

Clause

A **clause** is a group of words that contains both a verb and its subject.

Phrase:	our vacation (lacks a verb)
Phrase:	ended abruptly (lacks a subject)
Clause:	our vacation ended abruptly
	subject verb

A **main** (or independent) **clause** states a complete thought and can stand alone as a sentence. A **subordinate** (or dependent) **clause** cannot stand alone as a sentence.

The audience applauded loudly **until the actress left the stage.**
           main clause   subordinate clause

Restrictive and Nonrestrictive Elements

A phrase or clause is **restrictive** if it is essential to the meaning of a sentence. A **nonrestrictive** phrase or clause is not essential to the meaning of a sentence.

Always separate nonrestrictive phrases or clauses from the rest of a sentence using commas, dashes, or parentheses. *Never* use punctuation to separate restrictive phrases or clauses from the rest of a sentence.

Restrictive phrase: Margaret Atwood's novel ***The Handmaid's Tale*** has been adapted as a film.

Nonrestrictive phrase: Julie's father, **David Proule,** is an English teacher.

Restrictive clause: Barbara wore the dress **that her husband gave her on their fifth anniversary**.

Nonrestrictive clause: Philip Thomas—**who won this year's essay contest**—is in Grade 10 at Twelve Cedars High School.

GRAMMAR — Sentence Types

Sentences can be classified according to their structure and their function.

Sentence Structure

There are four types of sentence structures: **simple, compound, complex,** and **compound-complex.**

A **simple sentence** contains only one main clause (one subject and one predicate).

Lightning pierced the darkness.

A **compound sentence** contains two or more main clauses.

Lightning pierced the darkness, and Alicia yelped in surprise.

    main clause   main clause

A **complex sentence** contains one main clause and one or more subordinate clauses.

As lightning pierced the darkness, **rain began pounding on the metal roof.**

    subordinate clause   main clause

A **compound-complex sentence** contains at least two main clauses and at least one subordinate clause.

Because the rain showed no sign of letting up, **Alicia began looking for pans to**

    subordinate clause   main clause

catch the water dripping through the roof, and she found a bucket and two plastic containers under the sink.

    main clause

Sentence Function

Sentences can be classified according to their purposes. Writers use **declarative sentences** to make statements, **imperative sentences** to issue requests or commands, **interrogative sentences** to ask questions, and **exclamatory sentences** to make exclamations.

Declarative sentence:	Seatbelts save lives.
Imperative sentence:	Wear seatbelts at all times.
Interrogative sentence:	Will you risk your life by not buckling up?
Exclamatory sentence:	Driving without a seatbelt on today's highways is madness!

GRAMMAR Common Word-Use Problems

Pronoun Case

Subject Complements

Personal pronouns used as subjects or subject complements must appear in the **subjective case** while those functioning as objects must appear in the **objective case**. (Refer to pages 262–63 of this handbook for more information about pronoun case.) Problems often arise when a personal pronoun follows the linking verb *to be*. In formal writing, a pronoun used as a subject complement must appear in the subjective case.

Wrong:	The person you are looking for is **her.** (objective case)
Corrected:	The person you are looking for is **she.** (subjective case)
Wrong:	"It is **me,**" said the voice at the door. (objective case)
Corrected:	"It is **I,**" said the voice at the door. (subjective case)

If you find this formal usage stilted, try rewriting the sentence:

She is the person you are looking for.
"It is **Alex,**" said the voice at the door.

Compound Structures

Problems often arise when personal pronouns are used in compound structures.

Wrong:	Suzanne and **him** attended the art auction. (subjective form needed because the pronoun is the subject of the verb *attended*)
Wrong:	Caitlin asked Avery and **I** to attend it with her. (objective form needed because the pronoun is the object of the verb *asked*)

One way to avoid these errors is to imagine only the pronoun in the compound structure.

Correct:	. . . **He** attended the art auction.
Correct:	Caitlin asked . . . **me** to attend it with her.

HANDBOOK

We Versus *Us*

Problems can arise when *we* or *us* precede a noun.

Wrong: **Us** students raised all the money needed for the class trip.

Wrong: Two local businesses donated money to **we** students.

When choosing between *we* or *us,* omit the noun and choose the pronoun that is appropriate.

Correct: **We** . . . raised all the money needed for the class trip.

Correct: Two local businesses donated money to **us** . . . .

Who Versus *Whom*

Problems often arise when writers must choose between *who* and *whom.*

Wrong: **Who** are you waiting for?

Wrong: **Whom** is the best candidate for the job?

Wrong: This is the boy **who** I met at the party.

Wrong: Gayle is the person **whom** sold me this jacket.

When choosing between *who* or *whom* at the beginning of a question, answer the question using *he/she* or *him/her.* If you use the subjective pronoun *he/she* in your answer, choose the subjective pronoun *who.* If you use the objective pronoun *him/her* in your answer, choose the objective pronoun *whom.*

Who/Whom are you waiting for? Answer: I am waiting for **him.** (Choose *whom.*)

Who/Whom is the best candidate for the job? Answer: **She** is the best candidate. (Choose *who.*)

When *who* or *whom* appears in the middle of a sentence, look at the verb following the pronoun to determine whether or not it requires a subject. If so, choose the subjective pronoun *who;* if not, choose the objective pronoun *whom.*

This is the boy **who/whom** I met at the party. (In the part of the sentence following the pronoun, the verb *met* already has a subject—*I*—so choose the objective pronoun **whom.**)

Gayle is the person **who/whom** sold me this jacket. (In the part of the sentence following the pronoun, the verb *sold* has no subject, so choose the subjective pronoun **who.**)

When *who* or *whom* is followed by an expression like *I think* or *they know,* ignore this expression when deciding which pronoun to use.

The person **who/whom** I think is best for the job is Noelle. (Ignore *I think* and you will see that the verb *is* has no subject, so choose the subjective pronoun **who.**)

Pronoun Gender

The personal pronouns *he, his, she, her, it,* and *its* must agree in gender with their antecedents. Indefinite pronouns like *anybody, anything, each, either, everybody, everyone, nobody, no one, somebody, something,* etc. are singular, so writers must choose singular personal pronouns with which to replace them.

Wrong: Everyone is looking forward to **their** vacation. (The possessive pronoun *their* is plural, but its antecedent—*everyone*—is singular.)

There are three ways to correct this problem:

1. Replace the plural pronoun with *he* or *she* (or *his* or *her*).

    Correction: Everyone is looking forward to **his or her** vacation. (Because this is wordy, writers often choose one of the following revisions.)

2. Make the antecedent plural.

    Correction: **All the students** are looking forward to **their** vacation.

3. Rewrite the sentence to avoid the agreement problem.

    Correction: Everyone is looking forward to **this** vacation.

Pronoun Reference

A pronoun should refer clearly to the antecedent it is replacing. When a pronoun refers to two possible antecedents, the pronoun's reference is **ambiguous**. It is usually best to rewrite the sentence to correct the problem.

Ambiguous: Jerry told Luke that **he** had left their locker door open. (It is not clear whether *he* refers to *Jerry* or *Luke.*)
Corrected: Jerry told Luke, "I left our locker door open."

When a pronoun refers to an antecedent that is suggested but not actually present in the sentence, the pronoun's reference is **implied.** Although a modifier may strongly imply the noun that the pronoun refers to, be sure to include the actual noun in the sentence.

Implied: After biking all afternoon, Colleen returned **it** to the garage.
Corrected: After biking all afternoon, Colleen returned **the bike** to the garage.

Comparative Versus Superlative

Use the comparative degree when comparing two items. Use the superlative degree when comparing more than two items. (Refer to page 261 of this handbook for more information about comparative and superlatives degrees.)

Wrong: This is the **best** of the two soap detergents.
Corrected: This is the **better** of the two soap detergents. (The comparison involves only two items.)

Wrong:	Considering these four film versions of *Romeo and Juliet*, I think Baz Luhrmann's is the **more** interesting.
Corrected:	Considering these four film versions of *Romeo and Juliet*, I think Baz Luhrmann's is the **most** interesting. (The comparison involves more than two items.)

Adjective Versus Adverb

Use adverbs—not adjectives—to modify verbs, adjectives, and other adverbs.

Wrong:	After the tune-up, the engine ran very **quiet.**
Correct:	After the tune-up, the engine ran very **quietly.**
Wrong:	Janelle performed **good** in the part of Ophelia.
Correct:	Janelle performed **well** in the part of Ophelia.
Wrong:	Danny plays the guitar **real** well.
Correct:	Danny plays the guitar **really** well.

Use adjectives—not adverbs—as subject complements.

Wrong:	Jasmine looked **well** in her prom dress.
Correct:	Jasmine looked **good** in her prom dress.
Wrong:	All her classmates felt **badly** about Felicity's accident.
Correct:	All her classmates felt **bad** about Felicity's accident.

GRAMMAR Common Sentence Problems

Subject–Verb Agreement

A verb must agree in number with its subject. A singular subject requires a singular verb, and a plural subject requires a plural verb.

When two nouns joined by *and* form a **compound subject**, the verb is usually plural.

Heather and Jennifer **take** karate lessons on Tuesday nights.

compound subject plural verb

When compound subjects are connected by *or* or *nor*, make the verb agree with the part of the subject nearer to the verb.

Two knights or a bishop **is** all you need to win this game of chess.

singular verb

A bishop or two knights **are** all you need to win this game of chess.

plural verb

Indefinite pronouns often result in subject–verb disagreement, so writers need to remember which indefinite pronouns are plural and which are singular.

Indefinite pronouns that are singular	Indefinite pronouns that are plural	Indefinite pronouns that may be singular or plural
another, anybody, anyone, anything, each, either, every, everybody, everyone, everything, little, much, neither, nobody, no one, nothing, one, somebody, someone, something	both, few, many, others, several	all, any, more, most, none, some

<u>Neither</u> of the boys **was** in the classroom.

singular subject · · · · · singular verb

<u>Few</u> of the teachers **were** surprised by the announcement.

plural subject · · · · · plural subject

<u>All</u> of the cake **was** spoiled.

singular subject · singular verb

<u>All</u> the hockey players **were** sick with the flu.

plural subject · · · · · plural verb

Collective nouns are usually considered singular and, therefore, require a singular verb. (Refer to page 258 of this handbook for a discussion of collective nouns.)

A <u>crowd</u> **was** lined up in front of the cinema.

singular subject · singular verb

However, when the sentence emphasizes the actions of individuals, the collective noun is considered to be plural.

The <u>crowd</u> **were expressing** their opinions about the film.

plural subject · plural verb

Phrases that come between a subject and a verb are not the true subject.

<u>None</u> *of the three candidates* **is enjoying** the public debate.

singular subject · · · *phrase* · · · singular verb

The verb must agree with its subject even when the subject follows the verb.

There **is** only one <u>letter</u> for you.

singular verb · singular subject

There **are** three <u>people</u> waiting for you.
plural verb <u>plural subject</u>

Although they look plural, words such as *athletics, economics, mathematics, measles, mumps,* and *physics* are usually singular.

The <u>news</u> **is** not good.
<u>singular subject</u> **singular verb**

Pronoun–Antecedent Agreement

A pronoun must agree in case and number with its subject. (Refer to pages 262–63 of this handbook for a discussion of pronoun case.)

Singular antecedents require singular pronouns.

The principal arranged to hold the meeting in **her** office. (The singular pronoun *her* replaces the singular antecedent *principal.*)

Plural antecedents require plural pronouns.

The teachers shared **their** ideas with the administrator. (The plural pronoun *their* replaces the plural antecedent *teachers.*)

Indefinite pronouns such as *anybody, anyone, each, either, neither, no one,* and *someone* are singular and must be replaced by singular pronouns. (Refer to page 272 of this handbook for a more detailed list of singular indefinite pronouns.)

<u>Everyone</u> wrote a report on **his or her** favourite novel.
<u>singular antecedent</u> **singular pronoun**

Compound antecedents joined by *and* are plural.

<u>Keith and Ryan</u> built a rocket as part of **their** science project.
<u>plural antecedent</u> **plural pronoun**

When compound antecedents are joined by *or* or *nor*, the pronoun must agree in number with the nearer antecedent.

Either Graham or his two brothers will share **their** lunch with Tim.
(plural *their* agrees with plural *brothers*)
Either the two brothers or Graham will share **his** lunch with Tim.
(singular *his* agrees with singular *Graham*)

There is one exception to the rule above. If one antecedent is female and the other is male, rewrite the sentence.

Wrong: Either Sue or Juan will bring **his** stereo to the party. (This makes no sense since *Sue* is feminine and *his* is masculine.)

Corrected: Either Sue or Juan will make sure there is a stereo at the party.

Misplaced Modifier

A **misplaced modifier** results when a modifying word, phrase, or clause is placed too far away from the word it modifies. A misplaced modifier appears to modify a word other than the one intended.

Wrong:	Terri discovered that she had not missed the bus **happily.**
Corrected:	Terri **happily** discovered that she had not missed the bus.
Wrong:	The camper surprised a bear **wearing pajamas.**
Corrected:	**Wearing pajamas,** the camper surprised a bear.

Dangling Modifier

A **dangling modifier** results when the word being modified does not appear in the sentence.

Wrong:	**At the age of seven,** my doctor removed my tonsils.
Corrected:	When I was seven, my doctor removed my tonsils.
Wrong:	**When tired,** exercise can increase blood flow and make you more alert.
Corrected:	When you are tired, exercise can increase blood flow and make you more alert.

Run-on Sentence

A **run-on sentence** is two or more sentences (main clauses) written as a single sentence.

Wrong: <u>Rick hurried toward the stairway</u> <u>he had no time to wait for the elevator</u>.

          main clause   main clause

To correct a run-on sentence, do one of the following:

1. Rewrite the sentence as separate sentences.

   Rick hurried toward the stairway. He had no time to wait for the elevator.

2. Use a semicolon (or, if it is appropriate, a colon or a dash) to join the two main clauses.

   Rick hurried toward the stairway; he had no time to wait for the elevator.

3. Use a conjunction to connect the sentences.

   Rick hurried toward the stairway because he had no time to wait for the elevator.

Be careful when using transitional expressions like *also, however, therefore, meanwhile, moreover, for example,* and *in fact.* None of these transitions can function as conjunctions, so they should be preceded by a period or semicolon.

Comma Splice

A **comma splice** is a type of run-on sentence in which two sentences (main clauses) are separated by a comma. A comma cannot join two main clauses.

Wrong: An owl hooted in the distance, the sound sent shivers up my spine.

To correct a comma splice, follow one of the three suggestions given for correcting run-on sentences.

Sentence Fragment

A **sentence fragment** is a group of words that is punctuated as a sentence but expresses an incomplete thought. Sentence fragments may lack a subject, a verb, or both.

Drove all night long. (lacks a subject)

The winner of the competition. (lacks a verb)

Running and jumping in the grass. (lacks both a verb and a subject)

Sentences that begin with a coordinating conjunction (e.g., *and, but, or*) may contain both a subject and a verb but are technically fragments because the conjunction does not link one idea to another. The result is an incomplete thought:

Fragment: But Jan was very tired.

Corrected: We intended to stay later, but Jan was very tired.

Sentences that begin with a subordinating conjunction (e.g., *before, until, because*) are fragments if the subordinate clause is not followed by a main clause.

Fragment: Because the car ran out of gas.

Correct: Because the car ran out of gas, we were late for the movie.

Although sentence fragments are grammatically incorrect, writers often use them intentionally to achieve a particular effect. Fragments can convey a sense of realism (especially in dialogue) or emphasize a particular detail or impression:

Rowan had never feared the dark. **Until now.**

Sentence fragments can be used to generate excitement by quickening the pace of a piece of writing. Several of them can have the opposite effect, slowing the pace down by emphasizing the repetitive quality of an experience.

While intentional sentence fragments can be very effective, *unintentional* fragments can make writing appear careless and can lessen the overall impact of the message.

Double Negative

A **double negative** occurs when two negative forms are used in the same construction.

Henry didn't see nothing. (If he did not see nothing, he must have seen something.)

In standard English, the modifiers *barely, hardly,* and *scarcely* are considered negative, so they should not be used with other negative words.

Wrong: Charlie got barely no sleep.

Corrected: Charlie got barely any sleep.

HANDBOOK

Avoid double negatives except in the following instances:

1. You wish to capture in dialogue the sound of casual speech.

   The suspect shrugged his shoulders and muttered, "I ain't got nothin' to say."

2. You intend a positive meaning.

   The burglar was not unfamiliar with the holding cell. (Meaning: The burglar was very familiar with the holding cell.)

Consistency of Verb Tense

The tense of a verb establishes the time of the action being described. When a passage begins in one verb tense and then shifts to another, a reader can become confused.

I **thought** I **was going** to be late for my job interview. Just as I **saw** the bus drive off,

past tense   past tense   past tense

Chris <u>pulls</u> up beside me in his new car and <u>offers</u> me a ride.

   <u>present tense</u>   <u>present tense</u>

Although writers may switch verb tenses intentionally to create a particular effect, it is usually best to select the most appropriate tense and to maintain it throughout the piece of writing.

I **thought** I **was going** to be late for my job interview. Just as I **saw** the bus drive off, Chris **pulled** up beside me in his new car and **offered** me a ride.

Sentence Variety

A passage that contains many similar-sounding sentences can be tiresome to read. The following are three ways to add variety to writing:

1. Use a variety of sentence structures rather than relying on simple or compound sentences. (Refer to pages 267–68 of this handbook for a discussion of the various sentence types.)

2. Vary the openings of sentences.

   Helen, embarrassed by Trevor's cruel remark, ran crying from the room. (begins with the subject, *Helen*)

   Embarrassed by Trevor's cruel remark, Helen ran crying from the room. (begins with a participial phrase describing the subject)

3. Invert sentences to avoid having too many that follow the common subject-verb-object pattern.

   Common: The discovery of penicillin was one of the most important scientific advances of the 20th century.

   Inverted: One of the most important scientific advances of the 20th century was the discovery of penicillin.

Parallelism

Words, phrases, clauses, or sentences with similar grammatical structures or functions are said to be **parallel.** Errors in parallelism occur when elements in a series are not expressed in the same grammatical form (e.g., single words are not balanced with single words, phrases are not balanced with phrases, verbs are not balanced with verbs, etc.).

Not parallel: During our hike, we heard the chirping of birds, the chattering of chipmunks, and the sound of leaves rustling.

Corrected: During our hike, we heard the chirping of birds, the chattering of chipmunks, and the rustling of leaves.

Not parallel: Suffering from a migraine, Cynthia turned off the phone's ringer, darkened the room, hung a do-not-disturb sign on the door, and she tried to sleep.

Corrected: Suffering from a migraine, Cynthia turned off the phone's ringer, darkened the room, hung a do-not-disturb sign on the door, and tried to sleep.

Redundancy

Redundancy occurs when the writer says the same thing twice. Effective writers use as few words as possible to convey their meaning.

Redundant: Greg **quietly whispered** the location of the hidden bracelet.

Corrected: Greg whispered the location of the hidden bracelet.

Redundant: Celine **very quickly hurried** through the supermarket's bakery section.

Corrected: Celine hurried through the supermarket's bakery section.

Redundant: Everyone in the group **cooperated together** to complete the task.

Corrected: Everyone in the group cooperated to complete the task.

Point of View

Point of view is the perspective from which a piece is written. There are three grammatical points of view: **first person** (*I* or *we*), **second person** (*you*), or **third person** (*he, she, it, one,* or *they*). A reader can easily become confused when a passage switches from one point of view to another.

My friends and I took a first-aid course last spring. During the course, you learned

third person · second person

how to dress wounds, apply splints, and give CPR.

Although some writers may intentionally switch points of view to create a particular effect, it is best to choose the most appropriate point of view and to maintain it throughout the piece of writing.

My friends and I took a first-aid course last spring. During the course, **we** learned how to dress wounds, apply splints, and give CPR.

Proper Nouns and Adjectives

Capitalize proper nouns and proper adjectives.

Proper Noun	Proper Adjective
Canada	Canadian
Shakespeare	Shakespearean

Names and Titles of People

Capitalize people's names and initials that stand for names.

Sarah McLaughlin   Michael G. Tibbits

Capitalize titles and abbreviations of titles when used before people's names or in direct address.

Professor Jane Sampson   Ms. Tina Turner   Dr. S. Segal

Capitalize titles of high importance, even when they are used without names.

the Prime Minister of Canada   the Pope   the Chief Justice of the Supreme Court

Family Relationships

Capitalize words indicating family relationships when the words are used as names or parts of names. If the noun is preceded by a possessive word or by *a, an,* or *the,* it is not capitalized.

When is Dad going to be home, Mom?   My aunt gave me a big hug after the game.

The Pronoun *I*

Always capitalize the pronoun *I.*

My brother and I will be attending the party.

The Supreme Being and Sacred Writings

Capitalize all words referring to God and religious scriptures.

God   Allah   the Koran   the Bible   the Torah

Geographical Names

In a geographical name, capitalize the first letter of each word except articles and prepositions.

Continents:	North America	Asia	Africa
Bodies of water:	Lake Erie	Atlantic Ocean	the Gulf of Mexico
Landforms:	Rocky Mountains	Arctic Tundra	Sahara Desert
World regions:	the Yukon	Middle East	Central America
Public areas:	the Plains of Abraham	Fundy National Park	Red Square
Political units:	Province of Manitoba	France	Republic of China
Roads and highways:	Highway 401	Fourth Avenue	Erb Street

Directions and Sections

Capitalize names of sections of a country and any adjectives that modify those names.

The Prairie Provinces are Manitoba, Saskatchewan, and Alberta.

The population on the West Coast has increased over the past 10 years.

The East Coast town was hit by a terrible storm.

Do not capitalize compass directions or adjectives that merely indicate direction or a general location.

The wind is blowing from the east.   Take this highway north for 10 km.

Organizations and Institutions

Capitalize the names of organizations and institutions, including political parties, governmental bodies or agencies, schools, colleges, universities, churches, hospitals, clubs, businesses, and abbreviations of these names.

Liberal Party	United Nations	Forest Heights Collegiate
St. Joseph's Church	Louise Marshall Hospital	Rotary Club
Chapters	YWCA	UN

Events, Documents, and Periods of Time

Capitalize the names of historical events, documents, and periods of time.

World War II   Charter of Rights and Freedoms   the Middle Ages

Months, Days, and Holidays

Capitalize the names of months, days, and holidays but not the names of seasons.

June   Saturday   Labour Day   fall

Races, Languages, Nationalities, and Religions

Capitalize the names of races, languages, nationalities, and religions.

Asian   French   Portuguese   Hinduism

HANDBOOK

School Subjects and Class Names

Do not capitalize the general names of school subjects. School subjects that are languages are always capitalized. Do capitalize the titles of specific courses and of courses that are followed by a number.

geography   English   World History   Mathematics 100

Capitalize class names only when they refer to a specific group or event, or when they are used in direct address.

Only seniors will be allowed to attend the Senior Prom.

Structures

Capitalize the names of specific monuments, bridges, and buildings.

Peace Tower   Burlington Skyway   CN Tower

Ships, Trains, Airplanes, and Automobiles

Capitalize the names of ships, trains, airplanes, and automobiles.

Titanic   *Orient Express*   Concorde   Corvette

Bodies of the Universe

Capitalize the names of the planets in the solar system and other objects in the universe, except words like *sun* and *moon*.

Saturn   the Milky Way   Halley's Comet

Note: Capitalize the word *earth* only when it is used in conjunction with the names of other planets. The word *earth* is not capitalized when the article *the* precedes it.

Abbreviations

Capitalize the following time abbreviations: B.C., A.D., A.M., and P.M. (or a.m. and p.m.). Capitalize certain other abbreviations: Ont., TV, NHL, Ph.D., SOS.

First Words

Capitalize the first word of every sentence.

There are more students in Grade 10 this year.

In general, capitalize the first word of every line of poetry. (In some modern poetry, lines do not begin with a capital letter.)

My friends believe in golf, address the ball,
however bent, to an appointed place.

"Golf" by Alden Nowlan

Capitalize the first word of a direct quotation.

> Rebelling against his imprisonment by King Minos, he declares, "Minos may own all else, but he does not own the air" (177).

Capitalize the first word in the greeting of a letter. Also capitalize the title, the person's name, and words such as *Sir* and *Madam.*

> Dear Sir or Madam: Dear Dr. Stemeroff:

Capitalize only the first word in the complimentary close.

> Yours truly,   Sincerely,

Capitalize the first word of each item in an outline and letters that introduce major subsections.

> I. Animals
>   A. Dogs
>   1. German Shepherd
>   2. Collies

Capitalize the first word, the last word, and all other important words in titles. Do not capitalize conjunctions, articles, or prepositions with fewer than four letters.

Book Title:	*Romeo and Juliet*	Short Story:	"Bearing Up"
Newspaper:	*The Globe and Mail*	Song:	"O Canada"
Magazine:	the *Atlantic Monthly*	Television Series:	*Friends*
Play:	*Pygmalion*	Work of Art:	the *Mona Lisa*

Note: The word *the* at the beginning of a title and the word *magazine* are capitalized only when they are part of the formal name.

MECHANICS   Punctuation

Period

Use periods after declarative and imperative sentences.

> I shall be there this afternoon.   Close the door.

Use a period after an indirect quotation.

> He asked about the population of Canada.

Use periods after abbreviations.

> T. S. Elliott   Jr.   Mr.   i.e.   Alta.   St.   A.M.

Note: A two-letter provincial abbreviation without periods is used only when it is followed by a postal code.

> Kitchener, ON N2M 4R9

Use a period after a number or letter in an outline.

I. Winter Sports
    A. Skiing
        1. Downhill
        2. Cross-country

Note: No period is used if the numeral or letter is enclosed in parentheses.

In numerals use a period between dollars and cents and before a decimal.

$4.93   3.865

Use periods following certain units of expression.

Good morning.   Good night.

Question Mark

Use question marks at the end of interrogative sentences.

Are you going?   It will be a long trip, won't it?

Note: Do not use a question mark after an indirect quotation or after a courtesy question in a business communication.

He asked if I was feeling well.   Will you please see that I am kept informed.

Exclamation Mark

Use an exclamation mark at the end of an emphatic word, phrase, clause, or sentence.

Wonderful!   What a surprise!   I can hardly believe it!   That looks great!

Comma

Use a comma after every item in a series except the last. A series consists of three or more words, phrases, or clauses.

We found some nickels, dimes, and quarters in his pocket.
She darted up the stairs, along the hallway, and into her bedroom.
I laugh, I sing, and I dance.

Use commas after the adverbs *first, second, third,* and so on, when these adverbs introduce parallel items in a series.

There are three ways to stay healthy. First, eat nutritional meals; second, exercise regularly; and third, get plenty of rest.

Use a comma between two or more adjectives of equal rank that modify the same noun.

She chose the bright, shiny, expensive bike.

Note: To decide whether adjectives are of equal rank, try placing the word *and* between them. If the *and* sounds natural, and if you can reverse the order of the adjectives without changing the meaning, then the comma is needed.

Use a comma to separate an introductory word, phrase, or clause from the rest of the sentence.

> Yes, we will be attending the birthday party after all.
> During the winter, many retired people take holidays in warmer climates.
> When you decide whether or not you are going, give me a call.

Use commas to set off words or groups of words that interrupt the flow of a sentence.

> She was, however, able to qualify for the team.
> The novel, to be quite honest with you, brought me to tears.

Use commas to set off nouns of direct address.

> If you really understand the problem, Andrea, you should have no problem solving it.
> Arron, you have made the team.

Use commas to set off the speaker's tags used with direct quotations.

> The coach said, "The bus will be leaving in five minutes."
> "We shall be leaving," the coach said, "in five minutes."

Note: Do not use commas with indirect quotations.

> The coach said that the bus would be leaving in five minutes.

Use a comma before the conjunction that joins the two main clauses in a compound sentence.

> Naomi seemed to agree, and no one else objected.

In dates, use a comma between the day of the month and the year.

> July 17, 1943   Monday, October 15, 2000

No commas are required when the following styles are used.

> July 1943   15 October 2000

Use a comma between the name of a city or town and the name of a province, state, or country.

> Regina, Saskatchewan   London, England

In writing an address as part of a sentence, use a comma after each item. (Note that you do not place a comma between the province and the postal code.)

> Halifax, Nova Scotia B3K 2Z1

HANDBOOK

Use a comma after the salutation of a friendly letter and after the complimentary close of a friendly letter or a business letter.

> Dear Shania,　　　　Yours sincerely,

Use a comma to prevent the danger of misreading or confusion if a comma is not used.

> Who he is, is not known.　　　　Outside, it was freezing.

Semicolon

A semicolon separates related sentence elements. It indicates a more definite break than a comma does, but a less abrupt break than a period does.

Use a semicolon to join independent clauses *without* a coordinating conjunction (e.g., *and, or, nor, for, but, so, yet*).

> Robin has submitted her assignment; Dale has not yet done so.

Use a semicolon to join two main clauses when the second clause begins with a conjunctive adverb (e.g., *however, therefore, furthermore*).

> I am a hard worker who takes pride in doing the best possible job; furthermore, my friendly nature would enable me to get along well with the rest of your staff.

Use a semicolon to separate items in a series if one or more of these items contain commas.

> My experiences as a babysitter and day-care worker have taught me that people who work with children must be caring, responsible, and dependable; that children need a safe environment where they can play, learn, and grow; and that parents need to know that their children are being well cared for and stimulated.

Colon

Use a colon to introduce a list of items. A word or phrase such as *these* or *the following* is often followed by a colon. A colon must be preceded by an independent clause and should not be used directly after a preposition or a verb.

> The following items were found in the box: newspaper clippings, postcards, and an old hat.

Use a colon to introduce a long or formal quotation.

> Farmer's understated account of the death of Icarus is also extremely effective:
>
> > Straight as a gull he fell toward the sea, but did not swerve in safety like a gull above the glittering waves. He plunged right into the heart of them, and their startled waters closed above his head. All that remained of Icarus were some feathers floating on the sea, while his father flew, weeping, in the sky, alone (44).

Use a colon between two independent clauses when the second clause explains the first. (Note that the first word following a colon is not capitalized unless it is a proper noun or the start of a quotation.)

> Notice that the light enters the drop in a straight line but leaves the drop having been bent by the water: this is known as refraction.

Use a colon after the greeting in a formal letter.

Dear Sir or Madam: Dear Mr. Pietraszko:

Use a colon between numbers showing hours and minutes.

4:15 a.m.   12:00 noon

Hyphen

Use a hyphen between syllables divided at the end of a line.

The hall can accom-
modate 50 people.

Use a hyphen in compound numbers from twenty-one to ninety-nine. Use a hyphen in fractions.

thirty-five   eighty-eight   three-quarters   five-eighths

Use a hyphen in certain compound nouns.

father-in-law   self-respect

Use a hyphen between the words that make up a compound adjective when the modifier is used before the noun. Do not use a hyphen when the compound adjective follows the noun.

well-known person   hard-working people   The highway was well paved.

Do not use a hyphen between an adverb ending in -*ly* and an adjective preceding the noun.

My neatly cut hedge was much admired by my neighbour.

Apostrophe

Use an apostrophe to form the possessive of singular and plural nouns. To form the possessive of a singular noun, add an apostrophe and -*s*, even if the noun ends in -*s*.

Jane's book   John Davis's hat

To form the possessive of a plural noun that ends in -*s*, add an apostrophe only. To form the possessive of a plural noun that does not end in -*s*, add both an apostrophe and -*s*.

the boys' jackets   the women's dresses

To form the possessive of an indefinite pronoun, add an apostrophe and -*s*.

no one's pen   everybody's responsibility

Use an apostrophe in a contraction to show where one or more letters have been left out. Avoid using contractions in formal writing.

can't = cannot   he'll = he will or he shall   Sam's = Sam is or Sam has

Use an apostrophe to show the omission of figures in a date.

the class of '99   the storm of '95

Use an apostrophe to show the plurals of letters, numbers, signs, and words referred to as words.

There are two *f*'s in the word *different*.　There are too many *then*'s in your sentences.

Quotation Marks, Underlining, and Italicizing

Use quotation marks to begin and end a direct quotation. Do not use quotation marks for an indirect quotation.

Bruno said, "My feelings are hurt."　　Bruno said that his feelings were hurt.

To punctuate a direct quotation, enclose the exact words used by a speaker or writer in quotation marks. The first word of the quotation is capitalized. Commas are always placed inside the quotation marks. When the end of the quotation falls at the end of the sentence, the period is placed inside the quotation marks.

"The dam has busted," screamed the worker.

He whispered, "I didn't know you cared."

Put question marks and exclamation marks inside the quotation marks if they are part of the quotation.

"How far do we have to go?" asked Shuna.

"Help!" cried the little boy. "I can't swim!"

Put question marks and exclamation marks outside the quotation marks if they are not part of the quotation.

Who said, "Practice makes perfect"?

How furious he was when she muttered, "I don't remember"!

Always put commas and periods inside the quotation marks.

The finance minister said, "This move will preserve Canada for the future."

"This move will preserve Canada for the future," said the finance minister.

Enclose the parts of a divided quotation in quotation marks. Do not capitalize the first word of the second part unless it begins a new sentence.

"I'd rather be at home," said the young girl, "than here at camp."

"I'd rather be at home," said the young girl. "However, I'm going to stick it out until the end of camp."

In punctuating dialogue, begin a new paragraph to indicate a new speaker.

"It's not being a hero," Dad said. "It's just a job that's got to be done. It's my job."

"You didn't have to be a SARtech, though," Mike said. "You volunteered. You used to be a cook."

Dad shrugged. "Don't worry about it. Nothing's going to happen."

When quoting passages longer than one paragraph, use quotation marks at the beginning of each paragraph and at the end of only the last paragraph.

> Here's how Jerry Linenger, an astronaut, described a space walk to his son:
>
> "Imagine this. You are in scuba gear. Your vision is restricted by the size of your underwater mask. Your fins, wetsuit, and gloves make you clumsy and heavy. The water is frigid; in fact, it is thickly frozen overhead with only one entry-exit hole drilled. Your life depends on your gear functioning properly the entire time. The further away you venture, the further away the escape hole in the ice, and the less you can tolerate any failure whatsoever.
>
> "There is no bottom. Up and down are confused. Your path is not straight, but rather around obstacles on a constantly convex, falling away, prime surface. As you round one obstacle, the next appears, and soon enough it is difficult to determine from where you came."

Note: Further guidelines for incorporating direct quotations into essays and research reports are outlined on pages 226–27 of this text.

Use quotation marks to enclose the titles of short stories, poems, essays, magazine and newspaper articles, chapters, television episodes, and songs.

Short story	"Moving Day"
Poem	"Identity"
Essay	"Flying Free: Icarus Stories Old and New"
Magazine or newspaper article	"Eye Spy"
Chapter	"The Whiteness of the Whale"
Television episode	"The Giant Panda"
Song	"Immortality"

The titles of books, newspapers, magazines, movies, television series, plays, works of art, and long musical compositions are underlined in writing and italicized in print.

Book	*Technical Communication*
Newspaper	*National Post*
Magazine	*Maclean's*
Movie	*American Beauty*
Television series	*The Nature of Things*
Play	*The Hitchhiker*
Work of art	Michaelangelo's *David*
Long musical composition	Wagner's *The Ring*

Use quotation marks to set apart a word that is being discussed; to indicate that a word is slang; to point out that a word or phrase is being used in a special way.

The words "accept" and "except" are often confused.

That movie was really "cool."

This new outfit should really "light up my life."

Parentheses

Use parentheses around words that are included in a sentence to add information or to help make an idea clearer.

> After taking her temperature, pulse, and blood pressure (routine vital signs), the doctor made Lang as comfortable as possible.

> Finally, the night before I had to present my project, I got to work. I researched, wrote up, translated, and created an attractive poster, all after dinner (because a *Family Ties* rerun was on after school).

Use parentheses to enclose letters or numbers labelling items in a series.

> The secretary for our club is allowed to (1) sign checks, (2) pay bills, and (3) make purchases.

Brackets

Use brackets to enclose any words or phrases that you have inserted into an otherwise word-for-word quotation.

> *Audubon* reports that "if there are not enough young to balance deaths, the end of the species [California condor] is inevitable."

Use brackets to enclose stage directions in a script.

> I'LL SPREAD THE LEAVES, ALL RIGHT MRS. PHILLIPS? HERE, I'M SPREADING THE LEAVES [jumping on the pile of bags, ripping one open and swinging it about]. HOW'S THAT?

Ellipsis

If you omit any part of a quotation, use an ellipsis (...) to indicate that something has been left out. If the part left out comes at the end of the sentence, some style guides suggest adding a period before the ellipsis.

> In A.D. Melville's translation ... we find that Daedalus is challenging the known limits of the universe. Rebelling against his imprisonment by King Minos, he declares, "Minos may own all else, but he does not own the air" (177). Daedalus wishes to break free of his world, and soar over the sea to return to Athens. He believes that he can escape the confines of his community.

Dash

Use a dash to indicate a sudden break or change in a sentence.

> Two teams—Vancouver and Toronto—made it to the Stanley Cup.

> The all-new T595 Daytona signals the dawn of a new era in Triumph's history—technology, looks, and performance at the cutting edge of motorcycle design.

HANDBOOK

Use a dash to emphasize a word, a series of words, a phrase, or a clause.

> Some high-tech companies—ones that are on the cutting edge of technology—are seeing their stock prices rise quickly.

> I think that one of these career choices—advertising, photography, or media—is my ticket to employment in the future.

Use a dash to show that someone's speech is being interrupted by another person.

> Why, hello—yes, I understand—no, I don't believe so—oh—of course.

MECHANICS · Abbreviations

Use standard abbreviations for titles immediately before and after proper names.

Ms. Robin Ashoona	Rev. William Lamont	St. Jude	Prof. Sylvia Chin
Dennis Hines, Jr.	Donald Lang, Ph.D.	André Surin, M.D.	Neil Coburn, C.A.

Note: Don't abbreviate a title if it is not used with a proper name.

Abbreviate given names only if the person is most commonly known that way.

> My doctor is a cardiac specialist.

> W.O. Mitchell is a well-known Canadian writer.

Use familiar abbreviations for the names of organizations, corporations, and countries.

RCMP   NFL   OHIP   CTV   YMCA   UN

Note: Use the full name with the abbreviation in parentheses the first time it is used in a passage.

> The National Football League (NFL) provides excellent entertainment. Players for the NFL are very skilled.

Use the abbreviations A.M., P.M., A.D., B.C. No., and $ only with specific dates, times, numbers, and amounts.

2:00 A.M. (or a.m.)   50 B.C.   A.D. 39   No. 15 (or no. 15) $100

Use Latin abbreviations sparingly.

cf (compare)	e.g. (for example)	et al. (and others)	etc. (and so forth)
i.e. (that is)	N.B. (note well)	P.S. (postscript)	

Note: Do not use these abbreviations in formal writing.

Use abbreviations for the names of provinces in tables, notes, and bibliographies (see second column below) and in postal codes (see third column below).

Province or Territory	Traditional	Postal Code
Alberta	Alta.	AB
British Columbia	B.C.	BC
Manitoba	Man.	MB
New Brunswick	N.B.	NB
Newfoundland	Nfld.	NF
Northwest Territories	N.W.T.	NT
Nova Scotia	N.S.	NS
Nunavut	Nun.	NT
Ontario	Ont.	ON
Prince Edward Island	P.E.I.	PE
Quebec	Que.	QC
Saskatchewan	Sask.	SK
Yukon Territory	Y.T.	YT

In formal writing, abbreviations for the following are not commonly accepted: personal names, units of measurement, days of the week, holidays, months, courses of study, divisions of written works, provinces and countries (except in addresses), and company names (unless the abbreviation is part of the company name). Note, however, that even formal writing allows metric abbreviations (14 kg, 8 cm, etc.); but avoid combining such abbreviations with numbers spelled out, as in ten kg.

William (not Wm.)	pound (not lb.)	Tuesday (not Tues.)
Christmas (not Xmas)	March (not Mar.)	science (not sci.)
chapter (not ch.)	Ontario (not Ont. or ON)	Company (not Co.)

MECHANICS — Writing Numbers

Numbers from one to nine are usually written as words: all numbers 10 and over are usually written as numerals.

    three   eight   60   506

You may use a combination of numerals and words for very large numbers.

    6 million   7 trillion

Use words, not numerals, to begin a sentence.

    Four hundred and eighty-seven students attend our school.

Use only numerals to express money, decimals, percentages, chapters, pages, time, telephone numbers, dates, identification numbers, postal codes, addresses, and statistics.

$6.25	47.2	5 percent	chapter 6
pages 36–39	9:00 a.m.	44 Warren Road	Highway 15
July 1, 1948	A.D. 123	a vote of 43 to 26	50 km/h

If you are comparing two or more numbers in a sentence, write all of them as numerals or as words.

The students ranged in age from eight to seventeen.

The students ranged in age from 8 to 17.

Numbers that come before a compound modifier that includes a numeral should be written as words.

We need ten 12-foot lengths to finish the floor of the deck.

VOCABULARY AND SPELLING Vocabulary

You can determine the meaning of many new words by using the three word parts: roots, prefixes, and suffixes. Following are definitions and examples for each.

Roots

As its name suggests, a root is a word from which other words grow, usually through the addition of prefixes or suffixes.

Root	Meaning	Examples
aud	hear, listen	audible, audience
auto	self	autobiography, automatic
bene	good, well	benefit, benevolent
bio	life	biography, biosphere
centri	centre	concentric, eccentric
chron	time	chronological, sychronize
cide	kill	homicide, pesticide
derm	skin	dermatology, taxidermy
duct	to lead or to make	induce, reproduce
form	shape, structure	conform, formula
geo	earth	geography, geology

Root	Meaning	Examples
graph	to write	autograph, pictograph
hydro, hydra	water	hydrophobia, dehydrate
magn	great	magnificent, magnify
man	hand	manual, manicure
micro	small	microfilm, microwave
mit, miss	send	submit, missile
path, pathy	feeling, suffering	pathos, empathy
photo	light	photography, photometer
port	to carry	porter, export
psych	soul	psychiatry, psychology
rupt	break	erupt, rupture
scrib, script	write	describe, scribble
sent, sens	feel	sentiment, sensation
tele	far away	telegraph, telescope
therm	heat	thermometer, thermostat
vac	empty	vacuum, evacuate
vid, vis	see	video, revise

Prefixes

Prefixes are those "word parts" that come before the root word (*pre-* means "before"). Prefixes often change the intent of the root word. The following are some common prefixes of negation, opposition, quantity, time, and space.

Negation or Opposition

Prefix	Meaning	Examples
a, an	without, not	amoral, apathy
anti	against	antibody, anticlimax
contra	against	contradict, contravene
de	from, down	deprive, demote
dis	apart, away	disappear, dismiss
il, im, in, ir	not	illegal, impossible, indiscrete, irregular
mal	wrong	malpractice, malfunction
mis	wrong, bad	misuse, misprint
non	not	nontoxic, nonsense
un	not	unable, unfair

Prefixes of Quantity

Prefix	Meaning	Examples
bi	two, double, twice	bicycle, biweekly
milli	thousand	millimetre, milligram
mono	one, single	monoplane, monotone
omni	all	omniscient, omnipotent
semi	half	semicolon, semiconductor
tri	three	triangle, tripod
uni	one	unity, unique

Prefixes of Time and Space

Prefix	Meaning	Examples
ante	before	anteroom, antecedent
circum	around	circumference, circumspect
co, col, com, con, cor	with	copilot, collaborate, compose contact, correspond
e, ex	out of	emit, exit
hyper	over, more than	hypersensitive, hyperactive
hypo	under, less than	hypothesis, hypoglycemia
inter	between	interfere, international
mega	enlarge, large	megaphone, megabyte
micro	tiny	microscopic, microbe
neo	recent	neoclassic, neophyte
post	after	postscript, postpone
pre	before	preview, prevent
pro	forward, in favour of	proceed, promote
re	again, back	review, return
sub	under, beneath	submarine, submerge
super, supr	over, above	supervise, supreme
syn, sym, sys,	with, together	synchronize, sympathy, system
trans	across, over	transmit, transport

Suffixes

Suffixes come at the end of words and root words, and they modify or extend the meaning of the word. Suffixes can alter the part of speech of the original word, e. g., create (verb), creation (noun), creative (adjective), creatively (adverb). The following are some common suffixes arranged according to the part of speech they signify.

HANDBOOK

Noun Suffixes

Suffix	Meaning	Examples
acy	state or quality	privacy, democracy
al	act of	refusal, rebuttal
ance, ence	state or quality of	resistance, emininence
dom	place or state of being	kingdom, boredom
er, or	one who	painter, navigator
ism	doctrine or belief, condition	Communism, alchoholism
ist	one who	federalist, dentist
ity, ty	state, quality of	captivity, clarity
ment	act of, process	contentment, amendment
ness	state of	restlessness, consciousness
ship	position held	friendship, dictatorship
sion, tion	state of being or action	depression, transition

Verb Suffixes

Suffix	Meaning	Examples
ate	cause to be	regulate, obliterate
en	cause to be or become	frozen, lighten
ify, fy	make or cause to be	amplify, simplify
ize	cause to become	publicize, idolize

Adjective Suffixes

Suffix	Meaning	Examples
able, ible	capable of being	agreeable, edible
al	pertaining to	political, natural
ful	full of	frightful, careful
ic	pertaining to	poetic, heroic
ish	having the quality of	foolish, Irish
lous, ous	full of, having	nutritious, famous
ive	having the nature of	creative, exhaustive
less	without	careless, senseless

Adverb Suffixes

Suffix	Meaning	Examples
ly	in a certain manner, like	slowly, lightly

VOCABULARY AND SPELLING Spelling

Spelling Rules

The letter *q* is always followed by the letter *u*.

quite   quality   quick   quack

Every syllable has a vowel or *y*.

left   im-por-tant   try   slow-ly

Use *i* before *e* except after *c* or when it sounds like the letter *a*.

believe   receive   neighbourhood

When a *c* at the beginning of a word is followed by *e, i,* or *y*, it is soft (like the *s* sound); otherwise, it is hard (like the *k* sound).

cent   circle   cyber   cart   cottage

For words ending in a consonant plus *y*, change the *y* to *i* before adding a suffix other than *-ing*.

bakeries   monies   crying   prying

Drop the silent *e* from a root word before adding *-ing*.

creating   reducing   casing

For one-syllable words with a short vowel, double the final consonant before adding an ending.

fitting   clapping   bidding

Spelling Strategies

Sound Strategies

Imagine the sound of the word or actually say it out loud. This strategy works well for words that are spelled exactly the way they sound.

humanitarian   reminder

Use correct pronunciation. You may spell some words incorrectly because you do not pronounce them correctly.

extraordinary   February   probably

Exaggerate hidden sound. Some sounds are difficult to hear when you say the word normally. Exaggerating these sounds can help you spell the word correctly.

interEsting   exHausted

Say longer words one syllable at a time.

mil-len-ni-um   me-te-or-log-i-cal   hy-per-bol-ic-al-ly

Think of another word with the same pattern.

    stealth—wealth   weight—eight

Visual Strategies

Highlight difficult letters.

    fraGility   existEnce   soCiable

Draw the shape or configuration of the word.

    greed   heirloom

Look closely at the spelling of a word, and then close your eyes. Visualize the word. Do this a few times; then write the word on a piece of paper and check the spelling.

Meaning Strategies

Break words into root words, prefixes, and suffixes.

    sandbox   cupboard   breakfast

Use related words to help you spell a word.

    nation   national   nationality

Use word origins. The following words are derived from the Greek word *bios* meaning "life."

    biology   bionic   biography   biopsy   biomechanics   biosphere

Tactile Strategies

Trust your instincts: if a spelling does not "feel" right, it probably isn't. Try writing the word several ways, or check it in a dictionary.

Mnemonic Devices

Use mnemonic devices: rhymes, puns, and word associations.

    two servings for dessert   alone in the desert   The principal is my pal.

Dictionary

Use a dictionary to help you check the spelling of difficult words.

Homophones

Homophones are words that sound alike but have different spellings and meanings. Homophones usually come in pairs, but they also come in groups of three or more.

    there/their   its/it's   to/too/two   buy/by/bye

Plural Nouns

A noun is singular if it names one thing. It is plural if it names more than one thing. Follow these rules when forming the plurals of nouns:

Most nouns form the plural by simply adding -*s* to the singular.

    lakes   impressions   performances

Nouns that end in *-s, -sh, -ch, -x,* or *-z* form the plural by adding *-es.*

glasses   splashes   watches   boxes   waltzes

If a noun ends in *-o* preceded by a vowel, add *-s* to form the plural. Some nouns that end in *-o* preceded by a consonant form the plural with *-s.* Others form the plural with *-es.* Check a dictionary to determine the correct spelling.

radios   silos   heroes

If a noun ends in *-y* preceded by a vowel, add *-s* to form the plural. If the *-y* follows a consonant, change the *-y* to *i* and add *-es.*

chimneys   monkeys   duties   parties

Note: For proper names ending in -y, just add -s.

Rileys   Murphys

For some nouns ending in *-f* or *-fe,* add an *-s.* For others change the *-f* to *-v* and add *-es.*

reefs   giraffes   loaves

Some nouns have the same form for both singular and plural.

trout   moose   Sioux

Some nouns form their plurals in irregular ways.

goose—geese   foot—feet   woman—women

If a compound noun is written as separate words or is hyphenated, change the most important word to the plural form.

sister-in-law—sisters in law   tenth grader—tenth graders

Possessive Nouns and Pronouns

A possessive noun is one that shows ownership or belonging. Follow these rules when using the possessive form:

If a noun is singular, add an apostrophe and *-s* to form the possessive.

Janine's hat   cat's paws   three dollar's worth

If a noun is plural and ends in *-s,* add just the apostrophe.

girls' teams   parents' car   players' equipment

If a noun is plural and does not end in *-s,* add an apostrophe and *-s.*

men's suits   geese's feathers   children's gloves

Do not use an apostrophe with possessive personal pronouns.

His essay was better than **hers.**   Those books are **yours,** not **mine.**

To form the possessive case of some indefinite pronouns, add an apostrophe and an *-s.*

Somebody's keys were left in my locker.   **Nobody's** experiment worked.

Index

Acknowledgments

Visuals

Page 18 Gianni Dagli Orti/CORBIS; Page 19 Mary Evans Picture Library; Page 20 Mary Evans Picture Library; Page 21 Duncan Smith/PhotoDisc; Page 22 Pat Hammond Studio; Page 23 © Buddy Mays/CORBIS; Page 36 SW Production/PhotoDisc; Page 37 © Jim Zuckerman/CORBIS; Page 39 Greg Agnew/CP Picture Archive; Page 41 PhotoDisc; Page 42 © Ross Ressmeyer/CORBIS; Page 44 © George Lepp/CORBIS; Page 62 Steve Cole/PhotoDisc; Page 65, 67, 68 Photofest; Page 90 Harnett/Hanzon/PhotoDisc; Page 91 Janis Christie/PhotoDisc; Page 92 top Hulton-Deutsch Collection/CORBIS; Page 92 bottom Steve Mason/PhotoDisc; Page 104 Mark Richards/Photo Edit; Page 105 PhotoDisc; Page 106 Ryan McVay/PhotoDisc; Page 107 Steve Cole/PhotoDisc; Page 108 Mary Evans Picture Library; Page 109 Jack Hollingsworth/PhotoDisc; Page 124 Steve Cole/PhotoDisc; Page 125 NASA; Page 126 © CORBIS; Page 127 Associated Press/CP Archive; Page 147 top *The Record*; Page 147 bottom *Hartford Courant*; Page 148 top *Hartford Courant*; Page 148 bottom Itsuo Inouye/CP Picture Archive; Page 149 *Hartford Courant*; Page 162 © Bob Rowan; Progressive Image/CORBIS; Page 166 Duncan Smith/PhotoDisc; Page 200 Jonathan Nourok/Photo Edit; Page 216 PhotoDisc; Page 217 Mary Evans Picture Library; Page 234 Jack Star/PhotoLink/PhotoDisc

Text

"Lochinvar" by Sir Walter Scott from POETICAL WORKS, published by Oxford University Press. "Love Me, Love My Dog" by Isabella Valancy Crawford, *Telegram,* 25 March 1880. "The Jeannie C." by Stan Rogers. Copyright © 1978 Fogarty's Cove Music. Used by permission of Ariel Rogers. "Bearing Up" by Matt Hughes from *Takes: Stories for Young Adults* (Thistledown Press, 1996). "Romeo and Juliet" from "The Contemporary File," copyright © 1996 by Twentieth Century Fox Film Corporation, from WILLIAM SHAKESPEARE'S ROMEO AND JULIET: THE CONTEMPORARY FILM Screenplay by Craig Pearce and Baz Luhrmann. Used by permission of Dell Publishing, a division of Random House, Inc. "Sonnet xiv" by Elizabeth Barrett Browning from SONNETS FROM THE PORTUGUESE AND OTHER POEMS. Copyright © 1992 by Dover Publications, Inc. "Oh Mother, Oh Mother, Where Is Happiness?" by Gwendolyn Brook from ANNIE, ALLEN. Originally published in 1949 by Harper & Brothers, New York. "Golf" by Alden Nowlan from *Playing the Jesus Game* by Alden Nowlan. Copyright © 1970 by Alden Nowlan. "The Underpainter" by Jane Urquhart from *The Underpainter* by Jane Urquhart © 1997. Used by permission, McClelland and Stewart, Inc., *The Canadian Publishers*. From Flaubert, Gustave *Madame Bovary*. Translation Copyright © 1969 by Merloyd Lawrence. Adapted by permission of Houghton Mifflin Company. "It's All Downhill From Here" by Jerry Linenger. Reproduced with permission of NASA. "Eye Spy—Biometrics: Your Body as Password" by John M. Moran. Copyright: The Hartford Courant. Reprinted with permission. "The Use and Abuse of Antibiotics" by Bronwen McCurdy. Reprinted with permission. *Canada's Physical Activity Guide to Healthy Active Living,* Health Canada, 1998. Reproduced with permission of the Minister of Public Works and Government Services Canada, 2000. "I Choose NOT TO Smoke … Please DON'T Make Me." Reproduced with the permission of Council For a Tobacco-Free Waterloo Region. "Ceremony for Decorations for Bravery" by Roméo LeBlanc. Reproduced with permission of Roméo LeBlanc. "My Life as a Procrastinator" by Jennifer Williams. Reproduced with permission of the author. "Reach for the Sky" by Bill Anderson. Reprinted with permission of the author.